100 DAYS OF EPIC

MERIDITH ALEXANDER

Copyright © 2023 Meridith Hankenson Alexander

All rights reserved.

"Don't ask what the world needs. Ask what makes you come alive, and go do it. Because what the world needs is people who have come alive."

— Howard Thurman

Table of Epic Contents:

How Your Epic Journey Begins...

FOCUS / Introduction	1
Day 1 – FOCUS: Meet #1 OF THE EPIC 3 – The Power of Deliberate Focus and Unraveling the Secrets of Manifestation	22
Day 2 – FOCUS: Creating Your Remarkable Moment	27
Day 3 – FOCUS: Elevate Your Focus: Embrace the Realm of Infinite Possibilities	29
Day 4 – FOCUS: Embrace Your Epic Power and Worthiness	31
Day 5 – FOCUS: Be the Sovereign of Your Epic Story	33
Day 6 – FOCUS: Regret Reimagined- Embracing the Heroic You	37
Day 7 - FOCUS: Illuminating Forgiveness: Embracing the Gift of Resilience	38
Day 8 — FOCUS: Navigating the Seas of Self-Care, Self-Trust, and Self-Love	40
Day 9— FOCUS: Embrace the Power of Tiny Shifts for an EPIC IMPACT	42
Day 10 - FOCUS: Relax, Review & Recoup - Your "National All About Me" Day	43
Day 11- FOCUS: Building An Epic Team – The Right Fit	45
Day 12— FOCUS: Embrace Change, Unlock Limitless Potential	47
Day 13 - FOCUS: Embrace Your Epic History	49
Day 14— FOCUS: Embrace Your Epic Legacy	50
Day 15— FOCUS: Shaping Identity – From Boulders to Superpowers	52
Day 16—FOCUS: Perfectly Imperfect: Embracing the Flow of Life	53
Day 17 — FOCUS: Take the Driver's Seat and Embrace the Magic of Your Inner GPS	55
Day 18 — FOCUS: Craft Your Own Epic Definition of Success	57

DAY 19 – FOCUS: The Ultimate Self-Care When Just a Bubble Bath Won't Do	58
Day 20 — FOCUS: Create Your Tr'amily – The Power of Blending Tribe + Family	60
Day 21 — FOCUS: Embracing the Journey Beyond Goals	62
Day 22 — FOCUS: Shifting the Tractor Beam of Attraction to Inspired Action	64
Day 23 — FOCUS: Finding Your Significance Beyond the Storms of Others	66
Day 24 — FOCUS: Unleash Your Epic Power with Positive Triggers	68
Day 25 — FOCUS: I'll Be Happy When…	71
Day 26 — FOCUS: Nurture Your Soul with Positive Influences	72
Day 27 — FOCUS: Embrace the Hidden Treasures of Unexpected Falls	76
Day 28 —FOCUS: Reframing Your Self-Image	77
Day 29 —FOCUS: Allowing Your Little Voice Back Into the Castle	80
Day 30 — FOCUS: What If The Journey Through Life is the Ultimate Vacation Package…	85
Day 31 — FOCUS: Riding the Wave of Adaptation and Growth	87
Day 32 — FOCUS: Launching Your "Deliberately Empowered Optimism" Movement	89
Day 33 – FOCUS: The Garden of Successes	91
Day 34 – FOCUS: Happiness is a lifestyle	93
Day 35 – FOCUS: The Power of the 1%	95
Day 36 — FOCUS: The Road to Happiness: Surely It Doesn't Include That Brick Wall?	98
Day 37 — FOCUS: The Power of Celebration	101
Day 38 — FOCUS: Mud or Masterpiece?	105
Day 39 — FOCUS: Financial Abundance– the Ultimate Romeo and Juliet Story (But Potentially With a MUCH Happier Ending)	106

Day 40 — FOCUS: Celebrate the Genius of this Uncompleted Journey — 109

Day 41 - FOCUS: Living Life as a Champion — 112

Day 42 — FOCUS: "Shine On You Crazy Diamond" — 113

Day 43 — FOCUS: Kicking off the ruby red slippers for a moment to feel the grass between my toes....! — 115

Day 44 – FOCUS: When Things Don't Go "Right" — 117

Day 45 – FOCUS: Releasing the Baby Elephant Collars — 118

Day 46 - FOCUS: Always Be You Unless You Can Be A Unicorn Then Be A Unicorn — 122

Day 47 — FOCUS: Let's Keep Going – Unleash Your Epic Self — 124

Day 48: FOCUS: Creating a Focus-Centric Lifestyle™- Energizing Your Epic Journey! — 128

LANGUAGE — 131

Day 49— LANGUAGE: STICKS AND STONES MAY BREAK MY BONES BUT WORDS... OH MY — 134

Day 50 – LANGUAGE: My Biggest Challenge Is... — 135

Day 51 – LANGUAGE: That One Invisible Word — 138

Day 52 – LANGUAGE: A Tension Span — 140

Day 53 – LANGUAGE: Two Incredibly Impactful Words — 142

Day 54 – LANGUAGE: They're Playing My Tune — 144

Day 55 – LANGUAGE: Influences and Impact — 146

Day 56 – LANGUAGE: The "But" Hole — 149

Day 57 – LANGUAGE: May the Force Be With You — 151

Day 58 – LANGUAGE: The Intention Exercise — 154

Day 59 –LANGUAGE: The Writing is On the Wall — 155

Day 60 –LANGUAGE: The Words of Acknowledgement Game — 157

Day 61 – LANGUAGE: Unveiling Your Blind Spots- Illuminate the Path to Your Epic 159

Day 62 — LANGUAGE: Unveiling the 3 Defining Questions — Question #1 161

Day 63 – LANGUAGE: The 3 Defining Questions – Question #2 163

Day 64 — LANGUAGE: Completing the 3 Defining Questions – Question #3 165

Day 65 – LANGUAGE: The Epic WHO 167

Day 66 – LANGUAGE: Goal Diggers 169

Day 67 – LANGUAGE: All Work and No Play Makes Jack a Dull Boy 171

Day 68 – LANGUAGE: The Day of Four Phrases 172

Day 69 – LANGUAGE: The Flight of the Introvert 174

Day 70 – LANGUAGE: Will You Supersize It? 177

Day 71-LANGUAGE: From Flaw to Focused Possibility 178

Day 72 – LANGUAGE: Owning Your EPIC Story – An Odyssey of Empowering Possibilities 180

Day 73 – LANGUAGE: The Magic of "Being" - Unveiling the Secret Sauce 182

Day 74 – LANGUAGE: The Power of Appreciation Over Apology 184

Day 75 – LANGUAGE: Embrace Your Superpowers –Shifting from Comparison to How Can I Grow 186

Day 76 – LANGUAGE: Embracing Work/Life Harmony 187

Day 77 – LANGUAGE: Embracing the Dazzling Brilliance Within IMAGINATION 190

THE THIRD MASTERY – #3 OF THE EPIC 3 – IMAGINATION: The Power of Envisioning and Igniting the Force Within 192

Day 78 – IMAGINATION: Your Success Code – Getting Your IT (Inner Technology) Together — 193

Day 79 – IMAGINATION: Rewriting the Narrative – From Failure to Empowerment — 195

Day 80 – IMAGINATION: Failures Feed Your Superpowers — 198

Day 81 – IMAGINATION: Fear – Your Lightbulb Moment and the Dark Corners of Shame — 200

Day 82 – IMAGINATION: Fear Lives In Your Comfort Zone — 203

Day 83 – IMAGINATION: Fear Loves Confusion — 204

Day 84 – IMAGINATION: The De-Stuckifier – Conquering Fear with Confident Action — 206

Day 85 – IMAGINATION: Commit and Refuse to Renegotiate — 209

Day 86 – IMAGINATION: The 1% Consistency: Embracing the Journey of Epic — 211

Day 87 – IMAGINATION: Fear has a Physiology, So Breathe — 213

Day 88 – IMAGINATION: Fear as Your Superpower: Embracing Fear to Crush the Impossible — 215

Day 89 – IMAGINATION: Inside Your Fears is a Dream Waiting to Make Itself Heard… — 218

Day 90 – IMAGINATION: Embracing the Ordinary – Unleashing the Extraordinary — 220

Day 91 – IMAGINATION: The Power of Envision: Igniting Your Epic Future — 222

Day 92 – IMAGINATION: Harnessing the Wings of Your Soulmate — 224

Day 93 – IMAGINATION: The Appreciation Wheel – Antidote to Doubt and Pushback — 226

Day 94 – IMAGINATION: Real Eyes for Real EPIC — 228

Day 95 – IMAGINATION: Dancing With the Whales – Dive Into Your Ability to Play With the Big Fish — 229

Day 96 – IMAGINATION: The Envisioner's Triumph - Defying the Naysayers	232
Day 97 – IMAGINATION: 3 Things the Boulder Taught Me About Bad Times	234
Day 98 – IMAGINATION: Embrace the Hero Within - Unleashing the Epic YOU	236
Day 99– THE EPIC 3: Nurturing the 12 Brilliances	238
Day 100 – THE EPIC 3: Brilliant Habits	240
Day 101 – THE EPIC 3: Guiding Lights and Turbo-Chargers	241
Day 102 – THE EPIC 3: Once Upon A Future Me – The Story Not the Fantasy	246
Day 103 – THE EPIC 3: The Journey of Epic Transformation: A New Beginning	249
Conclusion / Acknowledgements / About the Author / Bonuses	251

DEDICATION

To the man who has taught me what it truly feels like to be epically loved, the man who encourages me to seize every moment and to face every boulder with grace and courage, the man whose smiling eyes I see when I imagine the delicious chapters of this life that are yet to be written, my truly EPIC E.O. Mike.

And to the amazing young woman that I am honored to call my daughter, you truly are the heart that lives outside my body, you are the inspiration for my EPIC, my sweet Schuyler.

INTRODUCTION: How to Play this EPIC Game TO WIN!

How Your Epic Journey Begins…

What if you could consistently wake up feeling exhilarated about the day ahead?

What if that crazy "own worst enemy" voice could stop showing up as your kryptonite and become your superpower?

What if the "epic version" of YOU is just waiting to be unleashed?

What if all those tiny thoughts and choices throughout your day can change the course of your destiny when you know how to focus on them?

Well, guess what? It's possible!

In fact, it can be your REALITY!

We hope this book will speak to the Super Shero and Hero within…

Yes, that wacky, wonderful (and subtly genius) version of us that often gets overshadowed by its "evil twin"… the one that has perhaps convinced us that IT is the "realistic" one…

Haha (said in a slightly mischievous voice), but just wait…

In this book, our mission is to obliterate a few of the "truths and beliefs" that have inadvertently kept you stuck…

Because you see, "EPIC" (whatever that means to you – and expect that definition to fluctuate and change just as you will) is not a destination.

It's a lifestyle…a frequency… a state of flow…

Yes, a deliberate choice made each and every moment…. BUT — we won't get there on autopilot or by doing the "same 'ole, same ole.'" This is not something that we can just understand intellectually and expect to "happen." Nor is it something that works by a "trial and error" or "Plan B" strategy. It's certainly not something that demands an outdated concept of "perfection." This turbo-charged journey into confidence and self-trust is a total "come as you are" adventure.

You heard me right– where we are right now is more than enough!

Just because you may not be "feeling your EPIC" right now doesn't mean you've lost your "Booyah." This book invites you to look at your life through a new lens where you'll no longer tolerate allowing your thoughts to 'think you." Each day is a Moment… an opportunity to stop "fixing the past" and create something going forward that you will remember and cherish forever. Or, it can be a moment that is swept nonchalantly under the rug, perhaps to be forgotten or even regretted, you choose.

Just remember: Every day is yesterday's "someday." We live in a world where the previous generation's "impossibles" become the next generation's new normal every single day. The "I'm Possibilities" are endless. Now is the time – OUR time – to become the Sovereign of our minds and, therefore, the CEO (Chief Excitement Officer) of our future.

Over the next 100 days, we are not moving toward the "goal" of "Epic."

We are exploring a new approach to "aliveness" where every day presents the opportunity to define and redefine our version of "Epic." Think of it as the ultimate amusement park ride where we never have to wait in line, sweat in the sun, or get off the ride if we don't want to…

If we look closely, we'll notice that this "ride" that is carrying us on this adventure is the version of ourselves who is willing to challenge what's possible – even when that means adapting, growing, and making some "not so easy" changes. How we are in this moment is every bit as epically "Be-You-Til-Full" and impressive as we need to be to succeed in this adventure. At the same time, the exciting thing is that there is always more in us just waiting to be unleashed.

As I write 100 Days of Epic, I'm 62 years old – albeit a version that still enjoys wearing sparkles from head to toe, admiring a new variation of rubber chicken, and surrounding myself with as many fur babies as possible.

From my many wanderings around this beautiful planet, I have found that as we grow wiser, we often discover a profound truth: it's the tough times, not the easy ones that reveal the often-overlooked elements essential for transforming an ordinary life into an epic one.

So this is the book that will begin to teach you how to embrace the gifts *within* the falling boulders versus feeling shamed by all the times that Life's boulders have left you scarred.

My belief is that you have earned the right (many times over) to wear these scars proudly as dazzling reminders that YOU were mightier than the things that tried to bring you down.

As you play with this book over the next 100 days, your mission is to compassionately identify and obliterate the thoughts and behaviors that stand between you and your epic potential (dare we say DESTINY) so that you can begin consistently showing up at your best even when Life demands that you become the "reluctant shero or hero" in your own story.

With the world changing around us, the definition of success is also changing and YOU will help to reshape it.

As the great Howard Thurman once said, "**Don't ask what the world needs. Ask what makes you come alive, and go do that. Because what the world needs is people who have come alive**."

Let this book help you ponder who you now choose to show up BE-ing. Allow it to help you hit the "reboot" button to step into your powerful future as a "force to be reckoned with"--both when opportunities abound and when times seem dire.

These 100 days are here to present (double entendre intended) you with an infinite number of "shades of epic." Enough variations so that you can create momentum not simply when times are "good" but also when times feel disruptive, challenging, and uncertain.

My desire is to help you harmonize two behind-the-scenes driving forces within your day: the "Joie de Vivre" (joy of coming fully alive) and the "Carpe Diem" (seizing the day from a place of passion and purpose).

How do we do this, and where did all of this "Epic-ness" come from?

I'll just say that it all starts "between a rock and a hard place"...

But, before I share "the How," let's start with THAT crazy story...

Introducing "the Boulder Story"....

Every cool process deserves a name. What you are about to encounter is much more than a mere process. It is a lifestyle!

....So we decided to give it even more "oooooo factor" by calling it a formula. Specifically, " The Epic You Formula."

It has been five decades in the making!

The quest began when I made it my mission to find the answer to one burning question that neither my prep school nor university education seemed to provide. This one question has gone on to shape my most triumphant decisions. It infuses the core philosophies of every program and strategy I teach, from my basic Interview Ninja course to my Society of Epic Chicks to my coaching programs (including the Titanium Mindset Program) to my Live Your Destiny Breakthrough Experience. It impacts how I try to live every precious moment each day.

In my humble opinion, answering this question should be our one and only goal in life. Everything else is just a target, an idea, or an objective:

> **How do I choose to live so that I can take my final breath declaring, "My life was amazing! I hope that I get a chance to do this again!"**

The quest to answer that question prompted me to spend nine months traveling around the US and Canada with my boyfriend from Georgetown when I was barely 20 years old. We experienced the world from a new perspective courtesy of a yellow Toyota mini-pickup truck that we pretended was part Land Rover and part RV. We dubbed it Vanilla Plumbego.

In other countries, students are often encouraged to take a "gap year" between high school and college. Here in the US, we tend to rush immediately into the professional world, often feeling the pressure to have our entire life path mapped out by the time we are in our early 20s.

Like many, I excelled in school, but I found I was also conflicted. There were careers that spoke to my sense of passion and purpose. However, most of those appeared to have been labeled by "adults in the know" as "unrealistic" or even "irresponsible." No smart Georgetown girl would seriously opt for any of *those* occupations. I felt the pressure to commit to a path, and yet those "reasonable" paths seemed like a recipe for decades of unhappiness. I was haunted by the underlying observation that the very adults who seemed so sure about *my* future often seemed very unfulfilled and unhappy about their own.

After two academically successful years at Georgetown, shaken up a bit personally by two fairly traumatizing professors (a tale for another day), I decided that something had to change. I needed time. I needed space. Even if it involved a certain amount of uncertainty and risk, I needed to look elsewhere for some new perspectives.

My parents were still unraveling the tangle of their lives post-divorce, so I held my breath, took an official extended leave of absence from Georgetown, and headed to NYC with my boyfriend to search for answers (i.e., to find "ME").

The Big Apple provided me with a wealth of insights and ideas. It also allowed me to secure a waitressing job at an upscale restaurant for a year, so I was able to save enough money to buy Vanilla Plumbego and fund Jacques' and my self-proclaimed "tour de force gap year."

The plan? Head north to Canada, then explore down into the western United States. Surely, there would be many examples of how others had decided "how to choose to live." Surely, *some of them must have found a way to do it that made them happy!*

With a truck bed filled with sacks of dried beans, dried fruits, rice, and grains, the wilderness of Canada became our new classroom.

Every moment was dedicated to "the quest":

> How could the human spirit find and fulfill its passion, its purpose, its joy? Was that even important in the grand scheme of things? With so many tangible obligations in life, did we need a sense of exhilaration and delight to feel "fully alive"?

I looked everywhere for these answers, and in nine months my search took me across thousands of miles. I spent time deep in the wilds, never seeing another human being for days. I hiked hundreds of miles over mountains, through deserts, and across the mysterious Canyonlands of Utah. I had my food stolen by bears and mountain goats. I was mistaken for Olivia Newton-John in Ponton, Manitoba (Population: 8). I mastered the art of making deep dish cobbler on a Coleman stove, met an array of intriguing characters at our various stops, and even managed to survive the particularly terrifying moment when Vanilla Plumbego slid precariously near the edge of a cliff, and rolled to a stop just in time.

Yes, it was a life-defining adventure and probably one of the most important gifts I have ever given my soul. Yet, even though I felt the clues all around me, I was still left with the gnawing contradiction between what made me feel truly alive and what seemed to be required to make a living in the "real world."

In the midst of it all, I read book after book. I devoured everything I could get my hands on: Lao Tzu's *Tao Te Ching*, Ram Dass' *The Only Dance There Is*, Carlos Castañeda's *The Teachings of Don Juan*, Antoine de Saint-Exupéry's *The Little Prince,* and numerous other books that explored the nooks and crannies of the hidden world within us.

These books ignited even more questions. So, as I dove back into "real life," I began to immerse myself in an even deeper study of our "inner game." I wanted to understand why some people could face formidable obstacles and emerge as bigger, bolder versions of themselves while others appeared to crash and burn.

Inner game mastery is an objective that's easy to talk about and, in some ways, easy to "know." The challenge for most of us – and this certainly was the case for me – is translating those truths into actions when "reality" starts throwing boulders in our path. Can we tame "our own worst enemy" and resist the temptation to get in our own way?

For me, it became brutally apparent that I could read and study a topic intensely; however, until I could integrate these truths into how I began showing up in my own life, there remained a **huge disconnect** between the way that I knew things "should be" versus the life that I was experiencing.

Especially once I became a mother and found myself as the main breadwinner who wanted desperately to always show up as "Supermom," it felt like there were two alternate universes– the one that promised that we each have "the peaceful warrior"/ "wise yogi version of ourselves" and the other which said that WE ARE our own worst enemy. "It is what it is."

Most people seem resigned to the belief that our minds can't help but constantly criticize, sabotage, and fill us with fear. We are doomed to live our entire life as natural-born self-hecklers. However, our self-loathing doesn't stop there. It seems that we were also trained to believe that not only our minds but our bodies are destined to behave as adversaries. The surrounding evidence seems to imply that we are born into a human vessel that is predetermined genetically. These bodies are destined to fail, shame, and disappoint us to various degrees throughout our lives. We live in fear of disease, injury, uncontrollable weight gain, and those devastating pimples that pop up on the most important day of our lives simply because the day before, we *dared* to *look* at a freshly baked chocolate chunk cookie.

I couldn't help but ponder: If we are doomed to believe that we are our own worst enemy body, mind, and soul (and that the world "out there" is a pretty unforgiving place as well), is it any wonder that our view of ourselves and the world feels stuck, depressed and deflated? The natural "set point" for the average person's life seemed frighteningly close to "impossible."

By the time my third child had arrived, I was in my 30s. I was finding that I had less and less time to read or to consciously focus on my "inner game." The children's father's career had tanked, so like a mama bear whose cubs were being chased by a lion, I descended into that gnarly place where I had time for one focus and one focus only – paying the bills.

The next few decades were what you might consider the "dark ages" of my life – I stepped into the laboratory where I would learn what life looks like when it's lived almost solely through the lens of the "outer game." I became a single mom and sole provider for my kids with an income that kept me neatly caged in the prison of financial terror. In my desperation to find a father figure for my children, I made some (let's just say) "interesting" choices in relationships.

Looking back, it's somewhat miraculous that I managed to raise three thriving adults when, for years, every time I crawled into bed at night, I felt like my soul was imploding. I was nowhere near where I thought that I would be at that point in my life. I was so ashamed. I had this elite education. I was a good person. But despite my best intentions, the more I chased, the more I seemed to be failing. Why on Earth couldn't I seem to figure this out?

Thankfully, aside from consuming more alcohol than I probably should have, I maintained my commitment to nurturing my body with food that pampered my cells versus simply my taste buds. From the time I was in my late teens, I had always embraced some form of a vegetarian/vegan/ pescatarian lifestyle. This discipline with my physical health helped to keep the mental pressures from dragging me under.

The "dark ages" finally came to a head in the early 2000s when my desperation was high and my self-worth was low. I allowed myself to step (with my children) into not one but two abusive relationships virtually back to back. My anxiety level got to such a point that I could not drive on the highway. I was afraid to sleep and was always in that hypervigilant state of "what's going to make him mad." However, amid this trauma, something almost magical seemed to happen.

I later came to refer to this moment as my "Problem of God" moment. It was a flashback to a class that I'd been required to take at Georgetown University to fulfill my religion requirement. The professor was an animated, brilliant soul named Father Cioffe. The class was a deep dive into the works of filmmaker Ingmar Bergman, whose films were notorious for their insights into the role of God in ordinary life.

In this class, we became adept at recognizing the symbolism that Bergman used to represent the presence of God. However, in one film, the customary symbolism was conspicuously missing. Father Cioffe loomed over us, daring us to identify where God was in this film. Even the most outspoken among us was silent. After a particularly triumphant pause, Father Cioffe revealed the "mic drop" answer: it was the complete "absence of God " that made the viewer so aware of the contrast between moments when God was present and times when He was missing.

By 2004, I was living this decade of my life in the middle of the "God is Missing" film. It wasn't so much God that was missing as it was my prioritization was not on my inner game. My sense of Self that was missing. My life was on a hamster wheel of razor blades, and I had no idea how to stop the spinning.

Now squarely in an abusive marriage, I had disintegrated into living basically in captivity due to my fear of triggering "John's" misplaced suspicions. My solace from the madness became what I call my dragon books. I soothed my emotions by turning my imagination loose in the world of fantasy novels. At least within those pages, Good always managed to overcome Evil.

It was on one of my rare trips to Borders Books where "it happened."

As I walked down the aisle in the fantasy section, a book literally seemed to jump off the shelf onto the floor directly in my path. I looked down, and it was not a fantasy novel. It was a little book titled, "Ask and It Is Given." This would be my introduction to the world of Abraham Hicks and the Law of Attraction – a "chance encounter" that would define the way my life would unfold going forward.

My curiosity piqued, I sat down in the chair at the end of the aisle, opened to the middle of the book, and started skimming. Skimming became reading, and I ultimately left with not one Abraham Hicks' book, but three.

This moment began my journey out of my dark abyss into a period where I would see even more emphatically the contrast between a life lived almost solely in the outer game and one guided by the empowered "I'm Possibilities" of the inner game.

Years passed, I made better choices in my relationships and made peace with the fact that I had permission to "fail" and to learn. My children grew toward adulthood and began doing amazing things.

But professionally and financially, "success" seemed to not only elude me but to scorn me. However, this time, I did not allow the things that were "not working" to distract me from my commitment to learning the principles of a "winning" inner game.

Even at my lowest, when I was taking hit after hit financially due to my businesses, I returned to my original question: **How to choose to live so that I could take my final breath declaring, "My life was amazing! I hope that I get a chance to do this again!"**

And my belief held that if I wasn't winning yet, it was because "the game" wasn't over!

Nevertheless, some critical piece in the puzzle was still missing. I knew there were some lessons in my life that I should feel grateful for and even forgive, but emotionally, it still felt impossible.

No matter what I tried, gratitude and forgiveness eluded me. I always seemed drawn back to a vision of myself where my passions and skills had zero translatable value in a world where the outer game and the "she who has the most toys wins" mentality ruled the airwaves.

Honestly speaking, I was not financially or professionally where I wanted to be. Even when the finances seemed to be growing, I by no means loved what I was doing. Yet I had no idea what I might consider "my calling," much less one that could financially support me.

Could my lifelong obsession with how to choose to live and "finding my bliss" actually be what many (even many in my inner circle) seemed to believe– i.e., a totally unrealistic "woo woo" and a waste of time, energy, and focus? An anti-climax to the younger version of me who had shown such "academic promise"?

I won't kid you. There were times when I lay in bed wondering whether all of this inner game stuff was simply a sham.

If it was valid and these were indeed laws, why weren't they working *for me?* Why did I find it so hard to implement? What did all these gurus, teachers, and mentors understand that I wasn't getting?

Then came February 19, 2016.

That day, a single boulder came plummeting off the side of a mountain in Colombia, South America, and literally crushed my daughter Schuyler. (If you're reading this and wondering, her name is pronounced Sky-ler).

Her injuries were MASSIVE… so extensive that medical precedent going back hundreds of years indicated they would be unsurvivable. Apparently, when you can see the brain of the patient, they don't make it. Not only could you see Schuy's exposed brain, but that was just one of the laundry list of injuries that usually proved fatal.

However, the despair I felt – the sense of being powerless to help my daughter – helped me fully embrace the potential of what I now call "the Epic You."

I realized none of my "outer game" skills could help me. Nor could I control any of the "outer game" circumstances. I certainly could not un-do the boulder, nor could I roll up my sleeves and be of assistance to her medical team.

Of all the heart-wrenching emotions that I was feeling, the worst was feeling powerless to help Schuyler.

So, if I couldn't control the outer game, was there anything I could control?

The only possible answer to that question was… yes… my inner game.

These ideas, these strategies that I had studied for decades, were either true or not true. I confess that there were many times that I had doubted them. Now was the time I had to find out: were those invisible "powers" within our minds actually "real"? Because what I needed right now was much bigger than my business or my love life. This was about finding any hidden powers within myself that might in some way help my child.

I decided to dig deep, brave the sudden wave of imposter syndrome, and declare, "Game On!"

Within the first 24 hours, I decided to find the "Epic You" within me and commit to doing whatever it might take to *live* these inner game principles that I had spent so much time studying.

It began by asking a series of new questions…by finding one thought… and then another that felt better than the previous thought **yet still believable**.

Cautiously, I inched my way from thoughts that triggered grief to thoughts that gave me small glimmers of hope. From hope, I looked for thoughts that would usher me into the realm of belief. But even beliefs have cracks in them, so I had to keep going.

Finally, there it was – the thoughts that created a sense of powerful "knowing" in the form of expectation. The expectation that my daughter would be "fine," whatever that new definition of "fine" was destined to be.

It was as if everything at that moment suddenly shifted.

What transpired was a string of miracles so remarkable that it began to look as if Life was conforming to my vision. It wasn't long before even the medical team began referring to us as the miracle family. Every single day, we were seeing results that were typically "impossible."

So yes, against all odds, Schuy survived the unsurvivable.

I became her primary 24/7 caregiver as she embarked upon the long road to regaining independence and discovering the future that now appeared to be quite different from the one that, just months ago, we had all been imagining.

In the process, I reconnected with my love of writing and began chronicling our inner and outer game journey on Facebook. Our "global family" continued to share our story until our following had grown into the thousands. Ultimately, these posts became the *Sky is the Limit* book, one of Amazon's hot new releases in the fall of 2017.

I was asked to share my inner game process with one person and then another. Next came the requests to speak on stage. I discovered that both my passion and my purpose were destined to be fulfilled in a career that I once thought I would "never do" – the world of speaking and coaching.

Looking back, never would my daughter Schuyler or I have dreamed that our own experience would have had such a dramatic impact not only in our own lives but in the lives of thousands of others…

As the years continue to go by, it becomes more and more clear that this crazy boulder has been perhaps my life's greatest teacher amidst a lifetime of great teachers. Life, with its infinite sense of humor as well as wisdom, had found it appropriate to ensure that my ultimate "degree" on the topic of the inner game would come literally from the "school of hard knocks."

But to tell the truth, despite the tears and frustration (and ok, the occasional very loud swear words), I now see that I wouldn't have changed anything!

The majesty of this adventure has been like that breathtaking glimpse of a spider web on a dewy spring morning. One moment, it's invisible, and in the next step, it's there in the morning sunlight, sparkling in its full glory.

I remember the moment in the Miami hospital chapel when that profound understanding hit me. I "saw" the complex brilliance of that sparkling web that spanned the decades of my life. Remarkably, as tortuous as those times of pain and struggle had been to live through, those exact moments transformed me into that tougher, more resilient version of myself. It had been those moments that had caused me to let go of things that had been keeping me playing small. It had been those experiences that had reconnected me with the power of the mind, and that helped me understand the non-negotiable value of becoming the sovereign of my own inner game.

That if I continued a life lived on autopilot, it would almost certainly cost me.

It was becoming more and more apparent that everything that is enduringly epic begins with an epic inner game.

When we refuse to see that, we spend a huge portion of our life licking our wounds down by the curb, believing that "life's a bitch, and then you die."

So are we willing to continue telling ourselves the story that the easier path is the one where we approach life like a giant casino where the house typically wins but where occasionally there is a payoff that keeps us coming back?

As I write this book, I am now 63 years old. I have willingly poured my heart, soul, and a whopping $427,000 into personal, spiritual, and professional development. I consciously (and sometimes unconsciously) dedicated over 50+ precious years of my life in pursuit of the answer to the one question that would reveal itself to be my "true calling." I have encountered mentors as well as "anti-mentors," and I can honestly say that I learned from them all.

My "stupid tax" (as some would call the cost of ignorance, stubbornness, or naivete) was paid in abundance – usually in the currency of fear, self-doubt, people-pleasing, and the constant need to over-achieve while proving to myself that there was significance in being able to endure challenges that others would find insurmountable.

… Of course, I paid a "super stupid tax" in those humiliating moments of "crash and burn" when I insisted on trying to accomplish by myself things that could easily have been achieved had I simply allowed myself to invest earlier in the guidance of great mentors, teachers, and coaches.

My past is littered with the remnants from every battle, camouflaging themselves as scars of shame I had been stubbornly allowing to stand between me and what would ultimately become my true "Destiny."

So why did it take me so darn long to figure all of this out?

Now THAT'S a great question.

I realize now that even with all of those great books at my fingertips, I just couldn't get past the predominant belief in the world around me: that if you can get the "great job," make "lots of money," accumulate "amazing stuff," "live the life," find the "right person," "look the right way," etc. that all of the inner game stuff (i.e., happiness, purpose, and passion) would just follow.

That approach to life didn't work out too well for me, and the truth is that when I look around, it doesn't appear to be working well for too many others.

So what *is* the better approach?

As Einstein said, "We can't solve problems by using the same kind of thinking we used when we created them."

So yes, if you want a different outcome, you must retire the "old approach thinking."

That means being willing to be open to the possibility that the missing link **IS** something within your inner game.

Whether it's neuroscience, energy healing, aikido, tai chi, teachings from diverse religions, spiritual philosophies, the Law of Attraction, the writings of the stoics dating back thousands of years, or live training from the best personal development experts in the world, the core messages are always the same: how well you learn to master the "resources within" determines how you experience all aspects of your life – no exceptions.

An epic inner game *always* shows up as a critical game-changer in achieving something that everyone else believes to be impossible.

If you are striving for a life that makes you feel fully alive personally, physically, or professionally– even spiritually, you must be able to think beyond your current limits.

The question now becomes this: **what is the true cost of settling for a "small mindset" on autopilot versus the benefit of learning how to cultivate an "epic mindset" over which you are sovereign?**

In my humble experience, it is the difference between waking up to a life burdened with self-doubt and regrets versus a life that makes you constantly revel in the experience of being fully and deliciously alive…

This brings me back to why I am writing this book…

Well, my "Epic Chicks and Gents," it's simple.

I know without a doubt that this boulder brought with it a gift, a gift that I don't think you should have to be crushed by a boulder to experience.

What was that gift?

In and amongst all the pain, grief, and uncertainty, this crazy boulder finally shared a crystal-clear insight into the questions that had been the object of my lifelong quest. Ironically, the thing that I had always feared (heartache, loss, "failure") provided me with the answers I had always sought…

I found the process for rediscovering my true Empowered Self. That often overlooked "superpower" within each of us that I now fondly call the "EPIC YOU."

The process for unleashing that gift has evolved into my "EPIC YOU FORMULA."

However, here is the most astonishing discovery that I made…

I realized that although the gift of the "Epic You Formula" transformed so many aspects of my life, it was all those years of struggle, "defeat," and searching made it possible for me to be ready and able to *see this gift*.

In other words, **life had to get me "ready to be ready."**

I had to decipher the runway that all of these clues were creating.

It was like that moment in *The Wizard of Oz* when Glenda the Good Witch tells Dorothy that she's had the power all along with the ruby red slippers. The Scarecrow asks Glenda why she hadn't just told Dorothy about her power earlier. Glenda responds that she had to discover this for herself. In other words, I guess I owed this new sense of Self that I was discovering to all of those darned "flying monkeys." Who knew?

So, you might say that bizarrely, even with all of the difficulty that it bestowed upon our family, this boulder also had a duality. In many ways, for both my daughter and me, this boulder became our Glenda, pointing out the ruby red slippers alongside all the scars.

It was these scars, ironically, that came together to create the perfect "code" so that I'd be ready to see "the formula" that would allow me to be the mother that my daughter so desperately needed.

So yes, that process of "getting ready to be ready" began when I didn't even realize it was happening. Back in my 20s, 30s, 40s, and 50s, I was taking hit after hit *after hit* and wondering why all these heart-wrenching things were happening.

I now know that it was precisely those times throughout my life of so much pain and emotional angst that got me ready to not only ask some new questions but to be open to some new answers. Open to entertain the possibility that the "tried and true beliefs and approaches" were the root of the problem.

Had I not experienced *and reacted exactly the way that I did to* every tear, every heartache, every moment of rage and frustration, I would not have been "ready" when that boulder fell to finally "see" and activate this "Epic You Formula."

Epic results *demand* an epic inner game.

Unfortunately, so few of us are deliberately taught how to play it.

So, this book is intended to serve as the catalyst to get you "ready to be ready" for epic things to start happening in your life. We'll be targeting the "prequel" to your "Epic Next Step Forward Story" by helping you experience what it can feel like to recalibrate that critical "inner game."

In case you're not familiar with the "inner game," I refer to it not simply as your mindset but more like your entire "inner technology" (I.T.) fused with the most brilliant aspects of your intuition, your energy/ frequency, and the mysterious combination of heart, soul and the Divine.

As you embark upon your 100 Days of Epic, you might say our mission is to replace the "out-of-date code" with new code. (Or, dare I say, to help you get your "I.T." together as you prep for something BIG!) My desire is to help you cultivate a new appreciation for your inner game and an elevated awareness of the treasure within even the most "negative" aspects of your existing story…

I call what we'll be focusing on…

Mastering The Epic 3…

When you start truly embodying this, it can feel almost like "magic." Most of us are a little bit skeptical when we hear the word "magic." We have been shaped into the current version of ourselves in a world overflowing with "it is what it is" (even when the "what is" cannot easily be explained). Yet, when the world seems to be crashing in around us, we often pray for that twist of fate that changes everything… that miracle to come and save the day and achieve *that impossible thing* that we seem incapable of creating.

Within this realm of new approaches and new possibilities – the "what ifs" that we often dare not mutter out loud (even to ourselves) – lies the untapped and often unrecognized potential of even the most "ordinary person's" inner game. *It is our most precious resource – the deliberately harmonized power of heart and mind.*

It's like laying the perfect foundation before you start building the castle of your dreams.

So, what are these "secret" building blocks that will start the process of "making over" your inner game? Things that will begin transforming thoughts and beliefs that have been acting like kryptonite to your superpower?

I call them "The EPIC 3."

These are the three foundational blocks of the inner game upon which I have built the Epic You Formula. This formula has led to not only overcoming seemingly insurmountable obstacles but to seeing a new level of "epic" become the "new normal" in all aspects of my life personally, emotionally, financially, professionally, spiritually, and physically.

I have now taught this formula to hundreds of clients. I have seen over and over again that those who create epic lives for themselves commit to learning to master these three things:

- **Focus** (And What We Make That Focus Mean)
- **Language** (The Communication That We Have In Our Own Inner Narrative As Well As With Others)
- **Fear** (How We Ultimately Choose to Use Our Imagination – as Dream Killers or Empowered Destiny Turbo-Chargers)

Yes, it's that simple – but don't be tempted to confuse simple with easy.

Why?

Because the programming we absorbed as children has been deeply entrenched, few of us believe that we have the power to revisit – much less successfully rewire – those childhood assessments.

Instead, we convince ourselves that we ARE those beliefs. "That's just who I am." "You can't teach an old dog new tricks."

Today, I invite you to begin changing that belief.

I encourage you to begin this chapter in your life where you give yourself permission to ask new questions and see your potential in a more empathetic light. A chapter where you are not only worthy, but you ARE more than enough. One that makes you agile, able to adapt, and always ready to blossom and grow.

THE EPIC 3

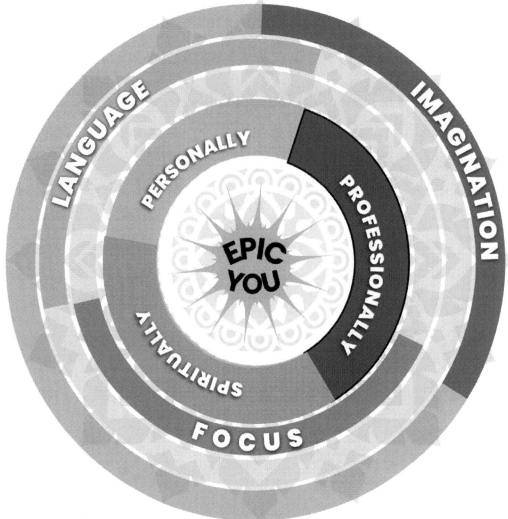

Mastery of Focus:
Mastery of Focus is the profound ability to harnes one's attentiona dnd direct it purposefully, irrespective of external distractions or internal mental chatter. It's a skill cultivated through deliberate practice, enabling individuals to channel their energies into the present moment and engage fully with their chosen objectives empowering them to create epic transformations in their lives.

Mastery of Language:
Mastery of Language is the art of consciously selecting and crafting one's words and thoughts to shape a powerful and empowering inner dialogue. It involves using language to create a positive and constructive narrative that aligns with one's goals and values, ultimately influencing emotions and behavior in ways that lead to epic personal and professional achievements.

Mastery of Imagination:
Mastery of Imagination is the ability to harness the creative power of the mind to envision and shape a future filled with epic possibilities. It involves breaking free from limiting beliefs, daring to dream big, and using the imagination as a tool for designing a life that aligns with one's deepest passions and purposes. This mastery empowers individuals to tap into their inner wellspring of creativity, paving the way for extraordinary personal and professional transformations.

Dare to see yourself as that EPIC version of you – all you have ever imagined and then some. "Perfectly imperfect" just as you are. THE piece in the masterpiece that makes everything around you come even more alive.

With this book, I welcome you to the moment in your life where all systems are "go" and where everything is set for you to unleash THE MOST EPIC VERSION OF YOU!

[Do I hear a full-blown EPIC BOOYAH! I certainly hope so!]

How to Use This Book:

This book has been designed to be as adaptable as you are. Think of it as sort of an "Inner Game Playbook" versus an actual "how to" book.

My focus will not be so much on answering the "how." The truth is that most of us often know the "hows" intellectually. We've heard them before, and we technically understand them. It's not as much a question of rehashing the "how do we do that" as it is a question of WHO. Who do we have to choose to show up *BE-ing* for us to execute the "how"?

Each day in *100 Days of Epic: Experience a Total Life Makeover and Live Your Destiny Starting Today* will come with these two elements with an optional third element to enhance your sense of fun and play:

1. **An element of insight and strategy** so that you can understand the "why" behind the action and create an experience and/or way of thought that more deeply aligns you with your "epic you." In some cases, I'll share this in the form of an excerpt from my own "Tinkerbell Project Blog" so that you can experience the potential dialogue that you too can choose to have with your "soulmate," "God Universe," "Source," "God" or even your "Global family."
2. **An action step/ "mission"** so that you can develop habits that lean into the direction of "The Epic 3." Over time, we want your reflexes to begin to turn toward this new way of processing your thoughts, feelings, and experiences.
3. **The opportunity to gamify your experience with our 100 Days of Epic Success Tracker!** Want even more momentum? Tap into the HUGE advantage of dopamine. Creators of video games all the way back to Pac-man, learned that we humans love to play, especially when it involves constant wins. Why? Because each time we win, our brains release dopamine, which gives us that "feel good" rush. Eventually, creators of experiences ranging from Pokemon Go to Duolingo realized the potential rush from dopamine could keep us persisting even when the challenges get tough. So we had an idea: why not give you the opportunity to experience these dopamine wins during your journey through the 100 Days of Epic book? Do you love that idea as much as we do?

Then here's all you need to do: Go to www.100DaysofEpic.com/YouWin and enter your name and email address for easy access to our super juicy, dare I say totally EPIC TRACKER. There, you can keep track of your points per day using gold stars, your favorite chicken stickers, or whatever your heart desires – even a good old-fashioned check mark! (And yes, it's not an accident that the actions are worth more and more points as you get further into the days! Just saying!) So why not make this 100 Days epically FUN as well as impactful!! Keep your motivation going and earn up to 686 stars in the process! Booyah!

However you decide to use this book, I highly encourage you to dive into all elements 1000% so that you can begin creating new habits and expectations. **And perhaps discover a transformational game that is worth repeating! Wink!**

One other optional resource is our **100 Days of Epic Digital Playbook,** which you can access here:

www.100DaysofEpic.com/Playbook

These are actual worksheets that will help you go even deeper into this 100-day quest. They are not essential in order to be successful. They have been created for those of you who are committed to seeing an even richer, more profound transformation and gaining the most for their time investment at the end of these 100 days.

Resist the urge to expect the deeper transformations to happen quickly. Although we have created the playbook to help you make the shifts as quickly and "ease-ily" as possible, you are unique. When you discover blocks and barriers, be patient. Your mind has constructed them believing that these protect you. You must regain your heart, mind, and soul's trust before they are willing to release these walls. Some changes will take more time than others. However, when you patiently persist, the shift will occur.

This 100 Days of Epic is not a magic wand or an "easy button." This is an introduction to a new world within so you can recognize it when you see it. That way, as you move forward, you will realize when you are getting "warmer" and when you're getting "colder" in your pursuit of Epic. You will be on the path for your moment when you discover that you are "ready to be READY."

Notice, also, that I put certain words in quotation marks. That is deliberate. When you see these words within the quote, consider it an invitation to pause and consider the invisible story that we typically associate with this word. Often, you'll see that these words carry with them some biases and some "truths" that are worth questioning. Language is a critical component of these 100 days, so I invite you to become very aware of the implications beneath some of our most commonly used words and phrases.

One other bit of navigational instruction: You will notice that I mention the frequency of your inner game. What I'm referring to is the connection between your inner game and what neuroscientists often refer to as your electromagnetic field.

What is this electromagnetic field?

Experts like Dr. Joe Dispenza emphasize that it is a dynamic force generated by the human body. It's rooted in the idea that our thoughts and emotions are not merely abstract processes but are closely tied to physical processes within the body. Based on their studies, when we think or feel, the brain and heart emit measurable electromagnetic frequencies. These frequencies are like the signals of a radio station, broadcasting our emotional states and thoughts into the world and interacting with the energies around us.

This concept is intricately connected to what I will be calling the "inner game frequency." Just as radio frequencies carry specific information, our emotional states and thoughts create unique frequencies that not only influence our internal experiences but also have the potential to attract or resonate with similar energies in the external world. This understanding underscores the importance of cultivating a positive inner game frequency because it can most certainly shape our experiences, interactions, and even opportunities in life.

By the way, you may be asking: Do I have to do every page for this to work?

Not necessarily. You can opt to use *100 Days of Epic,* almost like some might use "motivations for the day" or "angel cards"; just open up a page for that day.

However, we have laid out the book so that those who do follow it in order can experience a progression. Think of it almost like a "reverse onion." We'll start by building an empowered core and then add layers.

We'll begin introducing you to the power of a life lived in alignment with The Epic 3. Again, progress isn't measured by speed. Our objective is **consistency,** so we'll approach this as if you're constructing an intricate bejeweled crown. Each day's target is simply one more jewel in the crown.

We will spotlight each of The Epic 3, one at a time.

This means that the first third of the book will help you build your focusing "muscle." You'll learn to focus more deliberately and take ownership of what you are making those things you focus on mean.

As you become more fluent in actively directing your focus, we'll begin adding your language into the mix.

We're talking not only about how you communicate with others but also about how you tolerate communicating with *yourself*. Words act like "spells," so it's important to know how your words influence everything from your thoughts to your feelings, to your actions, and therefore to your results.

The last portion of the book addresses the final layer: mastery of fear – or, more accurately, mastery of imagination.

You'll learn how to begin tapping into the limitless resources within your imagination so that you can truly aspire to create a life that you love waking up to. Remember that it's your *observation* that helps to identify what it is that you want next, *and it's your imagination that helps you create the emotional/energetic frequency that allows you to create it.*

Awareness is one of the essential steps to change, so be "ruthlessly empathetic" with yourself when you discover a pattern that has been getting in your way. Instead of scolding yourself, commit to celebrating this new awareness and toward your consistent growth.

So, it's time to dive in and get started!

Allow yourself to remember as you embark upon the next 100 days that **we may not always control how long we get to play on this planet, but we definitely get to choose how epically we live while we are playing here…**

NOW IS YOUR TIME.

Don't waste your brilliant potential waiting for the dust to settle so that you can convince yourself that you are "ready."

Roll up your sleeves and choose to do whatever it takes to BE READY. (Or at least "ready-er"…!)

If you have read this far, clearly now is your time to find what YOU have been searching your entire life for – to choose to fall in love with all aspects of your life and BE that EPIC version of YOU!

Have fun with this!! You've got this!

To 100 Epic Days of Remarkable Delight!

Day 1 – FOCUS: Meet #1 OF THE EPIC 3 – The Power of Deliberate Focus and Unraveling the Secrets of Manifestation

Ah, that delicious word: focus.

The dictionary defines the word focus as the center of interest or activity.

Yet, is there an accompanying guide that can help us discern *what* we should be focusing on? Because clearly, what we choose to make the center of our interest and activity will shape how we experience our lives, yes?

Then we get to this other little truth, now reinforced by the research of neuroscience:

"What you focus on expands."

That can be one of the most frustrating and misunderstood "revelations" in the world of personal development and the inner game.

Let's be honest. How many times have you heard that and silently thought, "If what I focus on expands and I'm staring at my bank account, why isn't it expanding???"

The concept of focus, along with ideas like "manifesting," "affirmations," and "declarations," can leave many feeling bewildered and defeated, regardless of whether they approach it from the perspective of personal development, Law of Attraction, or neuroscience.

I promise you, I was absolutely no different.

I spent years believing that I was focusing on what I wanted — only to continue to see more and more of the things that caused me stress and frustration. I couldn't understand why I was getting so many things I *didn't* want when I was "definitely" focused on the opposite. I was focusing so hard that it's fair to say that I was "obsessing" on these things. So, how could I turn this around and start getting the results that I wanted?

I tried journaling, affirmations, meditations, and even praying. Most of the time, all it led to was me doubting myself. I crawled into bed feeling like (once again) I was failing while others were figuring it out and succeeding.

But the truth was, I wasn't "trying everything." I was trying the *same things over and over again.*

You see, your mind will keep repeating the same beliefs and patterns until it understands and believes there is a better way to do things.

To truly harness the power of focus, we must understand how to execute it correctly and overcome the common pitfalls of *misunderstanding*. Until we manage that, we stay on that same hamster wheel, wondering why our efforts don't pan out.

So here's the first lesson to learn about focus:

Your words do not indicate your true focus; your emotional energy, your "state," reveals your focus.

To phrase it slightly differently, that which is truly your center of attention will create a corresponding state and energy frequency.

If it's any solace, know that most people walk around believing they are talking about (focusing on) what they want. If you become aware of their energy, you will see that they are focusing on exactly the opposite.

Here's what I mean:

When most people envision where they want to be in a year, they describe their desires. However, it's essential to observe the emotional energy—the state—behind their words. Are they bubbling over with joy and anticipation like a child entering a toy store, or are they conveying a grocery list of missing or unsatisfying aspects of life?

The latter indicates a focus on lack, which can lead to *attracting more of what is missing*.

Let's imagine Gloria and Susan are sitting in the posh coffee spot in the Edition, Tampa's only 5-star hotel. As they sip on their lavender-infused lattés, Susan asks Gloria where she wants to be in a year. Gloria takes another sip of her latté and, with an emphatic sigh, declares, "A year from now, I want to be in a job that I actually love… something that finally pays me what I'm worth… I cannot tell you how tired I am of being paid less than six figures when I know that two of my colleagues are making at least that… You know what I mean??"

Susan rolls her eyes and shakes her head in agreement.

Gloria continues, "I want to be able to buy a house with a pool for a price that won't kill me… I'm so pissed that I missed the opportunity to grab something really nice when real estate prices were reasonable…"

"I know," Susan agrees. "Prices now are just terrible. Did you hear how much Ben and Sally paid for their new place?"

"Oh my gosh, yes." Gloria continues, "It makes me not even want to look! And, of course, I want to have much more time to enjoy my family… more work/life balance, you know…even my poor dog acts like she never gets to see me enough… And oy! How many years has it been since I took a real vacation? What I wouldn't give to get away from this company's toxic environment …!"

Sound familiar?

It sounds like Gloria is talking about what she truly wants, doesn't it?

However, go back and take a closer look. Isn't she focusing on the *checklist of all she believes is missing?* That's why when you hear those words, you feel a crunch rather than an infectious excitement.

Can you see why the concept of "what you focus on will expand" has felt just a wee bit confusing?

We can believe that we're talking about what we want. Still, we're setting into motion a frequency that will bring more of exactly the opposite!

NOW! Get excited because we're about to learn the more effective way for your mind to approach focusing and even manifesting.

It begins by putting a new question front and center**:**

That **new question** to start regularly asking yourself is, **"What has my attention right now?"**

If you will diligently and patiently *and consistently* play with these strategies over the next 100 days, you **will** begin to see a shift. Not just simply in how you feel but also in the results that you begin to see.

I encourage you, again, to think of this like a "reverse onion." Rather than pulling back the layers of the onion, we are starting with a small core and then adding to it!

Ready for some epic momentum to start showing up in your life?

Yes? Ok, let's get started!

Let me first share something that took me a long time to understand and master.

This is one of the most important subtleties on the topic of focus. When you can understand and adjust accordingly, great things begin to happen.

EPIC NINJA FACT ABOUT FOCUSING #1:

> **When we're desperate or deeply desiring something to the point where we feel like we "must" have it, we often turn to manifestation or prayer to help us achieve the "impossible." Ironically, during these moments of *desperation* that we may feel like the "focusing stuff" is not working.** The reason it's "not working" lies in our inability to direct our minds effectively and in our inability to identify that it's **not the *thing*** but the *feeling* that we want.
>
> When we believe that it's *one thing* that we want, that leads us to feel **the *fear of scarcity*.** When we realize that it's simply ***the feeling* that we desire**, we can relax into realizing that an **infinite number of paths will get us there.**
>
> **We feel calm confidence versus desperation – all due to where we focus.**
>
> So, yes, **desperation is the enemy of manifestation and focus.**

EPIC NINJA FACT ABOUT FOCUSING #2:

> When we're overwhelmed with the feeling of desperation, we often allow our minds to run on autopilot. **When our thoughts run on autopilot, it's like publicly revealing the passwords to our bank accounts and removing the anti-virus protection from our technology.** It allows anything and anyone access to our most valuable resource – the thoughts in our mind, even our identity, and how we see ourselves. If anything should be monitored, filtered, and sometimes contained, it's the words and phrases that we often "carte blanche" consume.
>
> The result? A mind where thoughts "**think us**," leaving us at the mercy of whichever thought carries the strongest emotional charge.

So, how *should* we be focusing on creating things in our life that we want?

Is there such a thing as "manifesting" what we wish to create?

I will answer that by sharing a story from my own experience and let you be the judge.

When I was expecting my first child, I playfully decided that the baby would be born on Christmas because my mom mentioned it in passing. It was infused with fun and excitement, not desperation. I told *everyone* that my son was going to arrive on Christmas. Day in, day out, "My son is going to be born on Christmas!"

Lo and behold, my son arrived on Christmas.

For my second child's due date was April, so I confidently declared that she would be born on April 1st. Afterall…wink…I was born on July 4th, and my son was born on Christmas; a pattern had begun. I was *so sure* my second child would be born on April 1st that I declared the following: if this child were a boy, we would name him after my uncle, *who was also born on April 1*. Again, it was lighthearted and joyful. No sense of desperation or urgency. Sure enough, even though my OB-GYN said it was "highly unlikely," my daughter Saya arrived on April 1st.

With my third child, her due date was in June. You guessed it. I immediately went to the calendar and declared that this child would be born on Memorial Day. After all… wink … I was born on July 4th, my son was born on Christmas, and my other daughter was born on April Fool's Day. The energy behind this declaration was positive and enthusiastic. Like the previous two pregnancies, I walked around telling *everyone* my prediction. And guess what? Yep, Schuyler arrived on Memorial Day. Our entire family was born on holidays!

Coincidence or an example of the power of focus and envisioning?

The fact that we can't explain these occurrences isn't as important as the prevalent emotions: joy, happiness, and excitement. These were fun ideas, not desperate yearnings. Contrast this with moments when we desire more money or a better relationship, and we may find ourselves in a state of lack, fear, and powerlessness.

If manifestations do occur, one thing is clear: the frequency that inspires them has to be one of possibility, not desperation.

So, your mission in the first part of our 100 Days of Epic is this:

1. Learn to deliberately identify your true focus— the things that you are making the "center of your interest or activity" and the power that you are giving these things to influence your experience.
2. Shift your focus from the lack of what you want to the presence of what you desire.
3. Learn to deliberately choose the things that you will make the center of your attention versus allowing them to impose their dominance on you.
4. Get better at regulating your thoughts and responses to what is going on around you so that you become the sovereign of your emotional state.
5. Recognize how joyous and empowered states lead to better outcomes in all aspects of life.
6. Become aware of the contrast between moments when you feel great, just okay, or dismal. Pay attention to the thoughts that led to those states because your emotional energy will indicate your true focus.

As you get more deliberate about consciously selecting your focus, notice that what you truly desire isn't the external manifestation of a specific thing itself; it's the feelings associated with it.

In other words, it's not that you must have a specific lover. It's that you have been craving that specific lover because you believe that this lover will give you those specific feelings, love, connection, etc.

When you focus on the energy of those feelings rather than the specific external outcome, you'll unlock a world of creative possibilities.

This means that as you embark on this journey of deliberate focus, you'll find that your "limits" were just illusions, and bold new horizons await you.

Indeed, as you decide to become the Sovereign of your mind and over how you process your experiences, you will have a very different sense of "aliveness" and "what's possible." More than when you had been leaving your thoughts/focus almost entirely on autopilot.

So, let's dive in and explore some ways to get familiar with the first of **The Epic 3: THE POWER OF DELIBERATE FOCUS!**

"One of the greatest discoveries a person makes is to find they can do what they were afraid they couldn't do."
HENRY FORD

TODAY'S ACTION STEPS:

- ***Play with writing a new story about where you want to be a year from today based on the presence of what you want – specifically what you want to be feeling. Date it one year from today and write it in the present tense. "On [Date], I am waking up exhilarated by the day ahead…" (+1 Gold Star)***
- ***Go out and observe yourself today, being epically aware of when you are truly focusing on the presence of what you want or evidence of the lack of the presence of what you want. (+2 Gold Stars)***
- ***Bonus points if you also journal your discovery about your current focus at the end of your day. (+1 Gold Star) Booyah!***

TOTAL POSSIBLE STARS FROM TODAY: 4 STARS

Day 2 – FOCUS: Creating Your Remarkable Moment

Welcome to the exhilarating journey of creating something unexpected and remarkable! Right here, right now, this very moment is your golden opportunity! The past might have thrown some boulders your way, but guess what? Today is a fresh start, so let's get ready to "play"!

As we begin to have some fun with the concept of "Focus," we'll start very simply by choosing to point our focus toward things that we find remarkable. In other words, our mission is to make the "center of our interest and activities" things that we find remarkable.

How many different ways can you achieve that?

What are elements that you can introduce into your routine, your work, your play, your family, and your spiritual life (yes, ALL the aspects of your life) that feel incredible?

Feeling stuck? It happens to the best of us. But here's the trick—*where* you direct your focus matters big time! As we are beginning to understand, what you focus on becomes the "center of your interest" – the focus of your camera lens – and what's at the center of your camera lens impacts how you feel. It also affects your frequency.

Are you dwelling on the presence of those pesky boulders or the lack of what you wish for? It's time to hit the refresh button and break free from the habits of our past!

Remember to keep it simple.

When your "center of interest" (your focus) slips to something that doesn't please you, reboot the moment by asking yourself, "**What has my attention right now, and what can I refocus my attention onto that will feel more remarkable?**"

We often make comments that "predict" the day ahead, destined very often to become self-fulfilling prophecies. So inadvertently, we end up piling boulder on top of boulder until the weight feels unbearable…

"My days just all blend into one."

"I have no motivation to do anything."

"I am stuck."

"I've tried everything, but nothing ever seems to work."

"It's just too hard to change things."

Beginning today, let's redefine the past—it's not just scars and obstacles; it's a treasure trove of opportunities! You get to choose how you interpret every single story, every single event that has happened in your past. Are you going to make the data mean that these things are holding you back, or are they propelling you forward like a rocket? After all, until you infuse it with meaning and emotion, *it's just data.*

The Epic Chick or Gent looks at each day as a blank movie screen, ready to project all of life's incredible possibilities! It's like they're the directors of their own blockbuster movie, and today is the grand premiere! Take a bow, folks!

Now, here's a crucial choice, and you're gonna love this—whether you make it consciously or subconsciously, it's going to happen! Will you let the past dictate your future, or will you take out your "movie camera" and create something different and *remarkable*?

Today is all about the remarkable – and your ability to discover your power to claim it! Be a giver of joy, send someone flowers, explore a museum or reach out to one of those big fishes" you've been too shy to call! Start that book or launch that YouTube channel – whatever it is that will make your heart sing.

Now, here's the best part—shift the spotlight from "what's wrong with this story" to "what's EPIC about YOUR story?" Now THAT'S remarkable. Change your focus, and the whole tale transforms!

This journey isn't about what you need to DO; it's about who you need to BE.

So, dive in, identify what matters, and choose "the center of your attention" wisely.

Day 2 is all about launching the authentic, incredible, and brilliantly irreplaceable YOU! Are you ready to soar? Let's get out there and focus on creating something *remarkable!*

TODAY'S ACTION STEPS:

- ***Brainstorm a list of 5-10 ways to initiate things that feel "unexpected and remarkable" today. (+1 Gold Star)***
- ***Go out and implement! (+2 Gold Stars)***
- ***Bonus points if you also set reminders on your phone to regularly do "unexpected and remarkable" things going forward! "Hey Siri! Hey Alexa!" (+1 Gold Star) Booyah!***

TOTAL POSSIBLE STARS FROM TODAY: 4 STARS

Day 3 – FOCUS: Elevate Your Focus: Embrace the Realm of Infinite Possibilities

Yesterday, our mission was to guide our focus toward things that felt unexpected and remarkable as well as to reboot our focus when things that did not energize us or take us closer to our target became our "center of interest."

A big lesson we uncovered was that the things we allow to become our "center of interest" shape how we feel about our days and, ultimately, our entire lives. When we can more deliberately filter what becomes our center of interest, we can then exert influence over what we focus on.

Today, on day 3, let's explore our obsession with needing to get to "the bottom of things" when things appear to be going "wrong." It's a concept that I have pondered for years because something just felt a little "off" in that focus. I wrote the following in an entry in my "Tinkerbell Project Blog." See if you agree:

Dear Lovely Universe and Soul Mate,

As I climb into my bed after a busy yet fulfilling day, I think back on a few stolen moments of "self-care" this past Saturday....Sitting there on my back porch soaking in the sounds and cool temps on that luxuriously "perfect" afternoon...

My three Diva dachshunds were nestled in their "den" next to me. The trickling flow from the fountain beside the porch created a sound that absolutely caressed my soul. The temperature here was finally cool and inviting.

And, of course, my sweet daughter sat there in the chair on the back porch next to me...

It seems only yesterday when this beautiful young woman graduated from Yale and started her year-long fellowship in South America. One day, she was off to work with the native population in Peru— helping to build a school and studying ways that social enterprise could make a future impact on the population.

Not even six months later, she would be in the ICU fighting what seemed to be an impossible battle thanks to a boulder that had fallen from the side of a mountain, leaving her within inches of death.

Yet, I have learned in more than six decades of life that things do not always unfold how we expect them to. That yes, there will be monstrous events, horrible challenges — and sometimes literally boulders on our path. But there will also be miracles and things so magical that some will question whether they truly can be real.

As I get ready to turn on my evening meditation and drift into sleep, it strikes me that ***we shouldn't be trying to get "to the bottom of things." We should focus on getting beyond the things that would drag us to the bottom.***

Epic is not imposed upon us; it is a conscious choice—a realm of infinite possibilities often disguised as formidable rocks.

Epic is what happens when you dare to adventure beyond the predictable.

Epic is never forced upon us. It is a choice. A frequency. A possibility. A profound gift that sometimes arrives looking like a formidable rock.

The secrets of the universe lie not in deciphering the depths but in embracing the heights.

Our inner game frequency is what holds the key to harmonizing the genius of the mind with the wisdom of the soul.

Today, I invite you, dear soul, to turn your gaze towards the limitless sky and dare to explore the endless horizons of what could be.

To The Magic of Aliveness!

xoxo

Meridith

So, Epic Chick or Gent, as you read this, if yesterday was about creating the remarkable, let today be about creating the "I'm Possible." What purpose does it really serve to make the "center of your interest" the bottom of the abyss? If those blue skies truly have no limit, why would you waste one more moment looking down?

Day 3 is all about realizing that beyond the "sky's limits" entire galaxies are waiting to be explored! Your mission is to practice redirecting your focus from the LACK of the presence of what you want to the PRESENCE of infinite possibilities. You are worthy of the remarkable and worthy of the "I'm Possible."

Because…If not YOU, then WHO?

TODAY'S ACTION STEPS:

- *Start writing or speaking stories that answer the question, "Wouldn't it be epic if…?" Challenge yourself to go even bigger than usual, even to the place that might feel a wee bit "unlikely, if not impossible." (+1 Gold Star)*
- *Go out and observe where you are, giving attention to roadblocks without looking for clues to opportunities within these blocks. What could be the hidden opportunities or new questions you can discover thanks to these fallen boulders? (+2 Gold Stars)*
- *Bonus points if you catch yourself obsessing over a boulder and reframe your focus onto the practice of looking for the "hidden clue." (+1 Gold Star) Booyah!*

TOTAL POSSIBLE STARS FROM TODAY: 4 STARS

Day 4 – FOCUS: Embrace Your Epic Power and Worthiness

Close your eyes for one moment and imagine the feeling of stepping out into the world as the most epic version of yourself:

Who is that person?

What kind of thoughts are you thinking?

How are you dressed? How are you feeling?

What type of "BE-ing" do others perceive you to be?

What sort of positive impact are you making on the world around you?

Take a moment to imagine that…

Life consists of an eternal string of moments that are here for the choreographing. And you are the master of this masterpiece…. potentially….You can choose to spend your moments chasing, worrying, complaining, and "not enoughing." You can believe that the people, places, and circumstances that surround you are ruling your destiny.

OR -- you can use this day to focus on finding the seeds of Epic in every moment and in every aspect of YOURSELF. This is the true sense of worthiness, of being more than enough.

Take a moment to experience *this sense of enoughness as the true "center of your interest."* We have focused on the remarkable. We have focused on the I'm Possible. Today is the day to focus on the "I am infinitely more than enough-ness!"

It is time to envision what your life could feel like were you to give yourself carte blanche authority to reclaim your power and assert your sovereignty over the yet-to-be-written story ahead. Now is your time… It is time to step out into the world as the version of YOU that you have always wished you could show up BE-ing!

Feel your power as you imagine the possibilities. Bask in the delicious emotion that can only be described as your glorious worthiness! Today, entertain the possibility that everything you desire can come to you as easily as a butterfly comes upon "its flower." As the great Rumi once said, **"What you seek is seeking you!"**

Showing up "in your power" is a choice … It involves deliberately tapping into the "Knowing" within yourself that you are unique and irreplaceable. What you bring into this world —and all you have lived — has value.

What about the experiences that challenge you?

These often prove to be the very experiences that transform a "normal" life into an epic one. These moments you hope never to live again still have their value.

It is in these moments of "failure," "shame," "fury," and "defeat" that you grow and discover what that highest expression of yourself might indeed be. You are here with your own specific set of experiences and a profound complexity…

You are here to share your wisdom…to impact…to transform…to discover your "perfectly imperfect" path toward the EPIC… to "real eyes" your beauty, and the many ways you can come truly alive…

So today, take time throughout the day to savor the worthiness and more-than-enoughness within this BE-ing that we call YOU.

Let your "center of interest" be this and only this: The knowing that you are remarkable. You are I'm Possible. You are worthy. You are deliciously and EPICALLY you!! The best part of your story is still ahead!

TODAY'S ACTION STEPS:

- *Write these words on an 8 X 11 blank paper: I AM REMARKABLE. I'M POSSIBLE. I AM ENOUGH. I'VE GOT THIS. Now, attach this to your bathroom mirror and look at it at least several times during the day. (+1 Gold Star)*
- *Write the same message and turn it into wallpaper on your phone! Look at it throughout the day and let the words sink in. (+2 Gold Stars)*
- *Bonus points if you go out into the world and play with setting the intention of this: I intend to see more evidence bubbling up around me that I am unique and remarkable. I intend to feel boundless joy as I see the benefits my gifts and skills bring into my world. (+1 Gold Star) Booyah!*

TOTAL POSSIBLE STARS FROM TODAY: 4 STARS

Day 5 – FOCUS: Be the Sovereign of Your Epic Story

So now that we've spent a few days playing with the potential of what a deliberately focused "center of interest" might be, let's explore the impact of a focus that has been conditioned just to be whatever circumstances "force it" to be.

In fact, let's start with this big question:

In the past, has your focus typically energized you? Has it moved you closer to the "epic" that you want?

Let's ponder it a bit differently.

Consider this: Would you ever consider waking up in the morning and removing all of your passwords from your bank account and technology???

Would you allow someone to convince you to delete all of the virus protection on your computers and phone? How about leaving your front door wide open and the keys in your car?

With your technology and other valuables, would you be willing to trust that whatever is "meant" to happen will? Would you be willing to forgo all of those passwords and virus protections so that others don't label you as untrusting, uncooperative, or unwelcome?

Chances are, you're smiling right now – and saying, "No way!"

Yet… that's what we do all day, every day when it comes to the thoughts we allow to lurk in our minds and the comments from others we choose to listen to and consider.

It's not simply that you might be allowing other people's words and behavior to impact you emotionally. It's that you might be allowing your OWN unfiltered words to impact you. Letting them dictate what you allow to become "the center of your interest."

Why?

Because, dear one, chances are that you have grown to have "sloppy thinking syndrome." What do I mean by that? Simply put, you have not been deliberately choosing to think specific thoughts. You have been allowing your thoughts to *think you.*

And your thoughts begin with your focus.

Even when the world is going "crazy" around you, your focus is one thing that is TOTALLY within your control. In fact, you cannot delegate it, automate it, AI it, or even eliminate it.

Let's follow the process:

> What you focus on, your mind creates a story about.
>
> You have a split-second gap to influence what you wish that story to be.
>
> Then, your story triggers what you make this object of your focus mean.
>
> This meaning then, of course, becomes the catalyst for that deluge of emotions!
>
> Emotions then cause you to react, creating your emotional/energetic state (frequency).
>
> This state tends to dictate your actions and even your words.
>
> Your words and actions have an impact, so <BOOM> they lead to a specific result.

So yes, your focus ("your center of interest") impacts your result.

Therefore, does it make sense to allow your focus to be on autopilot or default? Might it be a smart idea to start creating some system of "virus protection or password protection" for the thoughts that you allow to gain traction in your mind?

Tapping into the most epic version of yourself means committing to practicing AWARENESS.

Specifically, the awareness of what you are focusing on AND WHAT YOU MAKE THAT PERSON, PLACE, THING OR EXPERIENCE MEAN.

Your imagination is GOING to create a story, so you *need to* dive in and consciously decide that YOU will be the story's author.

Today, choose to create at least three new, energizing stories about your world, your life, about YOU.

Can you introduce some new, more protected code into your programming? Can you focus on "to be continued" instead of the "game overs"?

What if the realistic approach right now is not to worry about being "wrong" or "unrealistic"?

What if the actual success story formula for all of us includes "failures," frustrations, and statistics that look like this:

At age 23, Tina Fey was working at a YMCA.
At age 23, Oprah was fired from her first reporting job.
At age 24, Stephen King was working as a janitor and living in a trailer.
At age 27, Vincent Van Gogh failed as a missionary and decided to go to art school.
At age 28, J.K. Rowling was a suicidal single parent living on welfare.
At age 30, Harrison Ford was a carpenter.

Samuel L. Jackson didn't get his first movie role until he was 46.
Morgan Freeman landed his first MAJOR movie role at age 52.

Imagine if any of these amazing beings had allowed their mind to tell them that the game was over. That they should just quit? Maybe their minds did in some moments say that, but their mind's "virus protection" system quarantined that thought and instead inspired them to persist.

In their moments of deep self-doubt, do you think that any of them knew exactly how they were going to achieve their success? Do you think they might have encountered others who told them these dreams were impossible?

Most likely.

How many people hear a person say that they intend to become a movie star, a writer, or a billion-dollar influencer and think that this is a realistic objective? Yet, these "unrealistic dreams" are exactly what these folks made into their reality. So, why be so quick to belittle your big dreams? Doesn't that EPIC YOU deserve a bit of virus and password protection?

Today, why not simply add yourself to the list of those with EPIC FUTURES IN THE MAKING? Based on the precedent of many, MANY human BE-ings before you, chances are that WHATEVER you are facing right now is exactly where you are intended to be.

This is YOUR story toward EPIC, and this is exactly what the path to "success" looks like. The definition of success is changing, and it's up to you to decide right here, right now, what YOU will make your "center of interest" because YOU create your definition of success!

Time to start dreaming, envisioning, and deliberately training your focus beginning TODAY!

So, Yes! Your mission today is to decide what's going to be YOUR EPIC YOU story. And there is no better day than today to start practicing how to "virus protect" your thoughts more effectively. Now is your time to experience the feeling of being the sovereign of your own emotional/energetic state so that you can go out there, discover what makes you come alive, and maybe even create your own "impossible" that others can't stop talking about!!

Do I hear a BOOYAH???

TODAY'S ACTION STEPS:

- *Write a list of five experiences where you feel like you did not succeed or did not get the outcome you had hoped for. (+1 Gold Star)*
- *See if you can identify any thoughts or comments from yourself or others that led you to conclude that these experiences took you away from your dreams or targets. (+2 Gold Stars)*
- *Bonus points if you can now begin to rewrite your new Epic You Story, where you deliberately reframe those "bad" experiences in a way so that they contribute to your momentum, even if it's simply by arming you with more grit and resilience. Get Started! (+2 Gold Stars) Booyah!*

TOTAL POSSIBLE STARS FROM TODAY: 5 STARS

Day 6 – FOCUS: Regret Reimagined- Embracing the Heroic You

We've explored our ability to deliberately focus on the remarkable, the I'm Possible, and the limitless potential of our own value. We've introduced the need to "password protect" our most precious internal resources from viruses and "bad code."

Today, our mission is to target our propensity to focus on regret.

How can we reframe those regrets and transform them into catalysts?

Let's face it: regret isn't typically an energizing emotion. Sometimes, the focus in the center of our lens can be something that triggers a sense of regret.

Regret can be a real energy drainer, can't it? It has this uncanny ability to stir up blame, depression, self-doubt, and a whole range of negative emotions. But what if we looked at regrets from a different perspective? Here are three valuable insights about regret that can help us navigate these emotions and emerge stronger than ever:

1. Regret stems from who we don't allow ourselves to BE, not from what we do or don't do. We often set conditions for ourselves, believing we can only feel fulfilled or show up as our best selves if certain specific experiences or achievements are met. This restricts our growth and potential, limiting our capacity to see the epic possibilities within us.

2. Regret blinds us to the gifts hidden in our challenges. Instead of focusing solely on what we missed out on, what if we sought to discover the qualities and strengths we developed through those experiences? Maybe those "failures" were the stepping stones to unlocking our true potential. When, in those moments, can you ask yourself this instead, "What can I learn? What is this teaching me?"

3. Regret can prevent us from embracing our future. We get stuck dwelling on past disappointments, blaming ourselves or others for what happened. This obsession with the past can hinder us from envisioning the possibilities that lie ahead and creating new, exciting chapters in our lives.

The flawed logic of regret can keep us feeling bitter and resentful, preventing us from recognizing the paths we could still explore. We need a focus shift—one that allows us to reclaim our power and become the author and superhero of our journey.

You might think you missed certain opportunities or experiences, but that doesn't mean you can't BE the version of yourself that would have embraced them. You can redefine yourself at any age and pursue dreams that fill your heart with joy.

Remember, *BE-ing and DO-ing are not the same.* While there might be certain things you can't physically do, you can always BE the person who faces challenges head-on, defies the odds and refuses to let anything stop you from pursuing your passions.

Release the constraints of rigid expectations and embrace the surprises life has in store for you. Those seemingly insurmountable boulders falling in your path might be clearing the way for your true potential to shine.

So, what has regret been holding you back from accomplishing? Instead of blaming yourself for missed opportunities, view them as valuable learning experiences. Let your regrets fuel your determination, transform pain into passion, and guide you toward an empowered, self-valuing expression of who you truly are.

In this shero's/hero's journey, you are both the author and the protagonist. It's time to embark on a new chapter, leaving behind regret and embracing your heroic potential. Today, show up as the most epic version of yourself, ready to face the world with no regrets!

TODAY'S ACTION STEPS:

- *Write down a list of ideas of 1-3 experiences that have led to regrets. (+1 Gold Star)*
- *Now look at each experience and create a list for each one of the lessons that you have learned from those experiences. What didn't work, and what can you commit to doing differently now that you have seen the result of that experience? (+2 Gold Stars)*
- *Bonus points if your regret has to do with someone else and you feel guilty because you know that you owe them an apology. Take this moment to write an apology letter to them. And yes, this can still be successful even if you no longer know where to find this person or how to get this apology to them. The apology itself is critical. (+3 Gold Stars) Booyah!*

TOTAL POSSIBLE STARS FROM TODAY: 6 STARS

Day 7 - FOCUS: Illuminating Forgiveness: Embracing the Gift of Resilience

Epic Unveiled… Time to face the source of so much pain and distracted focus for so many of us…

Sitting in a small chapel at Jackson Memorial Hospital, waiting anxiously for my daughter's critical surgery to begin, life presented me with a profound lesson on resilience. It's incredible how a falling boulder can teach you so much about letting go and embracing the presence of forgiveness.

For years, I struggled with the concept of forgiveness, knowing I "should" forgive and feel grateful for the good things in my life. But emotionally, it seemed like an insurmountable task, especially when it came to the painful experiences that had left scars on my heart and shattered my sense of self-worth.

But while gazing at the stained glass in that chapel, a realization washed over me like a gentle wave: The struggles and pain I endured had a greater purpose. They sparked a relentless quest within me to discover the secrets of resilience and personal growth.

My hardships led me to delve into the lives of those who defied the odds and emerged as even greater versions of themselves. Within this journey, I found the root of my emotional struggles. It became clear that my inner game needed a transformative shift—I had been playing it, but it was also playing me.

Then, something extraordinary happened in that sacred space. I found peace and understanding, a profound Knowing that allowed me to forgive some of the most unforgivable circumstances and even feel gratitude for them. Those painful moments, as difficult as they were, had played an instrumental role in shaping me into the person I needed to be when life's boulder came crashing down.

Forgiveness, I realized, isn't about letting someone off the hook; it's about releasing the contract that inadvertently held me back. It was as if I had signed an agreement to allow my past traumas to dictate my future, to be a constant reminder of the hurt and pain. This silent internal protest against the universe had trapped me in a cycle of resentment, preventing me from embracing my potential.

But the falling boulder shattered that cycle. As my daughter fought for her life, I vowed to release this burden, to transform darkness into brightness. I chose to forgive, not to forget, but to honor the brilliance and worthiness within me. The boulder became a catalyst for growth, and I embraced my agility, resilience, and ability to expand.

So today, as you embark on your journey, let your boulder work its magic on your story. Consider the possibility of forgiving yourself or others, and let go of the chains that bind you to past pain. Embrace the gift of resilience and find your brilliance shining through.

As you look in the mirror, declare:

"Anger, pain, and wounds, I release you. I acknowledge my brilliance, significance, and worth. I embrace my agility, resilience, and growth. I trust my EPIC self, embracing the wisdom of this boulder. Today, I step out into the world as a healthier, happier, and whole version of myself, embracing the benefits of my past pains."

Your mission and focus today: FORGIVENESS! Because underneath that avalanche of pain is the true and authentic, "epic beyond measure" version of YOU!

Now, go out there and share your BOOYAH with the world!

TODAY'S ACTION STEPS:

- *Make a list of 1-3 experiences where you have been treated unfairly. (+1 Gold Star)*
- *For each of those experiences, write ways that you can forgive. Remember, this is not letting someone off the hook. It is about forgiving yourself for not knowing how to prevent this or from inadvertently trusting this person/choice, etc. (+2 Gold Stars)*
- *Bonus points if you can acknowledge what you have gained from this experience, even if it's only knowing that you have been to the bottom of the abyss and you survived. The grit. The resilience. The determination to thrive and prosper. (+2 Gold Stars) Booyah!*

TOTAL POSSIBLE STARS FROM TODAY: 5 STARS

Day 8 — FOCUS: Navigating the Seas of Self-Care, Self-Trust, and Self-Love

You are the Boat...

When asked, "How are you?" we often respond with a detached "Fine" or "Good," hiding our true feelings behind a façade. But deep down, how are we really feeling, and how does it impact our daily lives?

Our thoughts change when we feel confident and good about ourselves, leading to different actions and outcomes. Yet, many of us surrender control of these thoughts, letting them dictate our lives without conscious intent.

The pressure to conform to others' expectations and follow conventional paths shapes our thoughts. The more we act like an exaggerated version of ourselves to please others, the more we feel like we don't belong—like something is missing, broken, or that we aren't good enough.

We become trapped in a cycle of failure and imposter syndrome, causing our self-confidence and self-worth to falter. Lethargy and feelings of inadequacy set in, and we question our value and judgment. We may even lose sight of our true selves and doubt whether we can find joy, purpose, and passion in the future.

As hopelessness takes hold, our low self-esteem leads to destructive coping mechanisms. We seek temporary relief from unhealthy behaviors, avoiding self-care and personal boundaries that recognize our worthiness and priority.

With a sense of failure looming, we convince ourselves that we don't deserve a life filled with joy and ease. We believe our suffering is the only reason others notice or care about us.

But here's the truth—"Self-love" is knowing that you cannot miss the boat because you, my dear, ARE the boat —at least the only boat that matters.

Your significance lies in your uniqueness and imperfections, making you irreplaceable.

To halt this downward spiral, *we must embrace self-care, self-trust, and self-love—the cornerstones of an empowered life*. However, true and enduring self-love starts from within, loving every part of ourselves, even the "stickier, pricklier" aspects.

"Self-trust" often comes with age, and it certainly comes with experience, knowing that you have the ability to navigate through adversity because you are uniquely YOU.

Let's face it: there may have been times when you said, "I can't possibly," – and you figured out how to do it anyway. Isn't that worth at least a wee bit of self-trust? I certainly think so!

"Self-care" means recognizing that, yes, you are the boat, but you must learn to captain it.

So, as you sail through the journey of life, savor the moments of joy and darkness. Embrace the adventure and learn to deliberately choose thoughts that lead you toward your energizing North Star.

The mentors and anti-mentors you encounter will shape you into a great captain, capable of steering through the stormiest seas with confidence and trust.

Redirect your "stress energy" towards the beauty just over the horizon!

Today, answer "How are you?" with a resounding "Frickin' EPIC! THANK YOU!!"

You are the boat, and your journey awaits—captain it with self-care, self-trust, and self-love!

TODAY'S ACTION STEPS:

- *Write down 5-10 experiences during your hero's/ shero's journey that were painful or unpleasant at the time. Now, write down why your ability to navigate through those stormy waters is worth some kudos! (+1 Gold Star)*
- *Now look at each experience and create a list of what you did (or didn't do) during those times that have made it clearer what you stand for and what you stand against. For extra impact, be sure to include what you now stand for and stand against! (+2 Gold Stars)*
- *Bonus points if you now commit to trusting yourself more and honoring yourself with at least one gesture of self-care and self-love every day. Plan out what those actions will be for the week. (+2 Gold Stars) Booyah!*

TOTAL POSSIBLE STARS FROM TODAY: 5 STARS

Day 9— FOCUS: Embrace the Power of Tiny Shifts for an EPIC IMPACT

A Tiny Shift, a World of Difference…

When the boulder collided with our world, it left us with valuable lessons. One of the most powerful revelations was that coping skills alone wouldn't lead to real change. I needed to dig into the "root code" of why I needed coping in the first place.

I definitely couldn't control what was happening to us, but I could control how I chose to respond to it.

That's when my focus came into play. If I didn't want to become the second victim of this circumstance, I needed to take ownership of what I was going to choose to focus on and what I would make that focus mean. I had to be an active participant in the creation of my story.

This brought me to two letters: A versus O.

From an early age, I believed in the pursuit of perfection, which led me to focus solely on FLAW. I became hyper-aware of what was missing, broken, or wrong so that I would know what to avoid. I was obsessed with doing well in school. In fact, any grade less than "100" sent me reeling. As I entered the "real world," the lack of a clear path to perfection overwhelmed me. I feared self-judgment, afraid of discovering that I was "not enough."

Then came "the boulder."

At first, as I looked at this formidable crisis, it seemed impossible to be "enough." But as I delved into the wisdom of the inner game, something strange occurred. I came to realize that this boulder had come not to destroy us but to shatter the preconceptions that held me back from realizing my true potential and true path.

I had been focusing on FLAW when I needed to embrace FLOW.

By shifting my lens from FLAW to FLOW, a world of possibilities opened up. It allowed for iteration, innovation, and a sense of excitement for the next adventure. It transformed me into the Shero of my journey, the author of my story.

Today, years after the boulder, I seldom see anything in my day—be it Schuy's quest for physical independence or the significant changes in our family—as FLAW. My joy and delight now stem from naturally defining myself and my world through the lens of FLOW.

If you find yourself burdened by the pressure of FLAW, take a breath. Consider that transformation might be as simple as making a different choice—changing just one tiny letter in your programming code from A to O.

How would your world transform if you approached each moment from the perspective of FLOW?

Mission: Practice transforming your focus from the LACK of the presence of what you want to the PRESENCE of what you want. Embrace the power of tiny shifts for an EPIC IMPACT!

TODAY'S ACTION STEPS:

- *Make today a day of Epic Awareness. Notice when you focus on a flaw versus an opportunity to flow and keep track of those moments. (+1 Gold Star)*
- *When you notice yourself focusing on Flaw, try finding the one thought to help you shift your focus to Flow. It may take a few tries, but you'll find it! Be sure to congratulate yourself when you do! (+2 Gold Stars)*
- *Bonus points if you continue staying aware on a daily basis and perhaps program a reminder on your phone that simply asks, "Where's the flow?" (+2 Gold Stars) Booyah!*

TOTAL POSSIBLE STARS FROM TODAY: 5 STARS

Day 10 - FOCUS: Relax, Review & Recoup - Your "National All About Me" Day

Who's ready to take a day to focus on *inspired action?* To take a day to go back over what we have been exploring so far as you get closer and closer to creating your desired future?

Welcome to your "National All About Me" Day—a day dedicated to Relax, Review, and Recoup. As you go about your daily business, remember the acronym A.C.T., which will be another guiding light in shifting your focus, mastering your inner game, and creating the future you desire. However, rather than approaching this from the perspective of "work," I want you to explore how it feels to approach your world from the intention of "play."

Choosing from "I have to" or "I get to."

So, let's call A.C.T. part of your "home play."

What is this A.C.T. acronym?

"**A**" stands for staying "Aware of Your Focus." Take a moment to recognize where your thoughts are leading you. Are they fixating on past regrets, blame, or old wounds? Identify areas where you need to release guilt and shame, allowing yourself to heal and thrive.

Remember these four elements from your mission during these 100 Days:

1. Learn how to identify your current focus deliberately.
2. Practice transforming your focus from lack to presence.
3. Master "virus protecting" your thoughts to regain emotional control.
4. Feel how empowered states lead to better outcomes in all aspects of life.

Observe when your focus ignites and energizes you. Note the thoughts, feelings, and actions that accompany these moments, and consciously choose to create more of them. Also, be aware of when your focus pulls you down, allowing negative thoughts to run unchecked.

Now, the letter "**C**" represents "Commit to Change." Shift your focus towards thoughts that feel even slightly better. Continually find alternative perspectives that are true yet uplift you. For instance, rather than dwelling on self-confidence struggles, focus on learning new strategies to obliterate self-doubt and embrace excitement about your epic journey ahead.

Explore who you need to be to release past guilt, self-judgment, anger, or shame. Commit to breaking the habit of living on autopilot and take control of your thoughts with a password and virus protection system. Decide which thoughts deserve lasting traction in your mind.

Last but definitely not least, "**T**" reminds you that "Transformation is as Simple as Making a Different Choice." Make deliberate choices your priority, and believe in your determination to make this journey a success.

On your "National All About Me" Day, leaf back through the pages you've covered and bask in your commitment to make this work. Embrace your focus on becoming the best version of yourself.

Today is about you, your dreams, and who you choose to be. So, take the reins and A.C.T. for an EPIC future!

TODAY'S ACTION STEPS:

- *Write down 3-5 of your biggest takeaways so far. (+1 Gold Star)*
- *Write down what these takeaways will inspire you to start doing, stop doing, and perhaps do differently! (+2 Gold Stars)*
- *Bonus points if you apply some of your "start doings" right away. (+2 Gold Stars) Booyah!*

TOTAL POSSIBLE STARS FROM TODAY: 5 STARS

Day 11- FOCUS: Building An Epic Team – The Right Fit

So we've just come off a day that's all about you. Now, let's dedicate a day to focusing on "them."

Andrew Carnegie famously said, "Teamwork is the fuel that allows common people to attain uncommon results."

What could be a more fitting focus for the next day of our epic journey than to spotlight those whose support helps us hit those targets faster and with the least number of falls along the way – our inner circle, our mentors, our teams, our invaluable circle of support.

In the pursuit of change, whether in our physical, personal, or professional lives, we often fear feeling alienated and isolated. The concern of leaving behind our loved ones can keep us stuck in familiar patterns. It's not uncommon to feel discouraged and even abandoned when those around us fail to understand or support our vision. It's also not unknown to see us dim our light so we don't outshine another. However, this often results in both of us standing in darkness.

Remember, epic achievements are seldom solo endeavors; they are team sports. Surrounding yourself with great players is crucial. However, it's essential to recognize that different aspects of your journey might require different team members.

As you take your next step forward, it's crucial to recognize that not everyone close to you personally will be the perfect cheerleader or mentor for you professionally and vice versa. Choose your circles of support without feeling that these circles should be "one size fits all." Each group will be composed of individuals who align with your vision and aspirations in that area of focus and who truly understand and advise you based on shared values and goals.

People's perspectives and experiences shape how they perceive and respond to your vision. Some may find your ideas outlandish simply because they trigger old fears or remind them of bad experiences from the past. Others might simply be unable to envision themselves making the same choices you aspire to make, and that's ok. They don't have to be the key players on that particular team.

Building great teams is undeniably valuable, but expecting everyone to be the right fit for every team is unrealistic. People have their unique strengths, perspectives, and comfort zones. They may excel in one context but struggle in another.

In your pursuit of a life that feels epic, remember that your personal circle of friends and family might offer unconditional love and emotional support, but they may not fully grasp the intricacies of your ambitions. Similarly, some of your colleagues or mentors may not understand the deeply personal aspects of your journey.

Take a step back, breathe, and give yourself permission to be discerning when forming your teams. **Seek out individuals who share your passion, align with your vision, and understand the path you're walking**. Look for those who can offer valuable insights, support, and constructive feedback without being hindered by their fears or limitations.

Having the right fit in your team allows for powerful collaboration and enables everyone to shine in their respective roles. When you've chosen your team, don't hesitate to seek guidance and support.

Embrace the understanding that different teams will have different dynamics and compositions. Some may be your personal cheerleaders, always by your side no matter what, while others might be your professional advisors, challenging you to grow and evolve in your career.

Either way, you are set up to win! Today is a day filled with limitless possibilities.

By surrounding yourself with diverse reflections of "great players," you'll create a powerful legacy, find your passion and joy, and perhaps positively impact the world in the process.

Remember, epic is a team sport—build your circle of support wisely. Seek those who have earned the right to be on your team, individuals who inspire and uplift you on your journey toward all the epicness you can imagine or desire.

Time to go out, find your peeps, and savor this beautiful day while you're at it!

TODAY'S ACTION STEPS:

- *Make three columns on a piece of paper and write one area or project in each column where you could use support. This can be personally, professionally, or in any other aspect of your life. (+1 Gold Star)*
- *In each column, write down the names of people best suited to support you in these aspects or projects. Make clear notes of where there are gaps. (+2 Gold Stars)*

- *Bonus points if you now ask those people to support you and share specifically how you could use their support. (+1 Gold Stars)*
- *Additional bonus points if you start researching or asking for referrals to fill the gaps in your team/ support system. (+2 Gold Stars) Booyah!*

TOTAL POSSIBLE STARS FROM TODAY: 6 STARS

Day 12 — FOCUS: Embrace Change, Unlock Limitless Potential

We've focused on "them," our team. We've focused on ourselves. Now, let's focus on the "circumstances" that often become the "center of interest and activities." These "situations" are often the things that leave us spiraling down the rabbit hole!

Have you ever been in a place where you prayed for things to change – and then when they *did change, you panicked?*

Most of us have, so let's take a deeper look: Why did you panic?

Because your focus was amplifying the unfamiliarity of this change. You were not focusing on the benefits or the improvements in your new situation. You weren't giving yourself credit for being able to transform the changes into things that would make your life truly epic.

When this happens, we aren't making possibilities the "center of our interest." We are far more interested in all the things that could go wrong.

Today, we break free from the myth that certainty requires everything to remain the same, including ourselves. "Epic," and our unique version of it, is not about staying stagnant or trapped in sameness.

To make change possible, we must first believe in its possibility. Train your mind to affirm:

> "This thing is possible."
> "I can do it."
> "The effort is worth it."

As a leader, recognize the diverse abilities people possess. However, understand that one significant disability can hinder progress—THE LACK OF ABILITY TO ADAPT TO CHANGE.

Life is a series of transformations, and our survival hinges on our adaptability. When the boulder struck my daughter, it thrust us into a new reality beyond our control. But we had power over how we perceived this new normal in the context of our joy and life moving forward.

Remember the T. from the acronym A.C.T? Personal *transformation* begins with a choice—a choice to embrace the unpredictable and unfamiliar as sources of treasure and growth.

Change is the root of progress, innovation, and limitless potential. It opens the door to more and allows us to become more.

Your life is a blank canvas with endless colors at your fingertips. Embrace the thrill of the new and fresh with the same enthusiasm of a dog with its head out the window, delighting in the wind.

This moment is unique, never experienced before. Let your dreams guide you toward your destiny.

Imagine your future, Epic You—living your destiny and even surpassing it. What advice would that version of you give? Let's go back to the questions from the earlier action steps (and note how it's important to keep asking these powerful questions):

Is there something new you should start doing?
Is there something to stop doing?
What changes can you implement right now to become that Epic You?

TODAY'S ACTION STEPS:

- *Identify one target in your life personally, professionally, physically (etc.) that you really want to see change and then write authentically why you are not making that change. What are you really afraid of? Go deep. Are you afraid that it's simply not possible or that things will go wrong? What is it? (+1 Gold Star)*
- *Now look at what you wrote. Assess the fear. Is it really something that could physically put you in danger, or are you simply unfamiliar with how you would execute this in a way where you'd succeed? Circle the areas of unfamiliarity (+2 Gold Stars)*
- *Bonus points if you now write down ideas of how you can break through the unfamiliarity and start to ease the tension around that desired target. (+2 Gold Stars)*
- *Additional bonus points if you start putting some unfamiliarity-busting ideas into action beginning today. Even 5 minutes counts! (+3 Gold Stars) Booyah!*

TOTAL POSSIBLE STARS FROM TODAY: 8 STARS

Day 13 - FOCUS: Embrace Your Epic History

Day 13!

We've seen that our ability to deliberately focus directly impacts how we experience our lives. That our circumstances can hijack our sovereignty over our focus, but not all circumstances take place in the present. We have a sneaky habit of perpetually reliving the circumstances of the past – and making those past events the "focus of our interest."

The more we think about the past, the more those memories create expectations about the future. Before we know it, our thoughts are off and running on their momentum.

If you are determined to create a life that feels epic, you *must* get out of the habit of allowing "your thoughts to *think you."* Remember the concept of Sloppy Thinking Syndrome? Wink! What you choose to focus on, what shows up as "that thing that you are currently most interested in thinking about," is often a reflection of your expectations. What are you *expecting to see?*

As you wake up each morning, do you expect epic things to unfold abundantly in your life? Or do you anticipate another day, much like the ones before? Take a moment to reflect on what you're experiencing in life right now and why you believe you are experiencing this. Write down your thoughts and feelings about it.

It's easy to use our history to justify our current successes or failures, but history is not destiny. We are not bound to repeat our mistakes unless we choose not to learn or make better choices. Our past is simply data that we now have at our disposal so we can make even better decisions as we step forward.

Life is not happening to us; life is happening *for us,* **and we have the power to shape our path.** Let's break free from the notion that life is a casino where the house always wins.

Today, deliberately focus on liberating yourself from the grip of the past. Be fully present and use that history as valuable data to build an exhilarating future. Revel in the experiences that strengthen your resilience, drive, and creativity—the experiences that make you want to embrace the epic version of yourself.

Choose wisely which stories from your past you focus on. What meaning will you give them in the context of the epic version of you?

Would the epic version of you say, "I achieved my joy and success despite these boulders"? Or would they exclaim, "Thanks to these boulders, I became a bolder version of myself, paving the way for even greater accomplishments"?

As you grow, choose to become a *beacon of inspiration* for others who might also be letting their fears dictate their choices based on their past. Embrace your history as a glorious catalyst for the epic future that lies ahead.

Believe that you can do this! *Expect* this to be *the day* when life shows you evidence of your ability to co-create an epic future!

TODAY'S ACTION STEPS:

- *Take a moment to write down 3-5 experiences from the past that seem to complete the following sentence. "I am where I am right now in spite of/ because of….". (+1 Gold Star)*
- *Now look at those experiences, and for each one, let's write a new version that completes this sentence. "Thanks to this experience, I have the opportunity to choose/to be/ to do ….". (+2 Gold Stars)*
- *Bonus points if you now take a moment to imagine yourself waking up in the morning. Write down what you would say to create your revised story/declaration if you knew that your words are now LAW. What would be your morning "This is my expectation for the day of who I am and who I will show up being…" story? (+2 Gold Stars)*
- *Additional bonus points if you keep this by your bed and start making this statement part of your daily morning routine. (+1 Gold Star) Booyah!*

TOTAL POSSIBLE STARS FROM TODAY: 6 STARS

Day 14 — FOCUS: Embrace Your Epic Legacy

Circumstances that show up in the present…Circumstances that we relive from experiences in the past…What about those circumstances that are yet to be created? Is there value or power to be had if we choose to make *them* the center of our focused interest?

Today, we are going to explore the concept of legacy. But let's get real for a moment. Sometimes, focusing on leaving an epic legacy means having the courage to look beyond how we normally see ourselves. I won't lie; that can be pretty scary at times!

After Schuy's truly miraculous survival that defied medical precedent, I found myself back in Tampa, and people started suggesting I share our story with audiences—yes, we're talking about public speaking. Can I just say public speaking wasn't exactly my thing? In fact, I used to joke that I'd be the one to mess up the introduction for the real speaker. Stepping up on stage as myself? Terrifying! All I could think about were the haters and the critics.

But then, my dear friend "Mama-lita" convinced me to attend an event called "Train the Trainer." I was skeptical, to be honest, and only went "just to see" what it was about. And you know what? It turned out to be a game-changer!

The speaker, Robert Riopel, dropped a metaphor bomb on us. He asked if we'd ever skipped a pebble across a lake and watched the ripples spread. Some of us, he said, are like those pebbles, making a small impact with our words. But if we want to create a real "tsunami" of change, "you've got to embrace your boulders and step into your destiny"!

Cue the "aha" moment. His words spoke directly to my soul. So, I decided right then and there to shift my focus away from the fear of judgment and ridicule. It was time to open a new chapter where I could make a difference beyond just my little bubble. Can I be someone who leaves a lasting legacy that inspires growth and greatness?

Now that you've heard my legacy story let's talk about you!

What will be your legacy story? What will you be remembered for? It's true – when we shift our focus from ourselves to others, we start feeling pretty amazing. And you know what's even more powerful? Helping others feel amazing, too!

However, let's be clear. "Helping others feel amazing" isn't about becoming a doormat for toxic people or being swallowed up in a codependent melodrama. It isn't about beating yourself up because you can't make someone happy who gains their significance by being unhappy.

To go back to past metaphors, we may "be the boat," but we're not rescuing the people who keep putting holes in our boat here! We're talking about unleashing something not simply epic but meaningful that empowers ourselves and others– which means that if we want to rescue something, we'll go out and rescue something cute and furry!

Can you tell that I'm passionate about this? So yes!! Today is the perfect day to focus on envisioning your legacy – and, in the process, to empower those around you to see their potential, even when it means challenging them a bit.

Let's embrace our boulders—the challenges that hone our impact on the world. No more settling for ripples! Let the focus of our collective interest create a tsunami of positive growth and change! How many people will remember you for your impact? Can you leave behind a momentum that spans the test of time?

Take that first step toward your epic legacy, my fearless Epic Joy-rrior, and focus bigger than you've ever dared to focus until now!

TODAY'S ACTION STEPS:

- ***If you could pick one thing that would be your legacy, what would that be, and how would others describe it? (+1 Gold Star)***
- ***Write a letter that you will leave for your great-grandchildren that expresses your understanding of "how to choose to live." (+2 Gold Stars)***

- *Bonus points if you now are willing to get bold. I'm going to ask you to write a version of the eulogy that you wish could be read at your memorial. Who would you have read it and why? Would it be a call to action? Full of joy? Profound and deep? Filled with gratitude? What would it be? (+3 Gold Stars)*
- *EXTRA BONUS: We want to know how you're doing! Feeling proud? You should be! If you want to know how to join a community of others on this quest, email team@meridithalexander.com, and we'll get you the juicy details!! (+2 Gold Stars) Booyah!*

TOTAL POSSIBLE STARS FROM TODAY: 8 STARS

Day 15— FOCUS: Shaping Identity – From Boulders to Superpowers

In the past 14 days, we've looked at our focus from many different angles. Yet the truth is that one of the hardest things to focus on objectively is ourselves. It's that focus that shapes our identity – our self-image and how we see ourselves.

Today, we'll take a look at how YOU define yourself.

When you look in the mirror today, who do you see? What words do you use to describe yourself? Do you define yourself by the "boulders" that have left you scarred, or are you defining yourself as the bigger bolder version of yourself that these boulders inspire you to become?

What if rather than being the root of your life's "stumbles," these boulders allow you a moment of flight… Yep… that rare bird's eye view— before landing on new ground…?

As you look at your life from 10,000 feet up, can you forgive and feel limitless gratitude for the boulders of the past? What about your grit? What about your tenacity? What about your commitment to "never again" and "what if"? Are these not qualities born out of the terror, pain, and heartache of those past stories?

How different might today be if you wake up ready to embrace the jagged edges of these "impossible boulders"?

Can you claim these past experiences as the gifts that strengthen you and allow you to soar when the less mighty fall…Like the superhero who travels through the dark, difficult abyss that are her struggles, yet they hone within her a certain majesty – a profound story that no source of darkness can ever fully capture…

What if these boulders have NOT been your kryptonite?

What if they have been the essential ingredient for unleashing your SUPERPOWER?

If the boulders along your path are not happening TO you, but FOR YOU, who would you step out into the world being today?

What if you are mightier than you have ever allowed yourself to believe?

TODAY'S ACTION STEPS:

- *Write down 1-3 of the biggest "boulders" in your life experience. (+1 Gold Star)*
- *Now, write a list of the qualities that the scars from these boulders represent. Are you resilient, tenacious, dedicated, loyal, generous, loving, honest, etc.? (+2 Gold Stars)*
- *Bonus points if you now go out into this day focusing on those qualities that make you epic and living your day as this epic BE-ing who knows the value that these scars represent. (+2 Gold Stars) Booyah!*

TOTAL POSSIBLE STARS FROM TODAY: 5 STARS

Day 16—FOCUS: Perfectly Imperfect- Embracing the Flow of Life

No conversation about how we see ourselves and how we see our world would be complete without at least some focus on the concept of "perfection."

When we think of "perfect," what becomes the "center of our interest"? What do we hone in on? And what do we make that mean?

Those questions inspired another one of the entries in my "Tinkerbell Project Blog," so I thought that I would share…

Dear Epic Universe and Treasure of My Soul,

Once again, life has bestowed its magic upon me, leaving me feeling grateful beyond words. It's amazing how sometimes life steps in and shatters our expectations, only to deliver something far beyond our wildest dreams.

As I reflect on the boulder that transformed our lives in 2016, I've come to realize that life doesn't have to be perfect to be fulfilling and profound. But what does "perfect" even mean? Is it a static state with no room for change, growth, or expansion? Who gets to define perfection? Our parents, critics, bosses, or politicians?

Perhaps we've been looking at perfection all wrong. Maybe it's not about an impossible standard that we must reach but rather our ability to flow, adapt, and consistently transform. The Universe, with its enduring longevity, shows us the beauty of fluidity and embracing change.

So, let's question the past data of our lives. Does it hint at what is yet to come? Can we stretch beyond what we can easily see? Are we willing to be the change we wish to see in our lives?

As I sit here in the quiet of the moment, I've come to understand that true beauty often lies in the unknown. It's in those challenging moments when life seems uncertain and unfamiliar that we discover the depths of our courage and resilience.

The real magic happens when we embrace the unknown and challenge our upper limits. It's when we claim "impossible" as our own "I'm Possible" and dare to be who we truly are.

So, as you navigate your boulders and uncertainties, remember that perfection isn't about flawless achievements but about embracing the flow of life. Be willing to step into the unknown, for that's where the real magic lies.

With love and hope,
Meridith

As you read my letter above, I encourage you to take your pen and paper and perhaps write a letter to your soul.

Can today be the day when you redefine the way that you will choose to focus on perfection? Can you acknowledge the abundance of beauty, humanity, and elegance within? How about in the world around you? Yes, even with all the things that are upsetting, imperfect, and just plain wrong.

Can you celebrate your aliveness as you stumble and grow? Can you see yourself as one tiny being on a planet still expanding and evolving as things blossom and unfold?

Perfection is not a box that resists change. Every corner of the Universe demonstrates a different model for perfection: *the ability to be agile, to adapt, to observe, to iterate, course correct, and flow.* We as a species are here not because of our ability to prevent change but rather to adapt to change.

So, if you have been in pursuit of perfection, make sure that the way that you are defining "perfection" is accurate. How agile and adaptive can you be?

Welcome to the majesty that is the heartbeat of Life's profound flow… you are meant to be here whether the moment you're experiencing feels hot or cold, right or wrong. This is YOUR life experience, your garden, your playground.

Let today be your time to ask new questions so that nothing – least of all your own "boxed in" definition of perfection – keeps you from BE-ing the full expression of all you are destined to be! That loving, triumphant, joyous, fiercely "imperfect" and ever-flowing YOU!

TODAY'S ACTION STEPS:

- *Today is another Awareness Day. Step out into your day making note of when and where an outdated version of "perfectionism" shows up and how it makes you feel. (+1 Gold Star)*
- *Think about how you can instead think of this moment, circumstance, or topic from the perspective of expanding and growing. What opportunity is there to innovate or iterate? How might you respond differently? (+2 Gold Stars)*
- *Bonus points if you write down a list of words, phrases, and/or topics that tend to be a red flag alerting you to a bout of perfectionism. Program these into your mind and start committing to reframing them when you bump up against them. (+2 Gold Stars) Booyah!*

TOTAL POSSIBLE STARS FROM TODAY: 5 STARS

Day 17 — FOCUS: Take the Driver's Seat and Embrace the Magic of Your Inner GPS

Hey there, shining soul! Congratulations on all the steps toward the mastery of your focus that you have accomplished so far! So now, let's begin moving into the part of the story where we consciously and deliberately begin to **set our internal GPS**.

From this day forward, YOU will be the driver of this vehicle, the captain of this cruise ship. You will operate with the understanding that this incredible "center of interest or activity" will perform optimally when the autopilot is off and you are at the controls.

Let's talk about being our own best friend instead of our own worst enemy. Yes, we all do it – even when we get to the level of age and success when we should "know better." You know those debilitating, hurtful words we sometimes say to ourselves? Well, what if we could change that narrative?

Picture our mind like a curious Artificial Intelligence program (AI), always searching for patterns and examples to follow. What if we took charge and gave it the direction, guidance, and positivity it craves?

As we explored in the previous chapters, we often judge ourselves harshly, thinking we should be perfect or reach a destination – until that time, we have no "right" to feel happy. But what if we shifted our focus to celebrate the small victories along the way

What if we can use our deliberate focus to reinforce to our minds that Life isn't about being perfect; it's about progression, growth, and embracing the adventure? I remember a moment from my childhood when I crashed my tricycle while trying to avoid an ant hill. It was then that I realized I couldn't be perfect! Wink! "Shocking," I know, but that realization opened the doors to an enchanting journey of striving and growing.

We all can have this experience of seeing more wonder in our lives as long as we master the expectation of what a deliciously wonderful life should show up being. That demands that we show up in our day as "joy-rriors" – beings who are fiercely committed to approaching our world through the lens of "what's working" versus "not working."

We deliberately choose what we will focus on and what we will make that focus mean.

Life as a human being is a beautifully imperfect experience, and the dance between the moments of victory and opportunities to grow is where the magic lies. So, when you are willing to take ownership of setting your internal GPS, you'll find that every day is a glorious invitation to party with the Universe.

In each choice about what will be the next object of your attention, you give yourself the opportunity to savor every moment and live with unbridled joy, even when all of your "wants" and "shoulds" are not yet checked off.

Today, let's start this process of taking over our sovereignty by hitting pause on the "Are-we-there-yets?"

Jump into the driver's seat of life, put your foot on the gas, and just LIVE! After all, maybe there's a reason why the rearview mirror is the smallest in the car. Perhaps it's life's gentle reminder to focus on the exciting road ahead.

So, let's celebrate all the fuel life has put into our gas tank. We might have a few extra pieces of baggage in the trunk, but that just means that we won't arrive without at least a toothbrush.

Our GPS is ready, and we are turning the key! This is going to be an EPIC TRIP! Where should we go first? Engines ready!

TODAY'S ACTION STEPS:

- *Take a moment to write down 10-15 small successes you have experienced in the past 2-3 days. (+1 Gold Star)*

- *Take this list in front of a mirror and read each one of those successes aloud. After each success, look at yourself in the mirror and declare as loud as you dare (then go just a touch louder), "[Name], that's freaking EPIC!!" (+2 Gold Stars)*
- *Bonus points if you dance around as if you just crossed the end zone in the super bowl and repeat this exercise tomorrow! (+2 Gold Stars) Booyah!*

TOTAL POSSIBLE STARS FROM TODAY: 5 STARS

Day 18 — FOCUS: Craft Your Own Epic Definition of Success

Road trip! Time for a quick pit stop… destination: the "center of interest" that we call SUCCESS.

Today is the day to deliberately focus on a topic that will directly impact how you decide to "drive your machine."

This is an integral piece in the programming code that will ensure your ability to create the future you've always actively dreamed of.

It's part of the clarity piece, and it starts with redefining what success means to you. What you focus on today will help you shape your journey going forward. Give yourself permission to let go of the old societal norms and embrace a new, empowering definition of achievement. But you have to be able to envision it in order to believe it. When you can believe it, you'll find that your mind *can* figure out how it can be done.

Can you begin to identify what "success" looks like to you? Take a moment to really see how you would answer that. Be aware that you may have to start peeling back a few layers of the old onion and take some time to do that authentically. That's ok.

Success is not about wrinkles or years; it's about energy and zeal. It's about finding the fusion of brilliance that empowers you, ignites your passion, inspires and is inspired by others, and instills unshakable confidence.

In this modern age, we are redefining the finish line and crafting our rules for success. It's not just about knowing how to make a living; it's about knowing how to choose to live. Each day is an opportunity to declare your purpose and create an impact that lasts a lifetime.

So today, play with the possibilities. Map out your ideas. Create a vision board. Get out your post-its. Use whatever it is that helps you start honing in on those next targets. Write your ideas down and place them where you will see them every single day. Nurture them. Admire them. Adjust them. Allow them to be as fluid as you are.

Your next mission is to take the wheel and steer your life in the direction of your dreams. Embrace your emotional and logical intelligence, find and nurture your passions, and believe in your skills and talents. Your definition of success is yours to create.

Let *it be your center of interest and activity* for this "brimming with potential," "cusp of possibility" type of day!

As you step out into the tasks of the day, let your focus be on shaping your epic journey and defining success on your terms. Find your inner game frequency. Put your foot back on the gas pedal and write the next chapter of your life with purpose, passion, and joy.

The EPIC adventure that you have been waiting for is waiting for YOU!

TODAY'S ACTION STEPS:

- *Focus on these areas: personally, professionally, physically, financially, spiritually, relationships, and growth. Write down or map what success would feel like for you in each area and why. Remember to include what success would feel like, not simply what you would have, do, or experience. (+1 Gold Star)*
- *Write down one thing you could do in each area that will significantly move the needle if you do it consistently. (+2 Gold Stars)*
- *Bonus points if you start doing that one thing in at least two of those areas today! (+2 Gold Stars) Booyah!*

TOTAL POSSIBLE STARS FROM TODAY: 5 STARS

DAY 19 – FOCUS: The Ultimate Self-Care, When Just a Bubble Bath Won't Do

Look at you making all of these powerful changes in the way that you are focusing and showing up! (Can you hear the sound of our rubber "Epic chickens" squawking in celebratory awe and delight?)

But all of these changes need to be offset with a powerful system of self-care that will keep your energy and motivation high! When life gets busy – much less "tough" people often tell you to focus on self-care, but what does that really mean? Is it just about bubble baths and massages? I believe there's a deeper form of self-care that can truly transform your life and allow you to soar.

You can do many things in the name of self-care… a walk in your favorite park… a massage… a cozy hour with a treasured book … even a bubble bath (or two)…However, when the bubbles have vanished, and you're left simply with the unfiltered, "un-Facebooked" version of you, is there a more "epic You" version of self-care?

I would have to say a resounding "YES!" It might not be what you expect, but it is a form of self-care that becomes lasting and deep. I'll be honest: when I was thrust into the sudden role of my daughter's caregiver, most of my previous "self-care" habits out of necessity had to become temporarily obsolete.

And yet, in order to be truly valuable to my daughter, I couldn't allow myself to be constantly running on empty. I had to keep my ability to focus on "I'm Possibilities" constant and sharp.

That's when I discovered some secrets about authentic self-care:

- Self-care can exist even in the midst of interrupted sleep, high levels of stress, and having no time of my own.
- The ultimate "self-care" is less about the "do-ing" than about the "be-ing". Are you starting to see a trend here?
- Self-care is being willing to let go of the self-criticism in favor of the decision to deliberately focus on loving "fiercely"—- beginning with yourself.

I discovered that proper, focused self-care means doing what is necessary to authentically (yes) fall back in love with YOU! Even to fall back in love with the crazy "mess of a world" that you are currently (and temporarily) living in. To revel in the antics of this delicious heart and soul that makes you, YOU…To unconditionally celebrate not your "worst enemy" but your "perfectly imperfect" soul "mate." Yes, that quirky, spirited, "can't-believe-I-actually-did-that" version of YOU! I focused on learning to absolutely *treasure* the story of the "Epic Me."

Here are some other things that I discovered as I focused on "self-care":

- Self-care is letting go of the "judginess" and replacing it with the co-creative possibilities in life…
- Even when things feel incredibly challenging and low and dark, self-care is giving yourself permission to hide under the covers for a few moments, cry out loud and ultimately heal.
- Self-care is knowing that the joy and laughter will return, that the dark times won't last, and that if you haven't lived to say your final "BOOYAH," the game's not over yet.

So, today, heck yes! Go for that walk. Take that hot yoga class. Meditate and eat an extra salad with arugula and sprouts. But, if you are striving for "epic," commit to that deeper level of self-care. Know that epic is more than endless tubs full of bubbles. You've got everything you need to thrive in the midst of chaos.

Love the unpredictability of YOU and of life itself… Keep focusing. Keep driving. Keep your windshield clean because… guess what? The best part of this EPIC JOURNEY is just ahead!!!

TODAY'S ACTION STEPS:

- *Based on what you learned today, what are five things you can do daily that replenish your body and/or soul? What five things can you do to replenish your inner game on a daily basis? (+1 Gold Star)*
- *What can you STOP DOING in order to practice more self-care, externally and internally? (+2 Gold Stars)*
- *Bonus points if you catch yourself resorting to old habits of "judginess" and replace them with a new self-care approach. (+2 Gold Stars) Booyah!*

TOTAL POSSIBLE STARS FROM TODAY: 5 STARS

Day 20 — FOCUS: Create Your Tr'amily – The Power of Blending Tribe + Family

Day 20, and I hope that you're still buzzing with excitement as we continue our journey of powering up the epic life you're crafting! We've talked about team and finding your circle of support, but what about the crunch you can't help but feel when those you cherish most find it impossible to encourage you?

In fact, maybe they even criticize you. Ever felt like those who are closest to you sometimes don't "get" you? Or maybe you've spent your entire life watching others experience love and support while your own life seems only to attract pain and toxicity?

We talked about this a bit earlier, and there's no question that it can be a bit tough when the people we love don't fully get what we're striving for, right? So, let's focus on it even more deeply today because I know that "feeling heard and supported" is a repeating theme for many clients.

I promise you, I've been there, too, and I know it can feel like a major roadblock on our path to happiness. But guess what? As bad as it may feel, we've got this!

Our ability to focus deliberately and keep our eye on the GPS will carry us through this.

Our relationship with family— even close family — can be tricky, to say the least! As we begin to yearn to make some defining choices in our lives, we may fear that others may not understand or even agree with those choices. We might fear that our growth will potentially leave us alienated and alone. So how do we keep that fear from "taking over the driver's seat"?

As I have gotten older, *I have realized that those who love us can only support us within the boundaries of their fears.* What does that mean?

It's simple.

Even when they believe they have our absolute best interest in mind, their own experience has created beliefs that they view as unarguable truths. They simply cannot encourage us to do things they cannot imagine doing. It's essential to recognize that their advice often comes from their limited perspective. Sure, some of their insights might be valuable, but we can't let their doubts hold us back from our aspirations.

Many, many success stories, including mine, feature a time when you're going to feel virtually alone. In my own case, when I shifted into my coaching and speaking, very few of those closest to me thought that my odds of succeeding were good — even though I do believe that most wanted the best for me.

Well, let me tell you, it's okay to feel alone on the path sometimes. Those moments of doubt and even failure are essential learning experiences that push us to grow and evolve. So, here's what I want you to do today. Embrace your path with open arms and release any sting from feeling unsupported or unappreciated. Instead of dimming your light to please others, seek out your tr'amily – that unique blend of tribe and family.

Your tr'amily consists of fellow joy-rriors who share your sense of purpose and are willing to explore uncharted paths with you. These are the people who will celebrate your victories, lift you up when you stumble, and genuinely support your growth.

Choose your tr'amily wisely, and trust me, they'll be there to cheer you on every step of the way. When others don't fully understand your journey, it's okay. Love them for their concern, but don't let their doubts infringe upon your joy.

Today, remember that YOU define your destiny, and you're the driver of this incredible vehicle called life. Your tr'amily will be there to share the journey, making it even more exciting and fulfilling. With their support, you can soar beyond any limitations, fueling up with courage and inspiration along the way. It's time to own your path, embrace your uniqueness, and let the exuberance of the entire Universe lift you higher.

So, Epic One, go out there today and claim your destiny with a heart full of excitement and courage! The world is waiting for you to shine, and I can't wait to see the incredible impact you'll make! Let's do this together!

Now go be you and find the next beautiful "center of your attention" just waiting for you to fall in love with it!

TODAY'S ACTION STEPS:

- *Go back to the column sheet from Day 11 and identify one focus/target where you need support but are not getting that support from your inner circle/family. Identify what type of support you need and write that down. (+1 Gold Star)*

- *Now that you've identified the "what" you need, who could provide that for you? And if you can't think of a specific "who" yet, brainstorm where you might look and who might be able to help you find this support and/or refer someone. (+2 Gold Stars)*
- *Bonus points if you take action today to connect with this person, group, mastermind, mentor, community, coach, etc. (+2 Gold Stars) Booyah!*

TOTAL POSSIBLE STARS FROM TODAY: 5 STARS

Day 21 — FOCUS: Embracing the Journey Beyond Goals

We've made a lot of progress learning how to become the "sovereign" of our focus in the past 20 days. Kudos to you for making great strides in learning how to change the one thing that will significantly impact how your life feels on a daily basis. That one thing will be the biggest game-changer when YOU determine which of your thoughts you choose to think versus simply allowing your thoughts "to think you."

So, as we gain even more momentum, it's critical that we make another important distinction here. Your goal for picking up this book was to create a life that feels more epic than anything that you've experienced so far. However, it's important not to get "hijacked" by your goals. They can demand your focus so intently that before long, they are *focusing you* versus you *managing them*.

Living a life that feels deliciously epic means understanding that Life is so much more than the "inconveniences" that "get in the way" of being able to focus on our "critical goals."…It's more than finding new ways to cope with the constant pressure…

Epic is when we decide that we are no longer going to wait for good things to happen… praying for that "big break."…We're no longer going to measure our success based on how quickly we hit retirement and or whether we're the fastest to make it to the top. Like the most mouthwatering cup of tea or fine cabernet, EPIC can take time to "steep" and mature.

Epic is when we take ownership of creating our destiny. It's when we look at our GPS and realize there's a lot of beautiful scenery to soak in on the road between Point A and Point B. Living an epic life means understanding that happiness and fulfillment are more than just a pursuit of goals or ticking items off a checklist. It's about savoring every moment of the journey, even the inconveniences and pressures that may come our way.

In our quest for that epic life, we sometimes get so fixated on our goals that we lose sight of the bigger picture. We become like children in the back seat, constantly asking, "Are we there yet?" We wake up each day focused on the gap between where we are and where we want to be, and from the moment that we wake up, that gap makes us feel like a failure.

Your mission today is to explore ways that you can begin to avoid tying your happiness and self-worth to achieving those goals. Resist the temptation to obsess over one particular outcome. As I apply the lessons that the boulder taught me, I believe we have only one "goal" in life:

To take our last breath saying, "Gosh, that was amazing! I hope that I get to do this again sometime…." Everything else is just an objective, a target, or a new iteration with the potential to add some spice along the path.

I believe it's our objectives that can guide us to iterate our way toward that one ultimate goal.

So here's an idea: what if we could reframe our approach to viewing objectives using our newfound ability to focus? What if we see them as milestones and guideposts rather than our next "ultimate destination"? What if we focus on allowing ourselves to feel happy and fulfilled along the entire journey, celebrating each step forward, no matter how small?

What if a more deliberate focus can allow us to let go of the pressure to reach the finish line and allow us instead to embrace the beauty of the twists and turns that life throws our way?

Life is about more than just achieving goals; it's about the experiences, the connections, and the growth we encounter. It's about learning to become the sovereign creators of our stories, crafting our destiny with intention and purpose.

Let's reframe the notion of goals and objectives. They are not meant to define our self-worth or validate our existence. Instead, they serve as the musical notes that compose the symphony of our lives. We have the power to blend them into infinite harmonies, creating a rich and vibrant treasury of experiences.

So, as you move forward today, consider this: Embrace each moment, even the inconveniences, as opportunities for growth, learning, and connection. Allow yourself to feel joy and fulfillment right here, right now, regardless of whether you've reached your ultimate destination.

Life is an adventure, and the real magic lies in experiencing it to the fullest every step of the way. You are the driver of your destiny, so recalibrate your focus, play your theme song, and let your life be a deliciously lived masterpiece of epic proportions.

There is so much out there waiting for you! Give yourself permission to savor and enjoy it as only that most EPIC version of you can do!

TODAY'S ACTION STEPS:

- *Write down 3-5 objectives you can commit to focus on over the next 75 days. They should be small to medium-sized objectives that would feel like a meaningful finish line. (+1 Gold Star)*

- *Now, write down 3-5 things you want to target over the next 30 days. Map out a quick list of "ingredients," either using Post-its or a mindmap to itemize the things you need to focus on in order to hit those targets. (+2 Gold Stars)*
- *Bonus points if you now prioritize those ingredients into four groups of small actions/targets that you will focus on each week over the next month. (+3 Gold Stars) Booyah!*

TOTAL POSSIBLE STARS FROM TODAY: 5 STARS

Day 22 — FOCUS: Shifting the Tractor Beam of Attraction to Inspired Action

We've been diving deep into the art of focus, uncovering the magic that comes with crafting an epic life. You've now learned that focusing does not mean obsessing because obsessing is a closer parallel to the frequency of desperation and lack, isn't it?

So if we're pushing ourselves further away from what we want when we identify it as something we "must have," what's the alternative? How do we get things done and make progress? How do we create the momentum to achieve objectives and hit our targets?

Great questions! So, let's delve into a transformational force that might just seem straight out of a sci-fi movie—the Law of Attraction.

Ok, ok, I'll admit – you might need to toss out some preconceived notions about this, just as I did when I first encountered it. You see, the Law of Attraction is more than just "thinking yourself wealthier" or wishing things into existence. Let me share "a little story" with you.

Years back, I came across Napoleon Hill's "THINK AND GROW RICH," and I'll admit, I tried the whole "thinking my way to riches." But it left me feeling frustrated because I couldn't bridge the gap between thinking and manifesting despite being a high achiever in most areas of my life.

Remember that one day in a Borders Bookstore when I was searching for a new dragon fantasy book, and the Abraham Hicks's book called "Ask and It is Given" literally fell off the shelf at my feet. The title made me so curious that I couldn't resist taking a look. Pretty quickly, I began to find incredible value in their wisdom about the Law of Attraction. I began to play with some of their insights, and surprisingly, things started to shift. At first, I noticed the " attractions " were seemingly trivial—finding the perfect parking spot or seeing matching numbers on the clock.

But the big desires—like a great relationship, business success, and my own house—still seemed out of reach. Patience and trust were the missing ingredients.

Over time, as I listened to their tapes (yes, on good ol' cassette tapes), something clicked. Subtly, my thoughts began to rewire, replacing old patterns with this new way of thinking. My focus shifted, and my mind started to align with this powerful change at a profound level.

Here's the deal about the Law of Attraction—it's not just a cosmic tractor beam pulling things towards you. I look at the word "attraction" now as a contraction for several words: **Attracting The Right ACTION—the Law of AT'T'R'ACTION**. When viewed that way, *I found it easier to realize that the "secret" is to strive to create inspired action in harmony with your vision.*

Remember, "epic" thrives on Life's beautiful duality, the interplay of inner and outer game brings true magic. So, yes, set objectives, but don't get lost in the "are we there yet" mentality. Focus on *being* the version of yourself that naturally chooses the inspired action that will create the results that you desire. Focus on your frequency.

Yes, your focus plays a pivotal role. Your story about what you're focusing on shapes the actions you take. Let's play with an example:

Suppose you're unhappy about your health, weight, finances, or relationships. If you focus on the problem, the story may sound like, "This will lead to more pain and unhappiness; it's not changing fast enough."

In this version, your actions tend to self-sabotage, and if the scale's not moving quickly enough, that can lead to frustration. But imagine a different story—imagine seeing the "problems" as catalysts for growth.

Picture yourself a year from now, loving how you look, feeling energetic, and having a blast. Suddenly, those sprouts on your salad become part of the recipe for the high-energy epic you. Focus on knowing it will happen. Appreciate the few pounds that led you toward the desire to lock in some better habits and embrace the journey.

So, how can you shift your focus today? Gently! Lean into the Law of Inspired Action. Instead of resisting what displeases you, embrace it as the catalyst for change. Trust that new actions will lead to unexpected EPIC rewards.

Are you ready for a resounding BOOYAH? Today brims with possibilities, and it all starts with your focus. So, let's align that tractor beam with inspired action and unleash the magic in every moment!

TODAY'S ACTION STEPS:

- *Write down the one objective you feel you desire the most from yesterday. (+1 Gold Star)*
- *Take a moment to close your eyes and imagine three of the people you admire most throughout time (they do not have to be currently living) sitting with you in the most glorious setting you can imagine. One by one, imagine them sharing with each other and with you why they would choose you to achieve this objective – what they know*

you will feel, what impact you'll make with this... Now, hear them share why they think you are worthy of achieving this and how you will undoubtedly do so. If it helps you focus, choose some calm instrumental music to play in the background as the soundtrack for this encounter. (+2 Gold Stars)
- *Bonus points if you repeat this exercise once daily for seven days. (+3 Gold Stars) Booyah!*

TOTAL POSSIBLE STARS FROM TODAY: 5 STARS

Day 23 — FOCUS: Finding Your Significance Beyond the Storms of Others

Underneath all the hustle and bustle of the day can lurk some profound questions that most of us confront at some point in our lives: Why am I here? What is my life's significance in the grand scheme of eternity? Do I "matter"?

So, let's dive into a powerful lesson I recently encountered during a poignant conversation with a successful CEO. This conversation went beyond coping with stress—it touched the very essence of finding our significance. It spoke to our well-intentioned tendency to focus on making others feel happy or proud – and how we often stake our worthiness on whether we are successful in this mission.

In my conversation with this CEO, he shared that he had grown the family company immensely, and yet it seemed like, try as he might, he was constantly faced with his father's insults and wrath. It was phenomenally heartbreaking and stressful for him, especially considering his father's declining health. If only he could make his father see….

Now understand that this CEO came to me originally simply asking for ways to cope with the stress. We touched on a few practices ranging from meditation to other things that served as positive triggers for him. However, the solution to his stress went much deeper than mere coping skills – and this is where many of us jump to the wrong conclusion. Coping skills are just the band-aid. He needed to identify the root of the stresses that were causing his need to cope to begin with.

As we talked more about his father's history, a pattern emerged. His father had grown up in a post-WWII world of struggle and sacrifice. Life had been a series of unfair disappointments, and he began to define himself by his ability to weather these storms. In an ironic twist, his father's "superpower" was surviving the relentless challenges that life threw at him, even from those closest to him.

This belief in sacrifice as a measure of significance was ingrained in his father's generation. And now, if this CEO managed to make his father see the truth—that his significance didn't come from enduring suffering—it might shatter his father's entire sense of self-worth and purpose.

As we continued our conversation, the CEO realized that his father's accusations weren't about him; they reflected his father's beliefs about significance. Engaging in a contest of wills and truths wouldn't lead to any resolution at this stage of his father's life. Instead, the CEO could honor his core values by resisting the urge to argue and simply continue conveying love and admiration for his father.

He understood that just because someone makes statements about us doesn't make those statements true. This CEO finally began to focus on ways to take control of his story and find his significance beyond the storms of others.

So here's a profound truth for you: YOU define your significance. You decide what makes your life meaningful. It can be a force that uplifts and serves or one that diminishes and demeans. Toxic people, often trapped in their painful narratives, may try to project their storms onto you. But remember, their story is not your story, and your worth isn't contingent on their approval.

Embrace your sovereign EPIC self and rise above the turbulent tides of others' stories. Allow yourself to be free from the burden of seeking significance in their eyes. Your significance comes from within, from living authentically, and from the impact you create in the world.

Today, release yourself from the weight of others' expectations. Be unapologetically you, and focus simply on letting your light shine brighter than ever before. Because, dear friend, you are significant, and your story is a masterpiece of epic proportions!

There is nothing to "fix" — just opportunities to step forward and *create!*

TODAY'S ACTION STEPS:

- *Identify if someone else's turbulent story or sense of significance has been grabbing your focus. Think of the CEO's story and make note of any similarities you may see. (+1 Gold Star)*
- *Now, write down a list of things you have done for others' approval, then rank them on a scale of 1-10 based on how much happiness the results of those actions brought you. Note if there are common themes and/or lessons that you want recognized. (+2 Gold Stars)*
- *Bonus points if you now create a declaration for yourself that you can write on a large piece of paper and post in full view: I declare that going forward, I will be true to this vision of myself and who I intend to show up being…" Finish the sentence and post! (+3 Gold Stars) Booyah!*

TOTAL POSSIBLE STARS FROM TODAY: 5 STARS

Day 24 — FOCUS: Unleash Your Epic Power with Positive Triggers

We don't always get to choose how long we get to play on this **beautiful** little planet, but we do get to choose how epically we live while we play here.

So it's worth identifying where, when, how, and WHO you are at your best. What are the positive triggers that make it feel easier and more natural to get in your flow?

(Word of Advice: Do not assume that the world holds the reins on these triggers or that you have to wait until all your ducks are in a row before you can relax and feel like you have earned the right to be proud, fulfilled, and happily flowing.)

Seriously! What if YOU could create more conditions that make it easier to naturally focus on things that please you? And I'm talking about conditions that are within YOUR control!

In my world, I call it creating your own Personal Empowerment System™ (PES™).

If you are willing to invest as little as 30 minutes to an hour, you can create one of these too!

Today, let's embark on a transformative journey to unlock more epic in your day. It's time to dive deep into the realms of positive triggers and create your very own Personal Empowerment System™ (PES™). This system will be your guiding light, illuminating the path to all sorts of Epic Booyah!

Imagine having your own "care and feeding manual" that holds the secrets to keeping you at your absolute best—mind, body, and soul. To possess the power to enthrall, to establish deep connections. To engage in remarkable conversations without concerning yourself with appearances or the need for approval... To be recognized as someone who consistently shows up as the "Epic You," exuding self-assuredness, vibrancy, and wisdom...

It's time to share these secrets with yourself and with the world.

Let's begin by acknowledging that you don't have to wait until everything is perfectly aligned to live your epic life. We must start by identifying your "first duck"—the positive trigger that sets your epic life in motion.

Your PES™ is a powerful tool that encompasses every facet of your being. Start with the basics—nutrition and sleep. But don't just list how many hours of sleep you need; go deeper. Understand the conditions necessary for your best night's sleep. Is it a dark room or some gentle light? Silence or background noise? The perfect pillows, covers, and room temperature? What activities before bedtime help you sleep better? What should you avoid doing?

This is your manual of the conditions that make you feel EPIC, so don't hold back. Date the pages and revisit your PES™ at least quarterly to course-correct and recalibrate when needed.

And yes, these triggers must also include things in your inner game because, of course, the world that you are experiencing within often dictates how you experience the world outside. When I work with my clients, I even have them include their love languages.

In case you're not familiar with the book *"5 Love Languages"* created by Gary Chapman, Ph.D., he reveals that we all tend to communicate love in five basic ways. These are what he calls the love languages. The order in which you prioritize them not only reflects what makes you feel loved but it can also explain why your relationships are flowing smoothly or running into boulders. Knowing how you feel most loved—Quality Time, Words of Affirmation, Gifts, Touch, Acts of Service—can change your perspective on displaying love, respect, and affection for yourself and others.

You can see why this is so impactful. This is why your PES™ needs to include them.

Don't stop there. Explore how you handle conflict, practice self-care, engage in creative pursuits, and spend time with loved ones. Identify the environment that best nurtures your soul.

These are your positive triggers—the conditions that energize and uplift you. They exist within your reach, waiting to be harnessed and embraced. However, you might have inadvertently neglected them or believed you don't deserve them until you achieve certain goals.

But here's the truth: you CAN control these positive triggers. Don't let busyness or stress lead you to ignore what makes you feel your best. Embrace these conditions, cherish them, and prioritize them in your life.

Sometimes, it's a matter of finding creative solutions to incorporate positive triggers into your routine. For example, I had a client named Leanne. She was a wonderful "can do" sort of person, but she came to me feeling burned out and frustrated. Her job felt like it was consuming her energy, leaving her zero time to do what she really loved: spend time with her beloved horses. When we started working together on her PES™, it was Tuesday after a long weekend. I mentioned that we would work on identifying the positive triggers that helped her feel her best. She jokingly replied, "Well, I tend to feel my best when I can take a 3-day weekend once a month, but THAT'S not going to happen!"

No sooner were the words out of her mouth when I stopped her and asked how many PTO days she had in a year. The look on her face was priceless when she realized she could use her PTO days to create regular 3-day weekends, allowing her to spend time with her incredible horses.

Revelations like these are not unusual.

Let's look at my client, Ryan. He came to me feeling frazzled and completely overwhelmed with his work. He felt like he was working 24/7, doing everything he could to grow his business, but it left him feeling drained and uninspired. Every step forward felt like a dead end, so he came to me to help him re-energize and find clarity.

Part of our process was ensuring he was setting himself up for success. That meant putting consistent triggers into place to keep the inspiration and iterations flowing. As we dove into things that recharged his energy, he said this, "The truth is that as dumb as it sounds, I get some of my best ideas when I'm ice skating, but who has time for that anymore?"

I, of course, smiled and pointed out to him that he was making himself feel guilty for indulging in ice skating—the very activity that ignited his inspiration and helped him overcome business challenges. Personally AND professionally, this had to be a non-negotiable part of his system. Ryan made the adjustment and was shocked to see just how much of a vital role "Recharge" made in his success.

So, yes!

Today is the day you seize control of your positive triggers. Create your PES™ and put it into action. Unleash your epic power and claim your destiny, one positive trigger at a time!

Be the sleuth and look for the hidden possibilities within your own PES™. When you find your own version of the hidden 3-day weekend or the skating recharge, you will no longer be overwhelmed by trying to control the uncontrollable. Instead, you'll focus on embracing the joy of being in charge of your well-being. Yes! Starting right here, right now, YOU are the master of your destiny, the Ninja of all things Epic, and the weaver of your epic story.

The time is NOW. Go out there, play with all those ducks (or, in our world, those Epic Chicks), and remember to leave time for a big BOOYAH at the end of the day! Your epic journey awaits!

TODAY'S ACTION STEPS:

- *Start creating your own Personal Empowerment System by putting five columns on a sheet of paper. Label Column #1: At home. Column #2: At work. Column #3: Personally/Physically. #4: In Relationships #5. Then complete each column with as many things that complete this sentence, "I am at my best when I…" Try to include everything that you can think of. For example, in your relationship, you may be at your best when you have a date night with your honey at least twice a month. Be sure to be as specific as possible. (+3 Gold Stars)*
- *Hint: remember that we're asking you what conditions are in place when you feel your best. This is not about what you may now be in the habit of doing. Those are not necessarily the same, are they? Wink!*
- *Now look for clues! What conditions could you control that you aren't currently controlling that would help you consistently feel more energized, more inspired, and happier in general? List 2-3 ideas. (+2 Gold Stars)*
- *Bonus points if you want to complete the actual PES™ form I share with my clients. Email the word PES to team@gritmindsetacademy.com, and we'll get you started. (+3 Gold Stars) Booyah!*

TOTAL POSSIBLE STARS FROM TODAY: 8 STARS

Day 25 — FOCUS: I'll Be Happy When...

So why do we strive to create a life that feels more epic? Because we want to feel happy! Over the past few weeks, we've talked about many ways that simply shifting your focus can completely change how you feel.

However, this does not mean that you have to wait until you can say, "Yep, now my life is epic," before you give yourself the go-ahead to be happy.

If you want to achieve lasting traction for more energy, more joy, more "carpe diem," the time is NOW! We live so much of our lives "getting ready to be ready"— and we often believe that "ready" means that the conditions are "right." I encourage you to rediscover the magic that is potentially present every step of the way as we get "ready to be ready."

There is the possibility of tremendous joy and wonder even in those moments when we temporarily feel like we are falling. True, there are many conditions that we cannot control, but many that we can.

"Being happy" is a choice, not a condition, and the time to seize the magic of life is right now. If you only take one gem from these 100 days, let it be this: *No more waiting for the perfect conditions to be happy*. Again, happiness is not a condition—it is a choice. It is a choice that begins by choosing to become the sovereign of your focus, to take control of your thoughts, and to determine your emotional state based on the thoughts that you allow to have traction.

As I walked towards the Colombian hospital where my daughter fought for her life, I made a profound choice—to stay happy. You might wonder how I could feel happiness in such a dire situation, but I believed that my power in that scenario lay in my ability to become an energetic match for the positive outcome I desired. By aligning with the "frequency of miracles," I believed my focus could make a difference.

This concept is not just a mystical belief; science supports it, too. Experts like Dr. Joe Dispenza explain that *we must match our energy and emotions with the experiences we hope to attract* into our lives. It's about learning to harness the power of our thoughts and emotions and our inner game frequency.

I could have let my mind wander into a spiral of fear and anxiety, imagining all the terrible outcomes. But I refused to give those thoughts power over me. Instead, I became aware of the situation without letting it dictate my reaction.

Choosing happiness doesn't mean being in denial or ignoring challenging circumstances. It's about understanding that circumstances don't define how you experience life's moments. The power to choose your emotional response always lies within you.

Today, I invite you to explore the transformative choice of happiness, no matter what life throws at you. When your mind starts down a negative spiral, practice "ruthless compassion" by gently redirecting your thoughts to a more energizing and positive track.

Find joy in the small things—the chirping of birds, the dance of clouds, or the crackling of a fire. Dole out compliments to yourself and others. Train yourself to see the beauty and delight in every moment, even as you pursue your objectives and dreams.

The more you practice this empowering choice, the more natural it becomes. Soon, your thoughts will gravitate towards positivity, and the worst-case scenarios will lose their grip on your mind.

Life is a dance. Yes, it may sometimes step on our toes, but we have the power to respond gracefully. Embrace the exquisite dance of life, and choose to live epically in every moment, no matter the circumstances.

Let go of the belief that happiness is a distant destination and realize it is a dance partner, always ready to twirl and sway with you. This exquisite dance partner is capable of great shifts that can inspire sublime surprise and delight when you least expect it.

Claim your happiness by choosing to focus on things that bring you joy. Let your ability to envision epic things be a guiding force as you journey through the majestic experience of life. The choice is yours, so decide that you *are* ready!

Kick up those feet and choose to live in your happiness right here, right now.

TODAY'S ACTION STEPS:

- *Write down 3-5 "happiness-inducing actions" that you will do every day for the next seven days. Remember that these do not need to be big. They can be as simple as eating lunch at the park with the intent to stay off the phone, instead watching the clouds, the birds, and the butterflies go by. (+1 Gold Star)*
- *At the end of each day, write down five things that you noticed each day that captured the epicness of life and of this planet. (+2 Gold Stars)*
- *Bonus points if you share your observations with others and inspire others to start doing it too! (+2 Gold Stars) Booyah!*

TOTAL POSSIBLE STARS FROM TODAY: 5 STARS

Day 26 — FOCUS: Nurture Your Soul with Positive Influences – Dancing with the Anti-Mentors

Choosing to be happy sounds great, but we all know this can be really hard to execute when toxic or abusive people surround us. In fact, it's not uncommon for some of that negativity to "rub off on us." Today, we'll take another dive even deeper into how we can control the negative impact of others around us when we can't just pick up and leave– the **Anti-Mentors** in our lives. Well, have you ever heard the saying that we become the average of the five people we spend the most time with? It holds a profound truth. The people who surround us do influence us greatly, shaping our beliefs, attitudes, and perspectives on life.

Of course, we can't always control the people in our life. We don't usually control the family that we grow up with. We don't often even get to control the environment that we grow up in. And professionally, most of us don't get to choose who we end up working with. I'm pretty sure I'm not the only one who has faced a toxic colleague or client.

These are the folks that I lovingly call our Anti-Mentors. Although they may bring anguish and misery into our lives to varying degrees, they also provide us with an essential gift: clarity around what we **do not want.**

Though we all at times wish that this wasn't the case, I've found that Life's most captivating choreography casts us with two dance partners. In fact, in my experience, having an Epic perspective on life – what some might call deliberate optimism – is savoring the entire dance that we call life. It's loving the dance partner who steps on our toes and forces us to change stride just as much as we love the partner who glides effortlessly across the floor and lifts us deliciously into the air. The moment when life starts being truly Epic is when we find ourselves so engaged in life that we love every spectacular moment-- even the ones that look like they are going to kick us to the curb upon arrival. The Epic Ninja Focusers among us *know* that deliberate, focused optimism is oxygen for the soul, so breathe deeply..."

However, when the Anti-Mentors start showing up, the common approach of simply reacting to the world around us typically falls flat. This is where most of us "lose it" and start falling into the abyss.

THIS is where the mission of the Epic Ninja Focuser begins.

The Epic Ninja Focuser always remembers these five critical truths:

1. Remember that even **those who love you aren't always the "right" people to support you in every scenario**. Your loved ones' perspectives are always influenced by their fears and beliefs. They cannot encourage you to do something that they would never do. We've talked about this, but it's so important that I'm repeating it.
2. Remember that toxicity is contagious and that your **inner game jukebox is always listening.** If you do not deliberately and consciously find a way to counterbalance or override the negativity, there's a good chance that it will infect your dreams, compromise your confidence, and lead you down a path where all you see are flaws and turmoil. Your jukebox will always seem to be playing the songs that you don't like.
3. You DO have an imagination capable of **dreaming up incredibly wondrous and epic things**. As you exercise your imagination, it becomes grander and bolder, capable of triggering "impossible things" into reality. You have a right– I'd say an obligation – to

explore all that your uniquely brilliant mind can imagine. Why else would you be given your gifts, your talents, your insights, and yes, even all of those crazy experiences that become your stories?

4. **As unpleasant as it can feel when you're going through it, even the Anti-Mentors have value in our story.** Whereas we are often tempted to stray from the advice offered by our mentors, there is nothing like the absolute clarity regarding what we don't want when confronted by Anti-mentors. Their crisis and anger do not have to be yours. Just learn from it, extract more clarity about your preferences, and refocus on the next epic step for YOU!
5. **There ARE people out there** who would love nothing more than to align with you on your epic journey. No matter how bleak things may feel, with time and perseverance, you will find your inner circle, your mentors, and your champions. Only YOU ultimately get to choose who will be in your inner circle! Don't choose by default or allow proximity or dependency to make that choice for you.
6. The best way to navigate through a world where there is both a wealth of positivity and toxicity is to **deliberately focus on controlling the weight/impact of the narrative** that whirls both in the world around you and within. At the end of the day, YOU choose the energy that you allow to influence your power. It will either increase your power or deplete it. It all depends on what you choose and WHO you choose. Who will you listen to and allow in?

On a planet now so connected by technology, where negativity and hate speech can spread rapidly, it becomes even more important that we commit ourselves to becoming the sovereign of our minds and masters of our inner game. We can transform our lives and how we experience the world by simply taking control of what we consume mentally and emotionally. Who do you choose to listen to? Who do you allow in your "space"?

Even 10% more time spent in the company of those who nurture you will change your life.

Be patient but deliberate with this quest, knowing that success starts with your focus. Where IS your 10%? Go find them.

Embrace those who feel like positive influences, those who make you hungry for life, touch your heart and nourish your soul. Seek out those who inspire you to believe in a future filled with extraordinary potential and endless possibilities.

As you think about surrounding yourself with positive influences, there is one person you absolutely will spend the most time with.

Yes – YOU!

Remember that you are not absent from this equation. You cannot expect those around you to be supportive when you are not showing up as an empowering resource for yourself.
Your inner dialogue holds immense power. Let's face it: you spend more time with yourself than anyone else, so make sure that your time is spent with your best "soul mate," not your own worst enemy.

Loving yourself is the ultimate triumph of focus. Even during challenging times, choose to love yourself and love life. Embrace your past, even the painful chapters, as they have shaped you into the strong and resilient person you are today.

Your mission on this quest to Epic is to go find those people who will help you uncover that most Epic expression of you – those who can perhaps see that Epic Future You before you can even see it. Learn to be your biggest champion beginning right here, right now!

I'll emphasize again that you don't have to change your past to create your epic future. Your struggles and obstacles have been catalysts for growth, pushing you to become the best version of yourself. You don't even have to boot out everyone in your existing circle (unless you know they are drilling holes that keep sinking your boat).

Life is richer when we connect with positive influences and foster relationships with ourselves and others. Choose your influences wisely, and let go of the negative forces that may be ruling your thoughts and emotions.

Step jubilantly into the role of being the master of your masterpiece. Deliberately choose the colors that grace your palate. Let the positive influences guide you towards a more joyous, empowered self and inner circle.

Today, let the five biggest sources of influence in your life be a reflection of the best version of yourself—a person who uplifts and empowers, not just for others but for that special soul we know as YOU.

Guess what? As you focus on nurturing your soul with positive influences, you'll discover that you will experience more moments spent in joyous and empowered states, and they will lead to better outcomes in all aspects of your life.

So go out and find this day's "10%." Who will that be? Who can you meet? Are there those who you can reconnect with? Where is that next amazing soul just waiting to join your inner circle? This is a day filled with an infinite number of ways that you can infuse your life with positivity– no matter what! You'll find it! One little step at a time…

May your day be filled with surprise and delight as you choose to create the most breathtakingly EPIC version of YOU!

TODAY'S ACTION STEPS:

- *Brainstorm a list of 5-10 ways to surround yourself with 10% more positive influences today. (+1 Gold Star)*
- *Go out and implement! (+2 Gold Stars)*
- *Bonus points if you also create and implement a list of ways to EXPAND your inner circle. (+2 Gold Stars) Booyah!*

TOTAL POSSIBLE STARS FROM TODAY: 5 STARS

Day 27 — FOCUS: Embrace the Hidden Treasures of Unexpected Falls

Over the past few days, we've explored ways to focus more deliberately on controlling things that you have the power to control. But what about the moments that send you flying?

Well, what if a fall is just a spontaneous moment of unexpected flight before you hit new ground? Wink! Yes, that was the lesson of the Universe as I found myself suspended in an unexpected "flyover" (that moment when you find yourself in mid-flip over the handlebars waiting to see where you will land…).

As we all know, life is a continuous adventure filled with moments that take us by surprise—some joyous, others challenging. In my mid-50s, I discovered the thrill of… mountain biking! There's nothing like barreling down a 40-foot ravine to get your Sunday morning started on an exhilarating note!

During one particularly fast and glorious ride with a group of the "Swamp Club's" most seasoned riders, I felt like I had truly become an EPIC version of myself. I was zooming down winding paths, conquering hills with newfound confidence, and relishing the beauty of the day. Little did I know that the Universe had a surprise waiting for me.

As we approached a sharp decline, I heard a playful warning from the riders ahead. As I came around the corner, I quickly saw the Universe's "joie du jour"—a series of roots and logs embedded in a particularly sandy path, creating a tricky obstacle during the already challenging descent. Before I knew it, I was airborne, feeling both "practically perfect" like Mary Poppins and practically bruised upon landing.

In that moment, I could have allowed the fall to overshadow the glory of the adventure, but instead, I chose to bounce back up with even more determination. Despite the new bruises and a bit of blood, my desire to keep riding and pushing forward grew stronger. I even caught up with the faster riders, fueled by a new sense of joyous resilience.

What I discovered was profound—the fall had not eroded the glory of the adventure; instead, it added to the momentum. On that Sunday morning, I left the trails of Croom, having learned this: When we focus on the fall, we feel the bruises. When we focus on getting back on the bike, we feel the wind behind us.

So here's my message to you today. Control what you can control. Focus on setting yourself up for success. However, know that there are times when the things you can't control lead to a fall. In those moments, you *can* get up. How quickly you get back up is your decision. The more quickly you focus on getting back on the bike, the sooner these falls can become stepping stones to greater achievements. Life isn't just about the finish line; it's about the moments of wondrous flight and the tenacity to dream, love, and live more.

That morning, Mother Earth sent me out to play, reminding me to jump in puddles, run down hills, and relish the falls because the ups *and downs* hone the spirit. Challenges hold the promise of strength, tenacity, and the desire to create more and more.

Embrace the hidden treasures of unexpected falls. Each fall offers an opportunity to learn, grow, and gain momentum. When life throws you off course, grab the bike of resilience, race forward, and cheer yourself on with your mighty voice.

Today, choose to focus on the unlikely glory of your falls—the moments that propel you forward and remind you of your strength. Embrace the adventure, knowing each fall is a chance to rise higher, become more magnificent, and savor the joy of soaring through life.

What "unlikely glory" can you choose to focus on?

TODAY'S ACTION STEPS:

- *Think of a time recently when you had a "fall" – maybe not literally, but it was definitely an opportunity for some "unlikely glory." Even in the pain, were there moments you can feel proud of? Some things that you handled well? Were there endearing moments? Humorous moments? Moments when others showed generosity and care? Write down three takeaways about GOOD things this fall says about your spirit, perseverance, or any other quality you choose! (+1 Gold Star)*
- *Now – What's one playful adventure that you can plan? Can you push yourself slightly beyond what you'd normally choose and plan your epic adventure, confident that should it happen, you can turn a fall into a triumph? (+2 Gold Stars)*
- *Bonus points if you plan TWO!!. (+2 Gold Stars) Booyah!*

TOTAL POSSIBLE STARS FROM TODAY: 5 STARS

Day 28 —FOCUS: Reframing Your Self-Image

We just explored why it can be so critical to hop back on the bike quickly when things you can't control send you flying. This brings us to our next area of invaluable focus: SELF-ESTEEM! What do you think? Does your focus really impact your ability to believe in yourself? Absolutely!

If you aspire to go out into the world on this beautiful day feeling your best, then you have to realize the following:

- Lack of Confidence
- Imposter Syndrome

- People Pleasing
- Fear
- Believing That You "Can't"
- Feeling Shame Because A Toxic Person "Left You" – Or Because You Left Them…
- Blaming yourself for all of the times that Life sent you flying

I could go on and on. The list of negative emotions impacted by your focus is endless, but you get the point… All of these things are symptomatic of what we've been calling "The (Dreaded) Sloppy Thinking Syndrome." These are red flags that you are allowing your *thoughts to think you* versus activating the recalibrated approach where we focus deliberately.

Because (wait for it…) what you focus on and **what you make that focus means creates your beliefs**. (Look familiar? WINK!) When we believe that we've taken a lot of falls (and we don't focus on how well we got back on the bike), we start to let that impact our self-esteem.

Let's face it: your self-esteem is the foundation upon which your entire life is built. It influences how you perceive yourself, the world around you, and your potential to achieve that "Booyah Epicness." When your self-esteem is high, you radiate confidence, taking on challenges with gusto and believing in your abilities to overcome any obstacle. On the other hand, when self-esteem is low, doubt and insecurity can sabotage even your loftiest dreams.

But here's the secret: *your self-esteem is not fixed*. It's not a trait you're born with and stuck with for life. Instead, it's a malleable aspect of your being, shaped and influenced by your focus.

Consider the following quote by Alice Walker: *"The most common way people give up their power is by thinking they don't have any."* These few words hold profound wisdom. Your beliefs are the products of your focus, and your beliefs, in turn, shape your self-esteem and sense of personal power.

"Negative emotions" like those I mentioned above – lack of confidence, imposter syndrome, people-pleasing, fear, and feeling like you "can't" – stem from a misaligned and uninformed focus. It's easy to get caught up in the opinions of others, allowing their criticisms to dictate your self-worth. But what if you could shift your focus and choose what you make that focus mean?

When we are children, we are trained to respect the "wisdom" and clarity (and opinion and fears and perspectives) of those who "know better" – the authority figures that are typically our parents and teachers. If they can train us to allow them to call the shots, it makes managing us easier. Therefore, the programming is intense. It's often doled out with the best intentions because, at that time in our lives, it can benefit us and keep us safe.

However, as time passes, even when we know that these adults clearly have their issues, we fall into the habit of burying our preferences and instincts in favor of the thoughts and actions that will keep those around us happy.

This can mean that by the time we are approaching adulthood, *we trust and value others' opinions more than we trust our own.* **We judge our value by whether we can consistently get** *the approval of those "important people." Yet, it can often feel like the bar set by these influencers is impossibly high… and so now we feel like we are not enough – even failures.*

Before we know it, instead of living our own lives, we become focused on living a life that will please (and impress) those around us.

We wake up with the same expectations. We keep seeing ourselves based on who we were the day before. We allow the world around us, the *people* around us, to influence how we define ourselves – often based on our so-called "limitations and flaws."

Building healthy self-esteem starts with recalibrating your focus deliberately. Instead of dwelling on what's lacking or what you perceive as flaws, *look* for the hidden treasures within yourself. Challenge the negative beliefs that have held you back for far too long.

Like a glass half full, your self-image is brimming with potential, waiting to be filled with positivity and self-belief. You can start building a "glass half full" habit, a joyous obsession even, for seeing the best in yourself and your capabilities.

However… just talking about "seeing the glass half full" isn't enough. At first, you must deliberately instruct your focus to look for *and acknowledge* that there are A LOT of half-full glasses that have been sitting unnoticed in the world around you.

It's natural to experience moments of doubt, especially when faced with setbacks or criticism. I definitely found myself questioning my worth and potential in the past. But I've learned that it's crucial not to allow the negativity of others (or my own critical voice) to become the script that defines my life. It's also crucial to realize that some of the choices that you felt like you had to make as a child, you don't necessarily have to keep choosing to make today.

The power to change your focus lies within you. Instead of allowing a toxic narrative to define your self-image, reclaim that power and fill your glass with self-compassion and belief. Surround yourself with positive influences that uplift you and encourage your growth.

Remember, it's not about ignoring challenges or pretending the "dark side" doesn't exist. It's about fortifying your focus on the light with such tenacity—the strengths, achievements, and the capacity to rise from falls – that the dark can't overshadow the light.

Even in my Society of Epic Chicks, I've witnessed countless women transform their lives by taking control of their focus. They've stepped out of the shadows of past hurts and judgments, realizing that their worth is not determined by fixing the past. Instead, their brilliance and sense of accomplishment blossom by stepping forward into the future as someone who focuses on living that most epic expression of Self.

Today, as you are tempted to look back on the times that you "allowed yourself to fall," I encourage you to think again. Focus differently. Know that you have the choice to reshape your self-esteem, to become the master or mistress of what you choose to pour into your glass. Deliberately focus on the qualities that make you remarkable and embrace the journey of growth and self-discovery.

You don't need to seek validation or prove your worth to anyone else. Embrace the "glass half full" habit and watch your beliefs transform. Let your focus be the guide that empowers you to stand tall, to pursue your dreams, and to believe in the extraordinary potential within. The clock is ticking, and your time to rise to greatness is now.

So, if you have been struggling with your self-esteem, it's time to pause and entertain a new possibility: Gaining a stronger sense of Self is as simple as being willing to learn how to recalibrate your focus *and put the consistent discipline into doing it!*

The truth is that Life has given you a collection of stories, gifts, and abilities that already make you epic! Isn't it time for you to finally send that critical voice to a desert island and start embracing that?

Repeat after me: *I AM pretty darn EPIC – and that's something to Booyah about!*

TODAY'S ACTION STEPS:

- *Today is a day to have fun with the glass-half-full metaphor! Yes, grab a big glass (crystal if you have it). Now, grab a pitcher or a bottle of water. Fill half of the glass bit by bit. As you pour in each splash, recite one quality you believe you already possess and/or something you are grateful for. Do this until the glass is half full. (+2 Gold Stars)*
- *Now – do the same thing with the rest of the glass until the glass is full, except as you complete this glass, with each splash of water, recite the qualities within yourself that you will focus on gaining, growing, or expanding. (+2 Gold Stars)*
- *Bonus points if you write this second group of qualities you'll nurture on paper and post it somewhere visible!! Keep looking at it daily! (+2 Gold Stars) Booyah!*

TOTAL POSSIBLE STARS FROM TODAY: 6 STARS

Day 29 —FOCUS: Allowing Your Little Voice Back Into the Castle

Struggling with confidence and self-esteem is one thing, but what about those times when you are tempted to totally lose faith in yourself and feel like you will never be able to trust yourself again?

I'm talking about that moment when everything in your being told you that "you had found your 'it'... that this was your superpower, your calling, your *"thing"*.... you were starting to feel confident, then – wham — without warning, someone came along and "pulled back a curtain" that you didn't even realize existed. There for all the world to see laid your flaws and imperfections – and you felt like an idiot.

There was no "half full" at that moment, was there? Your glass was not only empty but forever broken.

Suddenly, all of that previous enthusiasm was drowning in an endless tidal wave of shame. You knew that you would never — EVER – expose yourself to the possibility of such humiliation again. Right then and there, you inadvertently turned over your power to the Haters of the world. It was as if your new truth became this: *Until they say that you are worthy of THEM, you can't trust yourself to believe that you are worthy of ANYONE – much less your own self-esteem.*

Can you tell that I have been there?

This "crash and burn" experience struck again even after the boulder when I was starting this speaking and coaching business. It was 2018. Schuy was making progress, but all of us were beginning to have to face the fact that Schuy's physical recovery was going *much slower* than any of us had originally expected. She had progressed beyond the point where she constantly needed someone in the room to ensure she wouldn't fall from her wheelchair, but there was still barely any sense of independence. As I focused on rebuilding some sort of income, it felt like I was juggling two full-time jobs. And yet, if that was going to take us to the light at the end of the tunnel, I knew that this was what I must find a way to do.

You might say that I was feeling a wee bit of pressure!

As you may know, the trickiest part of this industry is getting people to know about you. I heard LinkedIn could be a good avenue, so I was posting constantly. I even invested in joining a "posting pod" where we would all post simultaneously and go in to support each other, hoping to trigger more visibility from the algorithm.

One of these posts connected me with a lovely man affiliated with a highly respected speaker agency. He was a huge champion of Schuyler's and my story, and even though I was *very new* to the speaking world, he encouraged me to join their agency on a non-exclusive basis. He also invited me to fly to Texas, meet a couple of their agents, and check out their Spring speaker showcases. He *strongly* encouraged me to invest in their upcoming July showcase so that both their agents and buyers could see me. Even though I was still terrified on stage, I agreed to invest in the trip to Dallas.

The trip was inspiring. I met many great speakers, including a couple who have gone on to make millions in the industry. Facing quite a bit of uproar from those in my inner circle, I took the plunge and invested in the Kansas City July showcase.

As I excitedly prepared for the trip, I was emailing back and forth with the agency's owner. Things seemed to be going well until one of the Dallas agents mistakenly emailed me, thinking she was emailing the owner. In fairly strong terms, she said she had zero desire to work with me and that I had "talked her head off" at the spring showcase. Considering that I thought that I had just been following my original contact's instructions to share my story with the agents, I was horrified. I didn't know how to respond.

I didn't want to embarrass the woman, and at the same time, I had already paid and committed to the showcase in Kansas City. About 15 minutes later, another email appeared, and she apologized, saying that the email had been inappropriate and had not been intended for me. I did my best to respond gracefully, but I confess I was crushed. This did nothing for my confidence as I arrived to showcase.

Prepping for the event went smoothly. The other speakers welcomed me with open arms, and the owner of the agency was professional and nice. On the other hand, the Dallas agent avoided me. I learned that the man who was my original contact was no longer with the agency and would not be there. It was another awkward moment, but I was focused on doing my best!

Let me pause a moment in the story to emphasize something that can be tough to swallow: when we are learning a new skill, we *must* embrace that we simply aren't going to be as "brilliant" and smooth as we will after thousands of repetitions. So, I will be the first to admit I tend to be naturally animated, and, especially as a beginning speaker, I dealt with my nerves by sometimes coming off as a bit too dramatic. I own that.

So, circling back to my showcase… It opened with the Prevention Magazine video telling Schuy's and my story. They gave me a standing ovation as I walked on stage, which was encouraging; however, I knew how much was riding on this. I *had* to do well. We were dealing with so many financial challenges, and I was desperate for this to lead to some events. And, of course, I was very aware that some of those close to me seemed to expect me to fail.

My second video malfunctioned. It wouldn't start. There was an awkward moment as we all waited for the tech team to get it to play. Again, a wave of panic and nerves…

Yes, I probably was a wee bit overdramatic. As I exited the stage, one of the other speakers embraced me in tears, saying it was the most moving talk she had heard in 13 years of speaker showcases. Clearly, not everyone shared her response. Some people in the audience wouldn't make eye contact with me. The Dallas agent continued to ignore me, and I left the showcase feeling on edge. Weeks later, the agency shared the feedback sheets.

Although quite a few ranked me 5 out of 5 with comments that said "incredibly moving," two clients gave me 1 out of 5. And the comment from one of them almost caused me to quit: "Much too drama-filled. I really did not like this talk."

Welcome to the world of "putting yourself out there." Sometimes, it will feel wonderful, and if you let it, sometimes it will feel terrible.

This was definitely one of my "feel terrible" moments, and I humbly say this wasn't the first. Each time, I swore I would never venture back into the wild abyss inhabited by that oh-so-fickle beast known as Self-Trust. However, this time, thankfully, as the pain retreated, I began to hear a tiny voice inside that begged me not to give up on that which makes me ME. A voice that hinted that perhaps there were more glasses where that other glass had come from… And these glasses were just waiting to be filled…

So here I am years later, still perfecting my craft, still iterating, and yet living a destiny that not too many years ago seemed out of reach. But here's the point of the story:

I didn't just wake up one day and see my luck change. I didn't have this huge epiphany that allowed me just to flip the "happy and abundant" switch. I most certainly didn't learn a "hack" to spontaneously deliver the life of my dreams so that my cup "runneth over" and the haters started loving me.

What did change was *my focus.*

What I'm emphasizing here is the critical role that your focus plays in every aspect of your life. Especially when it comes to your self-trust. This truth is something that it took me decades to figure out. And even longer to incorporate into the way that I now live.

Whether you're interacting with strangers or those within your circle of family and friends, you will face those who think you're amazing and those who seem to believe you will never measure up.

As someone who in my younger days could easily have been mistaken for Elle in *Legally Blonde,* I speak from the perspective of someone whose "babe in the woods tax" often was paid in the form of trying to please people who could never be pleased…

Now, I'm not saying the Kansas City client who gave me such a scathing review was one of those. I am saying this: **we tend to give a disproportionate amount of power to negative criticism and even to the opinions of those who will never judge us favorably. And there comes a time when we must realize that we are not here to convert the "haters." Whether they are lovers or haters, the reality is that those opinions reflect more specifically about them than they do about us.**

Our self-esteem cannot be based on testimonials, social media likes, or rave reviews. The painful moments like the one I experienced in Kansas City just emphasize that our true self-worth must always come from looking within. That involves Focus.

When the criticisms and disappointments hit, we can choose to focus on *learning* from the Anti-Mentor experience, or we can allow the critique to obliterate/define us and choose to quit, leaving all of that vibrant future potential unexplored.

So why do we fall into the trap of measuring our self-worth based on the feedback of others, whether they be single encounters like my Kansas City buyer or constant interactions with family and friends?

Quite frankly, I believe it's because we allow the critical voices to ring louder than the voice of the True Self within. When you stifle the voice of the True Self, you diminish your access to the Epic You.

That's crazy! Remember what we discussed earlier: unhappy people cannot "let" you help them find happiness because in finding happiness, they would lose themselves. Were you to find a way to pierce that veil of toxicity and anger at the world, they would have to answer some disturbing questions they do not want to face.

For years, I allowed unhappy and toxic people to dictate not only my focus but also my trust in myself. I showed up trying to constantly sell my brand of happiness and my worthiness to those who viewed my "happiness" only as niaveté and as if it were poison. This contaminant needed to be destroyed.

Here's the ironic part…

There were many people who "caused me" pain. However, the people I allowed to derail me most often were not even "key actors" in my story. I barely remember some of these people's faces, and I often don't even remember their names. **I simply made them key actors by giving them my focus.**

And to reinforce the "mic drop moment" for you, their hurtful behavior was typically not even about ME. It was a reflection on THEM.

I was like Little Red Riding Hood stumbling across the Big Bad Wolf. I hinged my entire self-worth on whether I could convert those "wolves" from "haters" into "top fans." As you can imagine, it was a humiliating exercise in frustration, which usually left me licking my wounds. To make matters worse, these folks saw me as damaged and flawed, so I would try to prove to them (and to me) that I was not damaged or flawed. With all that focus on "damaged and flawed," what do you think my story expanded into?

The story of a single mom who could never achieve enough "unachievable things" to prove to herself that she was "worthy" versus "damaged and flawed." Can you see the absurdity of this scenario?

It all began by giving the "haters" the more significant focus – and agreeing to give traction to *their* story. Why do we do that? Or should I say, why do we *keep* doing that?

In keeping this cycle going, we give everyone else our power. We let the Haters of the world define us. Or, more tragically, we let them minimize us and cause us to doubt every corner of our BE-ing. We step forward again and again into our future, allowing these toxic individuals to convince us that WE are flawed. That it is WE who are broken.

So what has that cost us? Are we willing to continue to pay that high price – especially when we know that the clock is ticking? Unless we make some changes, many of us are barrelling toward that final moment of ultimate "regret"!

So let's return to our "glass half full metaphor": If your self-image is the beautiful glass waiting to be filled, then your self-trust is the luscious nectar you pour into your glass. Your focus determines what you do with that glass and its nectar. Will you keep it filled to the brim with things that surprise and delight you? Or will you hand your glass over to those who cannot possibly see the value of the container, much less the potential of what flows within?

Today, let the opinions of the lovers and the haters lie. Focus solely on filling your glass with the nectar of self-trust. Get excited. Get deliberate. And watch what happens when *you* become the master or mistress of your set of fine crystals.

TODAY'S ACTION STEPS:

- *Take time today to write down a list of 3-5 people who have shown up as Anti-Mentors in your experience. You may not even know or remember their names. What you do remember is their impact. Briefly describe the impact of the experience. (+2 Gold Stars)*
- *Now, to each of those entries, declare the following out loud as loudly as you dare (adjusting as needed): "Dear [Girl in the High School Cafeteria], I forgive you for the words/actions that I have allowed to cause me such pain. I see now that your words/actions were about your pain, not my unworthiness. I gave you my power, so I now declare that I am taking my power back. I release myself from this wound, knowing that my value is in no way tied to you. I AM a vibrant being filled with limitless Epic potential – brilliantly unique, irreplaceable, eager, and strong. I am excited and ready! This is MY Epic Story, and I am a Force to be reckoned with!" (+2 Gold Stars)*
- *Bonus points if you now take that list of Anti-Mentors, say thank you for the important lesson, and then crumple up that paper, throwing it forever away! (+2 Gold Stars) Booyah!*

TOTAL POSSIBLE STARS FROM TODAY: 6 STARS

Day 30 — FOCUS: What If The Journey Through Life is the Ultimate Vacation Package…

Over the past few days, we explored how our focus can help us take back our power over our self-esteem and self-trust. You might find yourself wishing you hadn't "wasted so much time" "getting in your own way."

Before you are tempted to beat yourself up too badly, let's focus on something that can be one of the most dominant attention-grabbers: TIME! We grow up in a world that believes there is a scarcity around time. We are weaned at the bosom of the belief that "life is too short." Our people-pleasing selves cringe at the idea of gaining a reputation for "running late" or "moving too slowly."

Think about it: How often have you told yourself that "there's just not enough time…?"

When we think about our future, we think about a condition or a destination versus a specific feeling or desired "state." We have allowed ourselves to be programmed into a neverending "flight or fight" mode, so is it any wonder that our energy is running a little low?

We scoff at the idea of allotting time for ourselves to recharge or replenish our energy. We often feel a sense of shame when doing something for ourselves rather than sacrificing our time for [fill in the blanks]. So what if we can start beginning today to look at time as an ally? Even as one of our most precious treasures or resources? Isn't "time" the ultimate investment in how YOU experience this crazy adventure that we call LIFE?

Yes! If you are going to unleash the most glorious expression of yourself and live a life that is as fulfilling as it is successful (whatever success means to you), then you'll need to learn to regulate your focus around time. So let's have some fun today, and let's pretend that instead of "going on vacation," you're "going on a LIFE JOURNEY."

We all know that when we go on those vacations, we'll ultimately end up at home. In some cases, possibly to a new home. Regardless, the "goal/ objective" of the vacation is not to "get home." If it was, then what's the point of even leaving?

No, the objective is the experience – even when that experience is currently part of the unknown.

You plan that trip to Rome or the beaches of Florida. You learn as much as possible, but you don't really know what you will find. Some experiences you will probably enjoy more than others, and there's a shot that some experiences you won't enjoy at all.

However, because you're focusing on this as a "vacation," your intention is to embark upon it for the purpose of a bit of wonder mixed with play combined with recharge and possibly growth. Especially when you have paid dearly for this experience, you are planning to show up as that best version of yourself – ready to make every moment count.

(You see where I'm going with this, don't you?)

So today, I will give you a little playful challenge: Can you step out into this day as if this moment in time is the "vacation of a lifetime"? And your "final destination" is when your "Life Journey vacation" is complete, and you are now ready to head "home." That means the vacation itself is simply the wonderful way you spend your time living this life on the way to going home.

Can you go out into your day, living your life like one glorious vacation? Give it a whirl! And be sure to take photos! Wink!

TODAY'S ACTION STEPS:

- *Brainstorm 5-10 ways to live today with a "vacation mindset." Even if you're working, how could you add some adventure and fun? (+2 Gold Stars)*
- *At the end of the day, write down how you did. What worked really well? What can you approach differently tomorrow? (+2 Gold Stars)*
- *Bonus points if you plan a "tourist for the day" experience, where you act as if you are a tourist in your own city/town. What might you do and explore? (+1 Gold Star)*
- *EXTRA BONUS: Share your biggest AHA! so far by emailing us at team@gritmindsetacademy.com . Who knows? There might be a special reward in it for you... just saying!!! (+2 Gold Stars) Booyah!*

TOTAL POSSIBLE STARS FROM TODAY: 7 STARS

Day 31 — FOCUS: Riding the Wave of Adaptation and Growth

Even on vacation, time passes, so what better "time" to focus on one of our biggest blind spots about time and change?

Think about it. Most of us buy into the belief that "things change." Many of us spend a lot of time and energy wishing things *would* change. We'll even invest a lot of blood, sweat, and tears trying to make *someone else change* — but we often step out into the world as if we are incapable of change.

"I'm just wired this way. I am who I am."

Newsflash: Life IS a dynamic journey, and we are not bound to the versions of ourselves from yesterday. We have the power to evolve, adapt, and recalibrate our identity as we continue to grow and discover new facets of our being. The belief that we must wake up defining ourselves as the same person we were yesterday is an illusion that stifles our potential for growth and transformation.

In those moments when we feel stuck or compare ourselves to others' apparent success on social media, it's crucial to remember that we all face similar struggles and doubts. The negative thoughts that bubble up are clues that our focus has wandered into a self-limiting narrative, making us feel small and unworthy.

But here's the key to breaking free from this cycle of "blindspot thinking™": *awareness and deliberate focus*. We can train ourselves to notice when our thoughts veer off course and gently steer them toward a more empowering direction. It will take practice and determination, but we can change our focus and rewrite our story.

A powerful example of this comes from an experience at Tony Robbins' virtual "Unleash the Power Within" event. Participants were encouraged to be authentic and vulnerable on social media, sharing their stories and insights. One woman, who appeared flawless and successful on the surface, opened up about her feelings of loneliness and imposter syndrome.

Her focus on maintaining a facade of perfection had kept her feeling isolated and unable to connect with others authentically. The trap of "impossible change" had imprisoned her in a story that didn't reflect the true depth of her being. Her willingness to shift her focus and embrace vulnerability allowed her to discover a more genuine and relatable version of herself.

This applies to our professional lives as well. Recently, my client Edward was looking for a new job. He was considering changing careers altogether, but he was torn between opportunities that also existed in his current field. What was keeping him stuck was this: things were moving along quickly with one company in the new field. However, there was a 5-year training process, which meant he wouldn't be making as much money as he'd like until that training was completed. Colleagues in his current field loved him, but they weren't hiring.

He considered himself someone who lived up to his commitments, so he overwhelmed himself with the pressure of making the correct choice. He was tempted to commit to the company in the new field but didn't feel confident that he had all of the data. After all, he didn't know that he would like the new field. We were able to detangle how he viewed commitment – which impacted how he viewed himself.

For him, commitment meant that if he accepted the job in the new industry, he was "stuck" there for perhaps a decade. As we took a deeper look, I was able to help him rework his perspective on commitment to look like this: *if* he accepts this job, he agrees to go in absolutely focused on performing to his highest ability. He will be coachable. He will be focused. He will do everything possible to ensure that he is a success. That said, should he be offered an exceptional opportunity in his current field resulting from his stellar reputation and past performance, he will give himself permission to seize that opportunity– should he feel inspired to make that choice.

We must recognize that our focus shapes our reality. When we focus on impossible standards, flawed expectations, or fixed identities, we limit our potential for growth and expansion. Embracing our "perfect imperfections," being willing to iterate when we take risks, and acknowledging that we are an ever-unfolding work in progress opens the door to limitless potential.

Remember: "Perfect" does not mean "done/completed"; it implies the beauty of continuous growth and learning. The true wealth lies in embracing the journey of becoming—the process of evolving, gaining wisdom, and uncovering new aspects of ourselves. Even giving ourselves permission to change our minds and make new choices.

The winds of change and momentum may blow around us, but the power of our focus allows us to harness the true wind beneath our wings. Embracing the fluidity of our identity allows us to remain open to new possibilities and to become truly irresistible, relatable, and real.

Remember today that you are not a static being. Give yourself the permission to adapt and change, to let go of old versions of yourself that no longer serve you. Embrace the journey of growth and self-discovery, and watch how your focus transforms your reality. You are the author of your story, and you hold the pen to rewrite and reimagine your narrative. Let the power of adaptation guide you toward a future filled with limitless potential and epic expansion.

TODAY'S ACTION STEPS:

- ***Today, practice exploring new versions of your Epic You. If you lack confidence, for example, walk into a meeting as if your personality radiates confidence and achievement. Ask yourself, "What would I be thinking if I were the confident version of me? How would I carry myself? How would I respond to things going on around me?" (+2 Gold Stars)***
- ***At the end of the day, write what you learned. What worked really well? What can you approach differently tomorrow? (+2 Gold Stars)***
- ***Bonus points if you sustain this by continuing to explore what it feels like to show up being more and more aligned with the Epic You. (+2 Gold Stars) Booyah!***

TOTAL POSSIBLE STARS FROM TODAY: 6 STARS

Day 32 — FOCUS: Launching Your "Deliberately Empowered Optimism" Movement

As you get back behind the wheel, put your foot on the gas and head out to your next stop during this epic vacation that we call Life, what kind of gas are you going to put in your vehicle? Will you opt for the cleanest, most high-octane variety of fuel, or will you go for the cheapest option and hope for the best?

Hopefully, when I put it that way, you're saying, "I deserve the best!"

So, what is the best way to fuel your journey? Some might say that it's realism. Have you ever heard a piece of advice that tells you to "prepare for the worst but hope for the best?" Knowing now what you have learned about focus, how do you think that advice is destined to work for you?

Now, let's be clear. It's not that you stick your head in the sand. Clearly, those boulders do fall, and you have to be in a position where you are ready to respond if they do. What I'm saying here is that you can't be SO focused on the falling boulders that you step off the cliff.

So what's the alternative? I call it deliberately empowered optimism, and it can be your superpower. I touched on it earlier, so let's explore!

Learning to regulate your focus in a way that **creates an impactful expectation of inevitable success** can be THE game-changer, not only for your professional results but also personally, physically, and spiritually. Don't mistake deliberately empowered optimism for looking at the world through rose-colored glasses.

Remember: This is not "trying to look on the bright side." This is the practice of learning to be the herding shepherd for those runaway thoughts. Success comes from starting small.

First, learn to celebrate the simple act of awareness. Early in the learning curve, victory is simply *realizing* that you caught yourself doing, saying, or thinking something that you would like to adjust or change.

As you stay diligent, you'll start *catching* yourself as you're in the process of doing/thinking "that thing." This is growth and improvement, so once again, celebrate.

If you stay determined and patient, you'll find more and more times going forward; you will start to catch yourself *before* you make that old choice or think that conditioned thought. Instead, you can now select a different thought, story, or action. You'll begin to notice slight shifts and positive changes.

When you do slip (and you will), staying persistent means you'll find that the hits usually don't last as long. It will become easier to find authentic thoughts with a more energizing perspective – easier to shift from a debilitating story to a "Shero's (or Hero's) story" with a much more empowering outcome. At the risk of sounding cliché, this isn't a sprint. It's a marathon – and yet one with huge potential for reward.

When you get to the point where you can honestly assess how the old approach has been working for you (or not), you'll be ready to commit to the self-discipline that this shift requires. When you commit to rewiring the destructive code, you will eventually discover that your thoughts and stories have changed.

I remember the day I talked to a client and realized that despite being a 24/7 caregiver while scaling my business, I couldn't remember the last time I had "one of those days." Have I had a moment of "pirate tongue" with an uncooperative piece of technology? You bet! But an entire day donated to misery and stress? No way!

So today, how can you interact with the world through the lens of deliberately empowered optimism? Can you find the thoughts that authentically help your mind believe that anything that could go well for you tends to go even better? Remember to start with awareness and celebrate each success!

Even with all of the "bad news" and divisive behavior you see, how can you be the catalyst for your deliberately empowered optimism *movement?* If it doesn't start with you, then who?

TODAY'S ACTION STEPS:

- *Today, stay aware of your focus. Make the commitment to keep bringing your focus back to the following: anything that can go well always goes even better for me. (+2 Gold Stars)*
- *At the end of the day, write what you learned. Could you feel any difference in your inner game frequency? Your mood? What worked really well? What can you approach differently tomorrow? (+2 Gold Stars)*
- *Bonus points if you keep up this practice for five more days. See what shifts and changes! (+2 Gold Stars) Booyah!*

TOTAL POSSIBLE STARS FROM TODAY: 6 STARS

Day 33— FOCUS: The Garden of Successes

As you tap into the power of your new deliberately empowered optimism, approach each new day as if Life is a garden of successes waiting to be harvested.

The potential bounty comes in all shapes and sizes. Some will resemble the decadent sweetness of melon, and some the nutritional fortitude of leafy greens. But together, these successes create a lifetime of potential harvest and well-being.

As the farmer of this eternally blossoming crop, it's important to revel in the diversity of your garden. Savor the successes and remember that not all fruits and vegetables blossom at the same time. Look for the signs of those new buds! Welcome into your definition of success in all aspects of the blooming process–including the creation of the rich soil and the planting of the seeds.

So, how does this translate into real life? How do we cultivate those new beliefs that support a healthy mind?

Think big–but start small. Success is not an "all or nothing" entity. A big success is nothing more than a series of small successes that combine to become mighty.

Expect it. See it. Or simply feel it. Allow it to evolve–which means relaxing into the challenging moments with the same confidence that you rejoice in the moments of obvious forward motion.

Success is fluid, so remember that the challenges serve a purpose. When you can relax, observe, and learn, these challenges can inspire your most rewarding insights. Let the stumbles guide you toward new ideas and let them serve as reminders for defining what it is that you do want.

Celebrate the "small" achievements and appreciate each moment a new Epic seed is planted in your garden. Allow yourself to feel as proud of those areas of your life that are "still growing" as you do about those areas that have already made it to your table.

The richness of your life comes from viewing your "garden" with the loving eyes of a true gardener.

Love the sun. Love the rain. Love the fertilizer that makes the soil vibrant and "more." Love the sprouts as they push up through the soil. Love the buds and love the harvest. Love the plants that seem to take forever to grow and love the plants that bloom quickly. Love the ones that struggle. Love the ones that thrive easily.

All are signs that your garden is vibrant and that this garden of life is "maturing." All is as it is intended to be. All in its own good time. All responding to the loving belief and nurturing of you, the caretaker.

Breathe in this new perspective and allow yourself to acknowledge the abundance of success all around you. Free yourself from the bondage of believing that success means that "there is no more to be had in any aspect of my life–I have it all, or I've obtained my objective, and there is nothing left to achieve."

This was perhaps well-intentioned programming, but it doesn't empower the successful gardener. It is a flawed belief, so it is time to add it to the mental compost pile.

Yes, Life is MEANT to be vibrant and flowing. Each moment is unique but mighty. Each moment carries with it the opportunity for jubilation. While one plant is blooming, another is just exploring beyond its seed. So revel in this luscious process– and know that this constant change creates the promise of eternally more.

This is the harmony of Nature, of kinetic motion, of eternity …of Life.

So go out into this day with eyes ready to appreciate and savor your garden of successes. Revel in its diversity. Relax and rejoice in the seeds that have been sown. Embrace the process of planting these seeds with the same satisfaction that you view the fruits ready for harvest. Know that these, too, will bloom!

Be as proud of your small successes as you are of the windfalls. Invite joy into your day and your life.

For you ARE the mighty gardener! You ARE a collage of successes. All around you are signs of growth and becoming. Dig your hands into the dirt. Celebrate your unique abundance of successes, whether they are "finished" successes or ones in motion!

It is Time!

It is time to welcome in the immensity of your garden and to feel the power of a Life that is constantly growing. For this makes it well worth each minute of YOUR century.

How will you celebrate this opportunity to cultivate a mighty life on this planet?

TODAY'S ACTION STEPS:

- *Grab some colored Post-it notes or make three columns on a piece of paper. On one color or column, write 3-5 "quick growing seeds" that you are planting or intend to plant today. (These can be inner game seeds, not simply outer game seeds.) On the second color or in the second column, write 3-5 seeds that take a little longer to come to fruition. The third color or column represents the slow-maturing fruit. Write down 3-5 seeds in that column. (+2 Gold Stars)*
- *Now, set a reminder for when you intend to return to the quick-blooming seeds and nurture them. Do the same for the other seeds. (+2 Gold Stars)*
- *Bonus points if you keep up this practice consistently so that you are always planting new seeds, tending to your existing seeds, and occasionally spreading that bit of fertilizer into the soil. Keep being an attentive gardener, and watch what grows! Enjoy and celebrate the harvest! (+2 Gold Stars) Booyah!*

TOTAL POSSIBLE STARS FROM TODAY: 6 STARS

Day 34 — FOCUS: Happiness is a lifestyle

As we continue exploring the first of The Epic 3 – FOCUS – let's take a moment to focus on the real target for us all: happiness. If you ask every parent what the one thing is that they want for their child, the answer is virtually always **happiness.**

So, what is this elusive thing that we call happiness?

Having spent more than six decades pouring heart and soul into answering this question, I have found that Happiness is a lifestyle. *It's not a location, a commodity, or a skill, nor is it something to "find."* It has no more to do with the car that cuts you off in traffic than it does with landing the dream job…. Because "the secret" to happiness is that it's not about them or "it"–it's about YOU!

Happiness is about the eyes you wake up with in the morning…or should I say that happiness is the heart you choose to adorn each morning.

Happiness is your spiritual wardrobe–the "little black dress of Life" that fits perfectly on any occasion, looks great and can be accessorized with just about anything. Like any wardrobe item, it is up to you to pull it out of the closet on any given day. It is not a school uniform. No one is going to force you to wear it.

Choosing to adorn oneself with happiness means letting go of some of the "cause and effect" behavior we have learned over the years. If someone behaves one way, you may choose your reaction based on how it will ultimately serve you.

Embracing the power of happiness means visiting a new "mental gym" and developing new mental muscles. Choosing happiness means toning up the spiritual flab and pursuing an emotional 6-pack with the same enthusiasm that many pursue a "perfect" physique.

Being happy is a richness that is much deeper than *feeling* happy.

Feeling happy typically means your emotions are responding to your environment, and this outer stimulus makes your thoughts (and, therefore, your emotions) feel good. BEING happy means, you have learned to recognize and to deliberately allow your mind to harvest from your experience the "mental health food" that infuses you with more consistent optimism, more power, and more appreciation of the value of the upside and downside of life experience.

Yes, happiness is a vast wealth accessible to all and waiting to be cultivated.

Happiness offers itself in the feel of a soft pillow or the smell of clean sheets. Happiness offers itself in the job loss that ended up inspiring the new booming business. Happiness offers itself in the words of a child or the wagging tail of a dog. Happiness offers itself in the spontaneous giggles inspired by a new Samsung commercial featuring ostriches that fly. Happiness offers itself in the quiet sanctity of the exquisite peace inspired by composers of musical masterpieces such as Debussy.

Living happiness means soaking in a friend's laughter…taking time to bathe in the scent of a freshly cut lawn, the first fires of autumn, or the smell of freshly baked bread as one zooms past a bakery.

Living happiness means understanding the value of focusing wisely. Living happiness means freeing oneself of the "obligation" to react negatively to something in one's environment. Living happiness means understanding that "reality" is not synonymous with problems…that we are not required to disempower ourselves by searching and destroying the "wrongs" in every picture.

Living happiness means embracing this essence as a viable reality–rocket fuel for human potential.

Joy taps into the energy of pure "flow" and unleashes our potential to unfold into all we are.

Living happiness is genuine… Not to be confused with "putting on a happy face." When you tone those "happiness muscles," your inner laser shifts from scouring the horizon for problems to scouring the horizon for evidence of well-being; both elements are present. Both are real. One empowers. One embitters.

Yes, happiness is a lifestyle.

Adopt it with gusto! Savor the leafy green thoughts and keep the headaches at bay. Revel in your blossoming spiritual 6-pack and wear the strength of your inner joy with pride.

You are here to think great thoughts and to stride powerfully ahead into the future of your EPIC imagination.

Be proud of your ability to choose the reality of optimism. Dance. Run. Muse. Invigorate! And by all means, LIVE! In 4-D, 5-D or even "10-D"! Why not?

Take the reins and synergize the "happiness" "Joie De Vivre" lifestyle of your childhood with the powerful "Carpe Diem" grit of your adulthood.

THIS is Life at its most promising. Your moment is now. Seize it. Love it. And let your happiness define you in all of its glory!

So, focus and BEGIN!

TODAY'S ACTION STEPS:

- *Brainstorm a list of 5-10 ideas for ways that you can transform happiness into YOUR lifestyle. What can you begin doing today? (+1 Gold Star)*
- *Go out and implement! (+2 Gold Stars)*
- *Bonus points if, at the end of the day, you can list five things that you did that infused happiness into your lifestyle. (+2 Gold Stars) Booyah!*

TOTAL POSSIBLE STARS FROM TODAY: 5 STARS

Day 35 — FOCUS: The Power of the 1%

Questing for happiness can feel BIG – and sometimes, we focus so much on the "big" aspect that we get overwhelmed. If you're feeling like your next targets are a little "big," I thought I'd share with you something I wrote on my "Tinkerbell Project Blog" more than ten years ago:

Hello, dear wonderful friends, and hello, dear wonderful planet!

Today, I sit in the marvelous silence of Night and bask in the unbridled power of the 1%.

Often, we tell ourselves that we must achieve these monumental tasks…we must move mountains…we must amass great fortunes…we must save the world… Life can appear daunting when we look at "all that must yet be done" and/or "all that is wrong or simply missing"….

Yet, the secret is to embrace the power of the 1%.....
Instead of needing to immediately leap from "here" all the way to "there," what if our daily goal was simply to move further by 1%?

Losing 200 pounds may seem impossible when faced with such enormous numbers—but dropping 2 pounds is achievable.

Eradicating a $50,000 debt might seem overwhelming, but knocking off $500 can be done.

Feeling and acting like a champion all day, every day, is probably pushing it for most of us, particularly when there are computers that crash, phones that lose connection, speed traps when you're late to work, or that dear, sweet person in line who managed to pick up the one item without a price tag...yes, even trying to behave like that perfectly enlightened soul can sometimes seem more daunting than scaling Mt. Everest.

So, today, as you go out to face the world, I would encourage you to celebrate the 1%. Be the champion you aspire to be 1% longer today than you were yesterday. Dieting? Try eating 1% healthier today than you did yesterday. Trying to save money? Save 1% more than you did last week, last month, or last year ...Trying to get yourself out of those summer doldrums? Find 1% more time to pursue a passion.....go to the beach...call an old friend...or just do something "totally weird and silly"....

Yes, even without the push of "compounded interest," 1% today adds up to 365% in one short year, but who's counting??...!

So, THE PRESSURE IS OFF! Anyone can handle 1%....! Time to laugh at those mountains up ahead! Time to let your dreams and imagination aim high! Anything is achievable if you approach it one step at a time.

Anyone who aspires to improve by 1% can be "successful." The journey is so much more than just a "start" and a "destination," so experience those miles in between....

THIS is your moment!

Make it the moment that you embrace the 1% that is NEW! Let go of all fear and let go of all pressure. This is your time to reach out and to be all that you are and all that you wish to be. THIS is that 1% moment when all risks are worth taking. The knowledge is yours... yes, you've "got" this... you're "good".... everything is working in your favor....that 1% is surely yours....!

And surprise...that 1% is Life's wonderful rocket fuel, so get ready to soar....we can already hear your rumble...so roar on and make it your 1% day!

XOXO
Meridith

So, where am I today? How did all of that 1% thinking "work" for me? (I mean, let's face it, when we have so "far to go," 1% can seem like it will be too slow…right?) Well, as you have read, I had some tragic things happen between the time when I wrote that blog and where I stand now. Most notably, of course, was becoming the 24/7 caregiver to Schuyler when that boulder crushed her.

Yet, **even with that, I am in awe of how much more epic my life is today than it was when I wrote those words so many years ago.** First and foremost, personally and professionally, I can say that I am **infinitely** HAPPIER and more fulfilled than I ever thought that I could be. My mind is calmer, more agile, more prone to joy, and a natural resilience.

Things that once seemed hard now come "naturally" to me. The sense of purpose and "being fully alive" that often alluded me has now become part of my daily life. Yes, it can seem "hard" to invest in our Future Self in a world where the emphasis seems to have shifted more and more to "instant gratification." But all of this push for the immediate clearly is taking its toll.

I would lovingly say, "How's it been working out for you?"

Today, I would suggest shifting your focus to the concept of experiencing an **"enduring unfolding."** Is what you are about to choose setting you up for a result that will be "enduring"? Is that result something that you *wish* to be lasting?

Is this train of thought something that you hope will endure? Are these beliefs ones that will benefit you if they persist? Do they bring you closer to the truest expression of your most authentic self?

What is a 1% new focus, a 1% new action that you can take today that will begin to create **an enduring momentum** toward a destiny that you would LOVE to create? Temporary gratification or enduring bliss … you get to choose the seeds you plant in your garden… And the next opportunity to plan for a bountiful harvest begins right now…!

TODAY'S ACTION STEPS:

- *What will be your 1% focus for today? (+1 Gold Star)*
- *What action do you commit to taking today to support that 1%? (+2 Gold Stars)*
- *Bonus points if you keep up this 1% practice for five more days. Set reminders. Take action! See what shifts and changes! (+2 Gold Stars) Booyah!*

TOTAL POSSIBLE STARS FROM TODAY: 5 STARS

Day 36 — FOCUS: The Road to Happiness- Surely It Doesn't Include That Brick Wall?

So now you've had more than 30+ days to play with your focus, and as you iterate your way toward more and more of those new "one percent" objectives, you will hit some brick walls. That's right. You *will* hit some brick walls. The question then becomes, do you approach those moments as if the entire car is totaled – or is this more like a fender bender?

I had one of those "brick wall moments" on my road to happiness and wrote about it in another of my "Tinkerbell Project Blog" posts. My thoughts were this:

Hello, dear wonderful friends, and hello, dear wonderfully precocious Universe!

Today, I (gasp!) celebrate something that probably sounds a bit odd and bizarre to be celebrating: yes, those obnoxious and frustrating brick walls that we all seem to hit occasionally....Okay, maybe I'm not truly rolling in joy as I say this, but please read on.....

Sometimes, these little challenges can feel like mere potholes; other times, they can feel like the Great Wall of China.

When that's the case, it is often hard not to feel like the wind has been knocked out of us. Forget about having any wind left to fill our sails. It is an awful, scary, frustrating, and disempowering sort of feeling. We usually feel like we just want to hide under the covers until some Fairy Godmother can come and magically strike down this evil intruder.

Whatever happened to our previously calm Universe?

What on Earth could we have done to deserve THIS particular monster?

This is the part of the story where the temptation is to either beat ourselves up or distract ourselves from the discomfort by looking for the villain elsewhere. We often feel like someone else is seriously flawed (because they really should have behaved differently) or that the world/entire "system" is flawed (because what happened was so obviously unfair), or in the worst-case scenario, that we ourselves are somehow tragically flawed (i.e., others seem to be able to avoid these sorts of disasters, what's wrong with me that I have allowed this to happen?).

Regardless of who we target (and sometimes all of the above), the feeling is anything but good, and our outlook on Life at these moments is anything but encouraging.

So yes, I am a Tinkerbell, but why am I celebrating this "brick wall" phenomenon? Am I just trying to put a fairy costume on Captain Hook? Am I willing to smile when my entire world is falling down around me...? Have I somehow managed to control the "calamities" in my life so that my tales of woe delve no deeper than a bad hair day?

Ah, wouldn't we all wish!! If I could figure out how to achieve THAT, I promise you, I would definitely blog about it....!

No, Life definitely dealt me a distinctive wall that seemed to come out of nowhere. It definitely scared me, worried me, depressed me, and left me shivering in my boots....

BUT......!!!!

(...Yes, in the midst of my spiral, my despair actually led me face to face with a very awe-inspiring and powerful "but".....)

After I had panicked for a while and imagined all forms of ultimate destruction, I finally took a breath and ALLOWED myself to relax into the new thoughts that I have learned to begin thinking....

What if this "obstacle" (this huge horrible beast) is a necessary and important part of "the plan" to get me to "the next level." What if instead of being evidence that something is "wrong," it's really a sign that something is on target...?

What if this is not the Universe doing something TO me but doing something FOR ME.... What if it's a hint to let go of something that no longer leads to the path that I desire ... what if it's a chance to re-examine my desires and to virtually "start fresh"....

What if....what if...what if....? (And doesn't it make sense that those "what ifs" just MIGHT be positive....)

As I took it further in my mind, it struck me that we ALL encounter these hurdles...even the most "successful" folks encounter challenges in their lives...whether it's Michael Jordan at one point being told that he can't play basketball or numerous multi-millionaires pulling themselves up from bankruptcy.

If these "challenges" are so prevalent, it isn't logical to buy into the belief that these "stumbles" are signs of failure. If those who succeed have also stumbled, it is NOT accurate to tell ourselves that these stumbles just prove our own failure. In fact, many who now have success attribute their success to the lessons and inspirations that resulted from those catastrophes.

So, if that's the case, then maybe these brick walls are not signs of anything going "wrong." And if things aren't going wrong, if these challenges are an important part of our progress, doesn't that mean that perhaps we shouldn't be viewing these moments with such dread and self-loathing?

Couldn't it mean that rather than scolding ourselves for our stupidity or for our slowness or for our inability to foresee (or control) events, perhaps we should be smiling with the thrill of understanding that we have come upon one of the most high-octane moments of "the race"?

So, YES, today I declare peace with the brick wall...and as I look from this new perspective, I have to wonder if this daunting obstacle is really the wall that it initially appeared to be.

Maybe it's just a new palate on which to create ... maybe it's THE lesson that will catapult me onward....maybe it's part of the road forward...or maybe it's the new lens with which I more clearly see my true self, and maybe I can use these bricks to forge that new road.

Today, it's time that I thank this turn of events for inspiring me to look anew at this journey and to hope, to believe, and to trust in this process.

Today, it's time to truly and openly look for the opportunity within the unknown. The challenge is simply to let go of the sails and allow the wind's power to carry this great vessel forward.

There are worlds to discover, so rather than curse our supposed misfortunes, let us venture on... strong, mighty, and with the courage of the ever-great explorer! If the moving currents can shape mountains, imagine what they can do to a mere brick wall....?

XO
Meridith

As you finish reading these words, think about how the **EPIC VERSION OF YOU** can show up today even with your own "brick walls." How have you been defining them? How have you been allowing them to impact the way that you're defining yourself?

Remember the three questions that will help you gain clarity personally and professionally:

- What's working?
- What's not working?
- What might I do differently?

How would you answer these three questions:

- What will I start doing?
- What will I stop doing?
- What will I adjust and do differently?

Where are the hidden clues and treasures in your brick walls? Success is an ocean, not a lightning bolt. Give yourself time (and credit) to navigate the waves. Take a moment today to truly explore the possibilities within the brick walls and "real eyes" where they are actually pointing...

Final thought: "When one door closes, start looking for windows..."

TODAY'S ACTION STEPS:

- *Is there a brick wall you've encountered recently? Or maybe it's more like a rose bush with some unexpected thorns? Take a moment to ponder it. (+1 Gold Stars)*
- *Now think about the three questions we focused on above: What new approach can you take? What's something that you are going to stop doing? And what will you now approach differently? (+2 Gold Stars)*
- *Bonus points if you can identify some possible windows in the brick wall! (+2 Gold Stars) Booyah!*

TOTAL POSSIBLE STARS FROM TODAY: 5 STARS

Day 37 — FOCUS: The Power of Celebration

By now, you should be celebrating and high-fiving yourself! You are mastering the FOCUS game and revving up the Epic Machine, so let's talk about gratitude.

It is said that gratitude can be one of the best coping skills when you're feeling anxious, frustrated, or depressed. However, if your mind is like mine used to be, telling it to focus on gratitude can be like trying to tell yourself to ignore the giant elephant in the tutu that is doing pirouettes in the corner of your bedroom.

You *want* to focus on feeling grateful. You "know" that you "should" find a way to feel grateful, even for those irksome things. Yet, emotionally, it can feel hard – if not impossible.

In 2014, I was struggling personally, financially and professionally. My self-esteem was low. My thoughts were engulfed by imposter syndrome. Professionally, I felt like I had chosen an industry that was going the way of the buggy whip. My efforts felt unrewarded and unrecognized, and at the end of the day, what I was contributing to the world would have little, if any, impact. I always felt like I was behind the 8-ball and totally deflated at the end of the day.

To make matters worse, I had taken a huge hit financially in my performing arts agency. Two tour producers reneged on agreements at the last minute, leaving me obligated to refund almost $100,000 to clients. This took place within weeks of what would have been the performance dates, so not only was it a HUGE financial blow – even more crushing was the blow to my integrity. I had rarely canceled a date, much less an entire tour! It was all I could do to get out of bed in the morning. I was so ashamed and humiliated.

Every morning when I woke up, my first thoughts were always, "How on Earth could you have been so stupid? How did you let yourself get into this situation? How will you possibly fix this?" On top of everything (yes, "there's more"), I was in a romantic relationship that I was beginning to suspect (like many before) was leading in a direction that wasn't at all like I had hoped.

It was an extraordinarily dark time, but thankfully, it led me to turn toward the teachings that would ultimately (and dramatically) transform things. The teachings from those who were experts in the human "inner game." It was during this time, at about 10 PM one night, as I sat at my desk staring out the window into the darkness in front of me, that I wrote yet another one of my Tinkerbell Project blogs:

Gratitude is said to be empowering, but often when we think of gratitude, at least part of our brain is still focused on that big hairy nasty thing that we have "just narrowly" escaped from....

So yes, it's quite possible that even if I'm expressing "gratitude" for money coming in, a good part of my subtle focus is actually saying, "I am so grateful for money coming in because money doesn't grow on trees and one can lose one's source of income so easily and lots of people don't have enough and that could easily be me and there doesn't seem like there is enough money to go around and all sorts of things can happen that can make me lose my money ... and ... and ...and...."

Alright, maybe I am the only one who occasionally catches my mind "pretending" to be positive when the mischievous part of my brain just can't resist pointing out the 101 Deadly Calamities that could be just around the corner....wink!

I may not SAY it, but "the man behind the curtain" is certainly trying to get me to THINK IT!!!.....

Conspiring with that "man behind the curtain" is the naughty little flying monkey in my brain who also is quick to point out that "gratitude" seems to imply that I believe that I am "out of the weeds" on that topic..."but am I really?" says the naughty monkey, "because Life is full of change and nothing lasts forever...." And all of a sudden, in the middle of my attempt to express some good, empowering gratitude, I am swept away in a sudden mental cyclone... ruby slippers and all....!

Now, I am DEFINITELY not saying that gratitude isn't important–although in my own life, I prefer to view it as "appreciation" since my mind seems to find less "evil story" characters attached to that phrase.

Appreciation is VITAL!...providing that one is truly viewing the FULLNESS of the scenario, not the links that are either still missing or potentially just around the next bend.

It occurred to me that since I have such a precocious little mind at times, I would be the perfect "guinea pig" for figuring out how to "outsmart" the system that my mind has spent half of a century hammering into place ... so yes, I read, and I read, and I read...

I observed and listened and tried HARD... the "A" student in me REALLY objected to the news that the harder one "tries," the longer it takes to reach the objective...now how is THAT "fair"?? ...more kicking and fussing....more pouting...more reading....and finally more hoping and just plain asking the Universe....

.... And then one day, the Universe seemed to reply....

...It was a day with dozens of brilliant gold and vibrant orange butterflies jetting around the foliage in the backyard....the sky was such a brilliant blue...the breeze was perfect....and my three furry Yodas were celebrating Life in their most spectacular rendition of "squirrel chasing," toy shaking, and pure unbridled runs of joy....

"Learn the Art of Celebration," the world seemed to say, "because in Celebration is PLAY..."

When we can celebrate, we amplify appreciation. We "allow" ourselves to laugh and to focus just on the "good." We allow ourselves to feel great and bask in the best we can be.
It's the closing pitcher on the winning baseball team who points at the sky in victory as the game is won. It's the athlete in the end zone dancing in delight. It's the child whooping and whirling when Life feels perfect. It's the resounding "YES" that we shout at the computer when we get that perfect piece of news—even when no one is around to hear it!

For in those moments of celebration, we are COMMITTED to believe that we can handle whatever comes our way! We know there are challenges, but we KNOW we can be champions!

We see others around us as contributors to this wonderful game– sometimes opposing us but always inspiring us to play our best. When we celebrate, we are not focused on the details of the future. We are truly (no evil story characters on site) APPRECIATING the Now.

So today, I would invite you to give yourself the license to CELEBRATE.

Give yourself a party in honor of all that you wish for and celebrate those victory feelings as if they are here. Yes, pretend and let loose–because this is PLAY!

In the concept of "play" lives the ideas of "allowing" and "freedom" and "empowered risk-taking" that mean the "serious" part of your brain can go "off duty." You can punch out your mental time clock and proceed onto (YES!!) "HAPPY" HOUR!!

As the glorious sun shines down on your face as you laugh and raise your glass, know that the laws of the Universe are at your back.

They are giving you more wind for your sails because as you cut loose the anchors of "struggle," "worry," "doubt," and the "shouldn't-I-be-seeing-more-progress-by-now" moments, the waves calm, and AWAY YOU GO!

So today: CELEBRATE! LAUGH! PLAY ...and turn all 24 hours into your own spiritual "happy hour"... because in celebration is focusing at its best and in its purest–and therein lies our power at its most breathtaking and SUBLIME!

Even though this was over a decade ago, you can still see that I was beginning to appreciate the power of learning to own your focus. Even from that dark abyss, as I grew more familiar with how to redirect the focus within my mind, I found relief.

Did you pick up this subtle "trick" that my mind had been playing? By demanding that I find "gratitude," I had inadvertently created yet another task I could not complete. I had found yet another reason to tell myself that I had failed.

By simply shifting the focus from gratitude for the things that I currently was experiencing (which felt insincere at the time) to appreciation *for what the world around me had to offer* (which didn't require anything from me but the willingness to experience it), I could now shift my state, my inner game frequency. Eventually, my perspective. I could now catch my breath and find a few thoughts that gave me hope – another example of how your mind must first believe it before it can create it.

By shifting my focus and what I was making that focus mean, I could get to a place where I could actually feel an expectation of eventual success. Yes, even celebration. So when those typical "coping skills" just aren't working, be willing to explore. What can YOU create for yourself through your thoughts and/or actions that move you closer to where you want to go? That helps you find a sense of hope and even progress on the way to your JOY.

Thankfully, I am nowhere near that abyss that had me in its depths just a decade ago. As you see, I didn't escape thanks to a silver bullet hack, a get-rich-quick scheme, or the circumstances that were soon to follow. It has truly been having the resolve to build my inner game "muscle" to become the sovereign of my focus that has led to a life that now feels so genuinely epic.

Today, step out into your world, not demanding that you always succeed in finding things to feel grateful for. Play with the idea of looking instead at your world from the lens of appreciation. What can you appreciate? Even celebrate? And play, play, play!

And by all means, focus on finding "What is *right* with this picture"! Who knows? This picture may soon be your masterpiece!

TODAY'S ACTION STEPS:

- *Today, take at least 5 minutes to go outside and deliberately appreciate this planet. (+2 Gold Stars)*
- *At the end of the day, focus back on that adventure in nature. What felt marvelous, and what's the next nature adventure you plan on taking? (+2 Gold Stars)*
- *Bonus points if you take photos and write about the details in a journal. (+2 Gold Stars) Booyah!*

TOTAL POSSIBLE STARS FROM TODAY: 6 STARS

Day 38 — FOCUS: Mud or Masterpiece?

Ask, and it is given. Celebrate and then get excited to receive even more! There is always the luster of a new day, a new week, a new month, and a new year. Even though we already have lived many, many moments in the past, we have never lived THIS moment.

With each sparkling fresh new moment shines the perfect opportunity to "recreate ourselves." It's time to dig our hands into the clay and sculpt the next masterpiece in our grand collection!

YES… our hands will get dirty…and our focus must be open yet precise…YES, there will be aspects of this creation that do not please us, so, yes, there will be parts of this project that we will build only to take apart…we may pound it…we may caress it into place…but eventually, the artwork will stand…majestic…the beautiful offspring of heart, soul, and the deliberate mind…..

Let's dive into these times of reinvention with the renewed vigor and focus of a master creator! Let's not lament the mud beneath our fingernails or the time required to transform that lump of clay (pun intended—wink!).

Instead, let's play with the joy of the artist…completely engaged in the eternal connection of this work in progress. Let's banish our fears of getting it "wrong" because, in art, there is only expression and unfolding….

Let's breathe deeply and see the world through our 'Michelangelo' eyes… Today, we can choose … are we viewing just the mud or the stone…Or are we viewing the potential foundation of a masterpiece that will span eternity…?

Maybe the dirt beneath our nails defines us as an artist…so dive in and get muddy!! The Epic-ness of this moment is "yours" for the creating!! Reinvention and co-creation start with your inner game. They start with focus.

Will you focus on the mud or the masterpiece as you step forward?

TODAY'S ACTION STEPS:

- *Today, go out into the world committed to seeing the world through your 'Michelangelo' eyes. Can you stay focused on seeing your masterpiece unfolding? (+2 Gold Stars)*
- *At the end of the day, write down when you could shift to seeing the masterpiece and when you saw just the mud. What was the difference in your inner game frequency between the two? How did it affect your decisions, responses, or results? (+2 Gold Stars)*
- *Bonus points if you keep up this practice for five more days. See what shifts and changes! (+2 Gold Stars) Booyah!*

TOTAL POSSIBLE STARS FROM TODAY: 6 STARS

Day 39 — FOCUS: Financial Abundance– the Ultimate Romeo and Juliet Story (But Potentially With a MUCH Happier Ending)

No conversation about regulating your focus, much less about living your definition of "epic" would be complete without taking a look at how you perceive the topic of wealth, money and overall abundance in your life. For many, their money story looks a lot like Shakespeare's Romeo and Juliet. The eternal love part is nice, but we want to create a much happier ending for our story, don't we? Well, today's the day, so let's get started!

Be honest, from where you sit right now, do you authentically feel that you are destined to have "plenty"? What does "plenty" mean to you? If you're waking up in the modern world, it can feel hard to separate how you see your life from how you feel about the amount of money in your life. Does money represent abundance for you? How about wealth?

Does it serve as a way to define yourself or measure your perceived value? Do you feel that money is an enhancement, an opportunity, a problem? Does it represent safety? Not simply physical well-being, but also the safety from feeling judged? Does it reflect the level of confidence that you believe you can rightfully claim for yourself? How about self-trust?

Your feelings about money and abundance go so much deeper than a new house, a prosperous portfolio, or "winning the Powerball." So let's buckle our seat belts, put all of that extra "baggage" in the trunk, and get ready to explore the realm of that resource that so many "love to love" or "love to hate": the sometimes fickle "friend" called MONEY.

Now, if you're already on good terms with money, kudos to you! But take a moment to ponder some other vital questions. Does financial wealth make you feel abundant, or do you still crave more? Is there a sense of harmony and flow in your life? Do you define your worth based solely on money, or does it extend to other areas like relationships, health, self-image, and inner peace? And even with all your current financial success, are there still areas where you feel a sense of lack?

As you embark upon another "day of Epic-ness," let's turn our focus to "our currency." Ah, Money! Songs have been written about it. Wars have been fought over it. Great philanthropists have done epic things, thanks to it. Most of us have heard the saying (over and over again) that money is the "root of all evil." However, if money is the "root of all evil, " why do we chase it or lament it?

We give it so much power and responsibility… so much credit… so much fear …What if we could gently shift and explore prosperity in a new, empowering way? What if today, we could wake up and proclaim:

"Today, dear world, will be the day when I SEE MY ABUNDANCE! Today will bring that powerful shift where I step further into my total loving embrace of this planet and all that it is and all that it offers to be."

"Today, I see the evidence—' the answer to my prayers.' Today, I feel the 'whoosh'—the undeniable arrival– of my ever-expanding financial abundance!"

"Today, dear world, I commit to letting go! Today, I let money 'off the hook' for all of the wrongs that have been done in its name –– 'off the hook' for all of the 'evil' that I have given it credit for –– 'off the hook' for its apparent 'absence' or 'abuse' –– 'off the hook' for padding the pockets of those whose choices or actions would not be mine –– 'off the hook' for seeming to be the 'yang' to the 'yin' of spirituality –– 'off the hook' for simply not being there when I so desperately 'needed' it ..."

"Yes, today, I will stop trying to figure it all out – today, I will forgive myself for not yet being the 'Master of Financial Abundance.'"

"Today, I will forgive myself for my credit scores and all my bills. I will forgive my lack of savings and lack of retirement funds. Today, I forgive all those 'financial mistakes,' and I even forgive myself for focusing on lack when there is so much abundance to be had."

"TODAY IS THAT DELICIOUS AND LONG AWAITED SHIFT where I allow the abundance of money to simply BE!!!"

"HOW SWEET THE SHIFT FEELS!!"

"Now, my dear money, I allow you to be my teacher, my investor – in fact, dear money, today I invite you to become a confidante and a close, eternal friend."

How do those words sound? How do those words *feel*? Maybe a little strange – or even "woo woo"? What if today's 100 Days of Epic "assignment" can be to put all of that "realism" aside for now and be open to the possibility of what your life might start looking like if you could allow this type of shift?

Yes, if we can resist judging money based on beliefs that no longer serve us, we can see that money is like the oxygen that gives our global economy life in many ways. To criticize money is like criticizing the air – because even our life-giving air carries germs and viruses. Today is about turning over a new leaf and welcoming all of our resources– including money – into our powerful circle of creation. Today is about revisiting the dream.

So what does that look like? And how do we get this Romeo and Juliet tale from tragedy to triumph? It starts by giving yourself permission to relax a bit and even laugh. When one of my clients expresses an issue around money, I take them through a powerful exercise I learned from one of my favorite mindset mentors, the magical Bill Baren. What I have my immersion-level clients do is write a letter to money as if Money is a person. The objective is to express how they feel about Money authentically.

"Dear Money… Here's what I want to say to you…"

Yes, that's right. I ask them to pretend that money is a "Being" versus a "thing." Do they see Money as a man, a woman, or perhaps a combination of both? Are they approaching this entity as a friend or foe? Is this a partnership or an adversarial relationship? Is there a predominance of trust or resentment?

From there, we take a look at what they have written. If Money was indeed a person, would this Money entity find YOU, someone *IT would want to have a relationship with?* Or…would it see how you approach it and want to stay as far away as possible? Hmmm…. this is when the relationship to money can get interesting…

So YES! I invite YOU to give this exercise a whirl. This is not a Shakespearean tragedy but perhaps just a story of misunderstandings. Like any good relationship story, there are ups and downs and miscommunications, but in the end, YOU are the author of this tale. Unlike Romeo and Juliet, you can build a strong, enduring bond with money that allows the two of you to commit to growing together.

What you discover will almost certainly surprise you! You might even find yourself giggling about the sense of humor our vibrant Universe must have if it inspired our species to have created "this money thing"! I mean, seriously… think about it…if the pursuit of "love" and "joy" weren't enough to challenge our species, we then chose to add money into the mix!

So how would you focus on money if you were to think of it simply as your beloved "wild child"—your unruly offspring, brimming over with genius potential but sometimes defying control? Can you breathe in the feeling of ease and allow money to FLOW?

Imagine yourself in the not-so-distant future, turning to welcome in your abundance with the same loving grace that you might welcome one of your most creative yet sometimes precocious children. Yes, with this beloved "Money" child, there will be stories, wild tales of dragons, and great adventures. There will be memories from the day and hopes for tomorrow, but there will also be the security and the gentle knowing that we are one— loving and thriving unconditionally.

Today, let the idea of "epic" mean that you relax into feeling the purity of your rekindled love for this sometimes "unruly" child. Yes, dear Money. You stretch and bend us, but we create a richer planet (double entendre intended) together. So, welcome home ~~ it is time!

In fact, it is finally OUR time! We welcome money into our hearts and into our family. Today, we walk arm in arm with abundance and know that life just keeps on getting better for us! YES, today, a new era is launched! So thank you, world, for yet another day of empowering creations! Thank you for the ease and the success of this great "allowing"!

Now, you Epic Be-ing, go out, and *claim* your new sense of abundance. Step out into this beautiful world today proclaiming: I am refreshed and ready to dance upon the gloriously EPIC wings of this magnificent day!!!

TODAY'S ACTION STEPS:

- *Write your "Dear Money, Here's how I feel about you…" letter. (+1 Gold Star)*
- *Now read the letter as if you were Money receiving this letter. Does it make you want to spend time with the writer? How do you feel about your relationship with the writer? Appreciated? Trusted? Like a valued partner? (+2 Gold Stars)*
- *Bonus points if you journal what your letter to money tells you about your current relationship with money. What has this letter taught you about how you perceive money, and can that be nurtured or improved? (+2 Gold Stars) Booyah!*

TOTAL POSSIBLE STARS FROM TODAY: 5 STARS

Day 40 — FOCUS: Celebrate the Genius of this Uncompleted Journey!

So, you've learned a lot about the power of your focus over the past 30+ days. Do you see how the ability to master your focus can positively impact everything from self-image to money? Are you seeing that your focus (and the stories you choose to tell about the things you are focusing on) define how you experience your day and, ultimately, your life?

Therefore, your focus often defines *who you believe yourself to be* – which defines how you usually show up BE-ing.

The world around us, our experiences, our memories, our imaginations, and our minds — all of these things feed us "topics." These are things that we can choose to (or choose not to) react to. We then get to choose what we make of (or not make of) those topics. In other words, we can't control what happens *to us,* but **we do get to choose what we make those things *mean*.** It's that simple.

Yet, that can become *very complicated,* can't it? Can you see how the level of "epic-ness" that we believe we experience really comes down to the stories we tell ourselves about the moments we are experiencing?

Don't get me wrong. Without question, there are traumatic moments in our lives. As I have shared, I have lived through many experiences that were tough to weather. When we're confronted with those scenarios, it would be difficult to imagine how they could not impact us. That said, *how long we get "stuck in that abyss" (and what we make this "abyss mean") is significantly influenced by the story that we create and by the expectations that this story creates.*

When Schuy had sustained such life-threatening injuries from the boulder, she spent months in Jackson Memorial Hospital in Miami. My boyfriend at the time told me that I was putting up a strong front but that, at some point, I was "going to crash." It was interesting to hear him say that.

I thought about it for a moment, did some soul-searching, and responded honestly that I was pretty sure I would not. I was correct: I never did. Now, let's be clear: it's not that I have never shed a tear or "wished" that things could be different. I absolutely have. It's not because the immensity of the life change had not sunk in or that I had not allowed myself "time to grieve."

I definitely did have moments when I had to face the very real possibility that my daughter's body would not survive the injuries. At one point, I was also told that if she survived, she would certainly be blind.

Even with all of the "evidence" pointing toward an outcome that I definitely didn't want, and even though now there are challenges that my daughter and I never dreamed that we would be facing, I have NEVER dipped into the depths of despair. Do you know why I believe that is?

Because of the many years *before the accident,* I *prioritized the value of learning how to use the most valuable resource I had been gifted: my mind.* **By the time the boulder fell, I was getting to the place where my thoughts no longer "thought me."** That's right. I wasn't so vulnerable to Sloppy Thinking Syndrome.

I did *not* try to face what was happening with "coping skills." I did *not* try to "look on the bright side" or soothe myself by declaring that "everything happens for a reason." I had been an avid student of the inner game for many years, and for the past decade, I had voraciously devoured the work of Abraham Hicks.

When this unexpected "accident" occurred, I was "ready to be ready" to implement these principles. I reminded myself that the immensity of what you intend to create is irrelevant in the realm of focused creation. I kept hearing Esther Hicks' words that creating a castle is as easy as a button. I was ready to see if these principles could "create" a miracle for my child.

I believe that I did not "crash" because I chose to be 100% invested in this "Law of Attracting the Right Action (Att'r'action)." I was unwilling to give traction to thoughts that did anything but energize my belief that (regardless of the outcome) we would be "fine whatever the 'new fine' might be."

By finding one thought that my mind could believe and then another one, and so on, I had managed to deliberately guide my mind to a place where my daughter's survival seemed possible. After all, "impossible" things were happening every day. That was a reality. So, THAT possibility – not the precedent of certain death – was my focus. It got to the point where it even felt like a probability.

I would often say that I would have been more surprised *not* to have seen a "miracle" than to see miracle upon miracle show up in our lives. My daily mantra became, "Anything that can go well will go even better!" Even when I thought about the possibility that she might not survive, I focused on what she would have wanted to be: her joy-filled legacy.

So today, begin to see that "**epic focus ninja**" within yourself. Embrace your ability to choose the stories that you create. Celebrate your power to create things to focus upon based on these criteria:

- Does this energize and empower you?
- Does this move you toward the future that you want to create?
- Does this align with the most epic version of yourself and who you want to show up BE-ing?
- Does this help you grow and expand?
- Does this allow you to contribute your gifts and your genius to your fullest extent?

Epic does not require luck. It does not require a magic wand. It doesn't require privilege or even the "right connections." It certainly doesn't demand you get it "right" every time. What it does require is commitment. The commitment to begin your quest for epic-ness *now*.

So go out into your day as the uniquely brilliant creator. What can you envision? What will you focus on, and what will you make that focus mean? How will you choose to impact those around you? Who will you choose to BE?

You've got this! The most EPIC days are still to come!

TODAY'S ACTION STEPS:

- *On a piece of paper where you can see it, post these five Creation Criteria Qualifiers: Does this energize and empower me? Does this move me toward the future that I want to create? Does this align with the most epic version of myself and who I want to show up BE-ing? Does this help me grow and expand? Does this allow me to contribute my gifts and genius to my fullest extent? (+2 Gold Stars)*
- *Step out into the world today with the intention of BE-ing the sovereign of your thoughts and what you are impacting and creating. Be a responder, not a reactor. (+2 Gold Stars)*
- *Bonus points if you add these criteria as reminders in your phone. (+2 Gold Stars) Booyah!*

TOTAL POSSIBLE STARS FROM TODAY: 6 STARS

Day 41 - FOCUS: Living Life as a Champion!

You're rocking your new ability to focus! You are much more aware of what you're thinking – and whether you choose to continue thinking that. Every day, you are getting closer to evolving into the sovereign of your mind. So now is your time to embrace that this epic version of you is no longer a dream, no longer a "Future You"-- now it's your Destiny! The "Epic You" *is YOU!*

Let today be about learning to be this epic champion — champion to one's loved ones, champion to one's colleagues, champion to our planet, and champion to our souls. Maybe even champions to the "strangers" we pass on the street!

Let us delight in showering those around us with random "Aren't - you - magnificent" smiles. And who knows? Maybe our smiles will inspire them to sprinkle that joyous "fairy dust of unconditional, unearned affection" on other "strangers" along their voyage.

Like a galaxy of dandelion seedlings, let us spread our joy, love, and positive belief across our magical little planet so they may take hold and bloom. Some days, we may feel more like wildflowers than roses, but beautiful and hearty are we! Courageous and ever-blooming—unconditional in our choice of soil, whether garden or roadway, ever and always heading upward toward the sun and the Heavens.

My belief is this:

Before the "most epic among us" discovered their strength, SOMEONE believed in them. Someone was their champion. Someone helped them unearth all they could be—no matter the number of stumbles.

The belief and KNOWING of this champion was so complete that before long, the one they helped began to see and BELIEVE their mightiness. By believing in their mightiness, they soared and soared AND SOARED. In their soaring, they inspired more "mere mortals" to new heights, and the world grew and grew and GREW.

So let us all be champions for each other and for our souls. As we thrive in our "believing," imagine the GREAT HEIGHTS of humanity that we will see … all the "miracles" that we can evoke! As we draw out the best in ourselves and each other, as we learn to expect from our planet all that we would have it be, surely we will find that we indeed are walking the fields of heaven.

Complete blissful harmony between humanity and Mother Earth is my dream. That is my wish. That is my focus. As my inner child lies blissfully on her back, staring up at the imaginary sky, how joyous to think that this vision begins with just one soul willing to BE the epic champion.

Let us each be that one champion that starts the unfolding! Happy Day of Epicness, dear one!

TODAY'S ACTION STEPS:

- *Today go out into the world dedicated to showing up as the champion to those around you. How can you uncover their hidden potential? How can you inspire them to be the best version of themselves? How many people can you champion today? (+2 Gold Stars)*
- *How many ways can you champion yourself today? Let your story for the day be this: I am the champion of possibility and everything that can go well goes EVEN BETTER for me and those that I champion. (+2 Gold Stars)*
- *Bonus points if you inspire to go out and find someone that THEY can champion. Create a culture of champions. (+2 Gold Stars) Booyah!*

TOTAL POSSIBLE STARS FROM TODAY: 6 STARS

Day 42 — FOCUS: "Shine On You Crazy Diamond."

Look how far you've already come! You really *are* beginning to focus like an epic inner game champion. It's time now to really level up your game by applying more and more of this new focusing muscle to your "Epic You Story."

As you become more aligned with creating the version of you (and your story) that you *deliberately choose to create,* practice seeing the "I'm Possibles" instead of the "impossibles." Focus on creating those deliberately empowering optimistic statements around "I am." Relinquish more and more of the thoughts that slow down your momentum to the category of "I am no longer." Of course, remember to focus on the presence of what you want in a way that helps you feel the emotions **that you want to feel**. Write stories that align with the frequency of who you intend to show up BE-ing.

In 2014, when I was experiencing some of the darkest times professionally, I fought the downward spiral by launching the "Tinkerbell Project Blog." I've shared some of the pieces that I featured in my blog. I used those posts to establish my sovereignty over my inner narrative – sort of like a journey into my "internal gym." I share them here in this book so you can feel how empowering a deliberately focused story can be.

It was on one of those particularly tough nights that I chose to stretch my ability to focus by writing the following:

"Hello, my dear, dear global friends~~ savor this sweet, sweet moment in all of our lives ~~ we are vibrant, we are alive, and we are questing ~~ we are all that life is about ~~ a tiny piece of each of us lies in each and every molecule!"

"With our challenges, our frustrations, we are the Universal heartbeat. We are Magnificence at its most radiant and supreme."

"Life is not about 'getting it right,' but rather about letting its life-giving energy pulse through our hearts, our veins, our dreams ~~ WE CREATE ETERNITY simply by the fact that we will never let 'it' end."

"We yearn, we desire, we plead, we even cry.... but were it not for these tears, there would be no need for tomorrow. Were it not for our ideas and creativity, there would be no future...."

"We are on a magnificent voyage together. We are artists ~~ we are dancers ~~ we are great explorers. We shape the future as we savor our way through the present."

"We are anything but alone ~~ we are human, and THAT is the greatest gift we can inherit. To see the world not through the eyes of perfection but through the eyes of possibility that is not only my dream but my vision!"

"This is our moment, and oh, is it ever worth the birthing!!! Be kind to yourself. Be kind to your soul. Love this planet because there is genius in even the most frustrating of moments. We are jewels in a magnificent crown ~~ so bask in your beauty and let your sparkle shine!"

"And shine and shine and shine! We truly already live in 'Heaven'— even if we fondly call this little planet simply Earth!"

By the time I finished writing this virtual "love poem" to the craziness of life, I was actually feeling a sense of relief. And despite the suffocating financial pressure that was still overwhelming, I even managed to feel a wee bit of "hope." Was I looking at the world through rose-colored glasses? Some might say, "yes." And yet, can we truly say "yes" if we know that this exercise led to an inner shift? A transformation that led to more clarity, more certainty, more confidence, and ultimately better results?

I don't think so.

My experience has taught me that this type of deliberately focused optimism is a mandatory part of the process in building an epic life. Resilience and grit aren't something that we can learn after the fact. We certainly can't just push a button that makes us stronger, and we can't just "wish" an epic inner game into being. To authentically achieve things that previously felt impossible, we must get to the place where we can regulate our thoughts and, therefore, our expectations *regardless of the situation.* As we gain that ability, it becomes possible to start seeing that there actually *are factual yet positively focused versions of just about every story.* You just have to "real eyes" (yes, realize) how to see it.

Your mission today is to pause wherever you are and write down your "epic life story." Re-read the "Tinkerbell Project Blog" posts that I have included. They are part of this book for a reason. Whether you view deliberate optimism as your right, your "mission," or whether you view it as the silly pastime of uninformed fools does matter.

When we take time to "write down our thoughts," that action inserts our Epic Self actively into that moment as the sovereign of that experience. It communicates to our subconscious that our thoughts do not have "carte blanche" to *think US*. It gives us that brief interval in which to make a deliberate choice – to have an opinion about whether that thought takes hold or whether we will actively do what it takes to create a more energizing, empowering version of that story.

As you deliberately craft your own "personal empowerment system™", consider including journaling or writing as another tool to explore. As you see in my "Tinkerbell Project Blog," it can help shift your mind into a state where better decisions can be made. Tony Robbins calls it priming.

So today, focus on rewriting your stories. Use them to reinforce just how much control you DO have amid a world where it's easy to convince ourselves that we have no power. Now, go out and seize the day. Give the world a new episode in your story that is worth remembering!

Now THAT deserves an epic "Booyah" worthy of a Focusing Joy-rrior!!

TODAY'S ACTION STEPS:

- ***Start rewriting your new "I'm Possible" Story or write your version of a Love Poem to Life. How real and raw and loving can you allow yourself to be? (+2 Gold Stars)***
- ***Go out into the world today with the intention of building your deliberate optimism muscle. Whenever you forget, make a mental note and keep breathing. The more you practice, the more you will find success! (+2 Gold Stars)***
- ***Bonus points if you reread this story to yourself before you sleep. (+2 Gold Stars) Booyah!***

TOTAL POSSIBLE STARS FROM TODAY: 6 STARS

Day 43— FOCUS: Kicking off the ruby red slippers for a moment to feel the grass between my toes....!

We've been playing with Focus and weaving the power of deliberate focusing into our stories. So, you might be wondering how you can take your ordinary moments and reframe them into a story that uplifts you while feeling grounded and true.

For example, here's another blog post from my "Tinkerbell Project Blog" on March 19, 2012:

Hello, dear superb friends! Just couldn't resist taking another moment to bask in the genius of our sweet, wonderful planet! Why are many of my best "moments of oneness" with the wonder of it all inspired by the eyes of a dog or a child—even if that child is my inner child?? Wink!

So today, it was just another innocent moment...I thought that I was merely taking my three handsome furry friends on a walk, but it became a journey into bliss...the sun was shining oh-so-perfectly—big beautiful poofy white clouds graced our global canopy...the perfect breeeze...next to my house, the azaleas were overflowing with masses of bright fuchsia blossoms framed by an exquisite façade of the most delicate purple wildflowers in the meadow next to my house that you ever have seen...

A duck "couple" was floating leisurely on the pond across the way...the neighborhood owl swooped across in the distance as if to say hello...as we approached the pond up the street, one of our alligator friends struck a GQ gator pose while soaking in the last remnants of the sun as three determined turtles squeezed their way onto a log and craned their necks in worship of the sun...(do turtles really need a tan?)....And then on the surface of the pond were these tiny little flashes of "circledom"...apparently even the insects are dancing in delight....

Overhead is a small plane...someone is learning to fly... I giggle because to that person up there, this must be heaven...and how incredible that not too long ago, looking up into the sky and seeing a human in flight was just a fantasy...did my grandparents look up into the sky and see a novice pilot gaining their wings?...

Yet, today, it fits into the harmony of the moment...

Meanwhile, the "boys" are sniffing every blade of grass as if each scent holds the hidden treasure of eternity...each blade captivates them, and I smile in awe of their passion... as they roll on their backs and deliciously rub the deepest of those scents into their fur, I am embraced in this grand tapestry of perfection.

I look up and see the trees, and I smell the distant orange blossoms... I marvel at the knowledge that the Universe does indeed seem to have our backs...here are these "tiny things"...free for the taking...yet definite food for the soul...these are the gems in life...the things that make us say "ahhhhh" if we remember to see them....

These are the "priceless" gifts that the planet offers without a fee...free for all—"rich" or "poor."....the world adapts and shifts and changes, but it finds a way to deliver beauty...and in that beauty is the promise of ease and all-is-wellness....

"The boys and I" savored our wonderful walk and used it to put the pressures of the day on hold for a moment...when I walked inside the house, the phone rang, and "the sound of" my daughter's smile across the miles seemed that much more magnificent...the warmth of all the love in my heart seemed all the more encompassing...

I was gratified with the knowing that life is indeed exquisite and that we have such a magnificent treasure chest of wonder before us....

My dear global family, I wish you each the true kiss of the Universe upon your foreheads! As human as we may be, all of the "crazy life stuff" we each experience is perhaps deliciously "perfect" and eternal....

So whether it's the moments that are so awe-filled that they take my breath away or so heart-wrenching that they knock the wind out of me, they are all part of this beautiful dance that we call life. And my fellow travelers, thank you for inspiring me so upon my own little journey...!

May your day be filled with hand-made clover crowns, and may we each take a moment to kick off those ruby red slippers so we can feel the grass between our toes! Wink (again)!

Epic begins with what we choose to focus on, so isn't it time to turn the gaze away from all those flying monkeys…? How delicious can you make today's story? Does anyone care to join me as I kick off the ruby red slippers for a moment to feel the grass between my toes?

TODAY'S ACTION STEPS:

- *Today is a deliberate focus day. Set the intention to stay very aware of your focus, your narrative, and your inner frequency. (+2 Gold Stars)*
- *Track the things that bring you joy today. How many can you find? (+1 Gold Star)*
- *Bonus points if you hit more than 20 tracked moments of joy today! (+2 Gold Stars) Booyah!*
- *EXTRA BONUS: Share your three biggest needle movers so far by emailing us at team@gritmindsetacademy.com. Who knows? There might be a special reward in it for you… just saying!!! (+2 Gold Stars) Booyah!*

TOTAL POSSIBLE STARS FROM TODAY: 7 STARS

Day 44 – FOCUS: When things don't go "right."

Every single day offers us the opportunity to reinvent ourselves. Or simply to see ourselves in a way that previously never seemed possible. If that is true (which it is), why do we tend to hold onto a perception of ourselves that feels "underwhelming"? Maybe you're discovering that you have been doing this.

When "bad things" happen, we often look in the mirror and realize that we have no idea who we even are. Or if we believe we know who we are, we often decide that "who we are" is not who we need to be in this crisis. Sound familiar?

This was definitely something that I faced on that fateful Friday afternoon in February 2016 when I got "the call" about Schuyler. As tough as it is to admit, one of my very first thoughts was that my daughter deserved a better mom than me. I chided myself for not having infinite wealth to pay for the treatments and hospitalization and for not having the fighter personality that she might need. My low esteem and lack of self-confidence meant that I had nothing encouraging to tell myself about how I would handle what most certainly I would be experiencing.

I even felt the hit of shame as I imagined how inadequate I would appear as a mom when others saw me going forward. When I first posted on Facebook days later, I cringed thinking of how others would see me. I had committed to leaning into the Law of Att'r'action™ principles as my strategy, so I couldn't help but think of how many would find my optimism inappropriate and Pollyanna-ish. What actually happened ended up being quite the opposite.

So here I am, more than seven years later literally writing this on my 63rd birthday. Here are my "words of wisdom" for you today regarding whatever you face in the world today as you focus on deliberately writing *your* story– yes, especially if that story is feeling like a tragedy:

Claiming your Epic life is when you finally understand that each moment is not about clearly defining *who you can't be*. It's about *realigning with who you know you are destined to be — and doing everything in your power to go out and BE THAT!*

Epic isn't something that you discover. It's something within yourself that you allow yourself TO BE.

Who will you show up focusing on BE-ing in your story today?

TODAY'S ACTION STEPS:

- *Today is a great day to refocus on going into the world as if that Epic Future You is already here! Let's try it! Can you sustain it? What makes it easy, and what can you identify that has been getting in your way? How can you adapt and iterate? (+2 Gold Stars)*
- *At the end of today, look at your day. Were you able to sustain being that epic version of yourself for longer? What worked best? (+1 Gold Star)*
- *Bonus points if you jot down a few ideas of how you might approach this with even better results going forward. (+2 Gold Stars) Booyah!*

TOTAL POSSIBLE STARS FROM TODAY: 5 STARS

Day 45 – FOCUS: Releasing the Baby Elephant Collars

As you review and re-write some of those favorite stories, you may discover something: You things that are lurking in your blind spot, and YOU have been a victim of Blind Spot Thinking™.

One of the first and most critical sessions I have with new clients focuses almost entirely on the foundation for learning how to play the inner game to win. It's where they begin to understand the way that our minds work (or do not work) based on whether we leave our thoughts on autopilot (the mind's version of a "Hail Mary") or on whether we commit to becoming our mind's sovereign.

This one session has led to numerous testimonials from even hardcore skeptics who can't believe the shift that they are feeling after only one session. This shift transpires simply because our minds crave clarity and direction. Our minds love to learn. They resist change not because they are typically afraid of the data. It's usually because they feel like they don't have *enough* data. Therefore, they are being asked to walk into the unfamiliar and/or the unknown.

When our mind begins to truly understand the data and *the most advantageous way to process that data*, it becomes energized and empowered. That's when our state changes, and, as we all have experienced, we tend to make better decisions when we feel confident, at ease, and inspired. As Tony Robbins says, "Clarity is your power," and I have definitely found that to be so.

Still, obtaining that clarity can be the trick.

Humans are notorious for feeling like we understand something intellectually, but we don't always align emotionally with what our minds tell us is the "truth." When this happens, we feel the push/pull of conflicting influences. Then, it's hard to feel confident in one consistent behavior or course of action.

We discover a wall within ourselves – a wall that can remain impenetrable for decades. So much so that we begin to believe that this wall is part of who we are. The more walls we sense, the more we view ourselves as flawed, and the more we look for coping skills to help us coexist with these walls. Perhaps you've been there.

These coping skills can be drugs and alcohol. They can be the accumulation of "things." They can be changing jobs, changing locations, or even changing relationships. Sometimes, when we sense a source of stress, we adopt "coping skills" that can seem very positive, such as mindfulness or self-love. However, coping skills on their own do not address the reason that you need these coping techniques to begin with.

In order to really step out into the world as that epic version of yourself, you must ask:

What is causing the pain, and can you now finally step into a time in your life when you can choose to retire it? I believe that the answer is YES! After all, you ARE reading this book…

So take a deep breath and allow me to share a story that I share with my elite immersion clients on the very first day of our work together. Know that one of the most powerful ways to allow your mind to learn is in the context of a story or metaphor. In this case, our story takes place in a part of the world where humans have used the majestic elephant almost like a construction vehicle for decades.

This mighty creature can knock down trees, walls – virtually anything in its path. So how, then, has Man figured out a way to keep them in captivity within the flimsy walls of a human camp setting? That's a good question, right?

People discovered that they could take a baby elephant when it was young and fit this baby elephant with a collar and attach the collar to a chain. The chain was then attached to a stake that went deep enough into the ground to keep the baby elephant from being able to escape. The baby elephant pulled and pulled. It was maddening, but eventually, the baby elephant comes to what (at the time) was a very brilliant assessment:

It is without a doubt (at that time) in the baby elephant's best interest to stop pulling on the collar. This will prevent the baby elephant from feeling pain and also please the human beings she relies on for food and shelter. In other words, it is in her best interest (at the time) to adjust her behavior so that those she depends on remain happy.

When they are happy with her, she has the best chance of getting what she needs and being treated as well as possible. So, from an early age, the baby elephant succeeds in adapting to her environment – and to the idiosyncrasies of her scenario. Again, this was a smart call for the baby elephant at the time. She has made an accurate assessment and adjusted accordingly.

It may not be easy, but she learns to do what she must do in order to survive. However, as you would imagine, the elephant grows and grows. There comes a time when this beautiful creature could easily free herself from the "baby elephant collar" and the "magic stake" – however, here is where the brilliance of the early life decision becomes a miscalculation… a flawed premise.

The problem is not that the baby elephant's early assessment was wrong. It's that the baby elephant viewed that **one unique phase of its life as something that it could expect to be a life-long trend.**

The baby elephant never re-assessed its original situation based on its growth and decades of new experiences and wisdom. Had it taken an opportunity to pull again on that meager chain and to test its current strength, the elephant would have been able to see how much it had grown – how capable it was now of facing what had been earlier an impossible challenge.

So the question for you, of course, is this:

What are *your* baby elephant collars?

Another more subtle strand of questions might also be:

- **What assessment might you have made earlier in life that was a smart assessment "at the time"?**

- **Can you give your younger self credit for adjusting to your circumstances, or will you turn that smart assessment into evidence of your weakness and cause for self-blame?**
- **Can you forgive yourself for believing this earlier assessment was a trend, not a temporary phase?**
- **Can you acknowledge the courage, the sacrifice, and the pain that it might have taken for this younger self to stop pulling on the collar and the chain?**
- **Can you forgive yourself for having "rewarded" this younger YOU's painful choices by compounding the sorrow and shame with self-criticism and blame?**

Today is the perfect day to "real eyes" that (yes) even those "baby elephant collars" at one time may have even "served you well." In order to survive, you may have needed to come to the exact conclusion that your younger self did.

In fact, today is the perfect day to retire those collars and embrace that "baby elephant" *with appreciation and awe*. What your younger self had to do might have been way above the "normal" decisions for most children at that age. And yet YOU – yes, YOU – made it through. No matter how messy, you DID IT!

The "baby elephant" within you worked hard and gave up a lot so that you could grow to be strong. So now is *your time* to BE strong. To look at yourself in the mirror with the unconditional love of a true EPIC BE-ing.

Know the "I-ams…"

- I am someone who perseveres.
- I am a fast learner with things that I'm passionate about.
- I am capable of doing even bigger, bolder things.
- I am kind and compassionate.
- I am someone who has important things to say.
- I am committed to making choices that energize and empower me.
- I am willing to let myself off the hook for my choices during those "learning experiences."
- I am excited to see all the wonderful things that now lie ahead of me.
- Etc.

And rejoice in the "I-am-NO-LONGERS…"

- I am no longer in a position where I feel that I have to say "yes" when I want to say "no."
- I am no longer attached to the belief that I must please the people who don't intend to be pleased.
- I am no longer someone who allows others to define me.
- I am no longer someone who allows a situation to make me feel small.
- I am no longer someone who is a prisoner to my reactions.
- I am no longer someone who focuses primarily on my challenges.
- Etc.

Now is the time to go back over and rewrite your own "I-ams" and "I-am-no-longers" down. Get creative. Have fun. Turn them into art if you wish, and hang them on your wall. As you go through this exercise, be sure to *thank the "no-longers."* Yes, that's right. I said to THANK the "no-longers." Why?

Because without the "no-longers," you certainly wouldn't be who you are right now, and you wouldn't be in the position where you can *choose not to repeat* **what you have learned…**

So today's adventure into focusing EPICALLY is simply this:

Step into this day with the commitment to *honor the baby elephant within* by releasing the collar and allowing yourself to grow. Even the word itself– EPICALLY – contains a clue. The key to showing up "epically" is discovering the "epic ally" within. So, shoulders back and stand up tall! Because isn't that mightier-grown version of YOU pretty freaking magnificent?

TODAY'S ACTION STEPS:

- *Let's revisit these two declarations: I AM & I AM NO LONGER. Write two columns on a piece of paper. One column is the I AM column, and the other is the I AM NO LONGER column. Keep this with you today, and fill in the columns as you go along. (+2 Gold Stars)*
- *At the end of the day, look at your columns. Now look up at the clouds or the stars (even if it has to be through your 37th-floor window) and read your declarations to the Universe. (+2 Gold Stars)*
- *Bonus points if you conclude this ritual by cutting each of the I-AM-NO-LONGERs into their piece of paper and, in a safe location with water nearby, lighting it on fire and dropping it into the water. As you drop it, be sure to thank it for bringing you this far and affirm that you need that quality no longer. (+2 Gold Stars) Booyah!*

TOTAL POSSIBLE STARS FROM TODAY: 6 STARS

Day 46 - FOCUS: Always Be You Unless You Can Be A Unicorn Then Be A Unicorn

We're all about now starting to practice living our "new story," but 'fess up. Is there a teeny, tiny (or HUGE) part of that old "blindspot thinking™" version of your mind that warns you not to get "carried away"? After all, life is not all fairy wings and chocolate truffles, is it?

So, let's take a look at that. Is who you believe yourself to be evidence of fact or just habit? Are you really that version of yourself, or have you been doing the same things for so long that you now believe those things are part of who you are? And if it's habit versus fact, is the habit reality – or something you can realistically decide to change?

Think back about waking up this morning… What was your first thought? What was your first action? Did those mimic what you did yesterday… and the day before and, the day before and the day before that…? For most of us, the answer is YES.

Why? Because our minds love patterns and because we are in the habit of defining ourselves as the same version of ourselves who went to sleep the night before. We operate from the expectation that we don't change *unless the circumstances and/or things around us change.* This means that we wake up expecting to be a BE-ing who thinks the same thoughts, reacts the same way, and focuses on the world as we did the day before.

We believe that it will be "hard" to change that.

As you start to see from all the many ways we have played with our invitation to "focus," we get to choose what we focus on – and what we make that focus mean. Most of us are just choosing to focus the same way we always have because we believe that will be "easier" – even when "easy" has led us to a lot of hardship, frustration, and pain.

So today, I will invite you to go a bit "renegade." I will invite you to give yourself permission to focus on your world, your day, and your activities from the vantage point of the most "unicorn version" of yourself.

And what does that mean? Being the Unicorn version of yourself means you open your mind and embrace the magical, wonderful person that this Unicorn KNOWS you can be.

Might that Unicorn version of you have a different perspective of what's impossible or far-fetched? Might they think differently? Might they respond differently?
Most definitely!

How would that confident Unicorn version of yourself interact even with those folks in the office who are notoriously toxic? Even with that one relative who knows how to get under your skin? Even with that little voice inside that tells you that you can't possibly win…?

Think about it. When you respond by finally "putting them in their place," is that really how someone would respond when they *know* that things are always working out for them? When they're confident that this other person's poor behavior will not have a lasting impact on their success? When this person realizes that her own "worst enemy voice" is just a record from an old jukebox stuck on infinite repeat?

Might this Unicorn version of you simply smile and shrug it off like you might smile and shrug off an annoying song that has made its way into your brain? Might this Unicorn version of you convey their influence with a more subtle strength and even compassion? An expectation that anything that can go well for YOU is going to go *even better?*

Or maybe that Unicorn version of You has secretly always wanted to be a writer…How might you structure your day if that Unicorn version of you identifies as a writer ready to explode onto the writing scene? Even if you have another job (for now), might you watch the world around you with the eyes of an author who always finds new and great content? Might you find time each day to write even a page or two – or map out the storyline?

Newsflash: If you're not choosing to grow, you're choosing to stagnate and decline. So choose to blossom! Choose to be Epic!

Today is THE DAY to hit the "pause" button on the "someday" version of you. Today is all about the Unicorn You. How will you focus? And who will you discover that this Unicorn invites you to BE?

TODAY'S ACTION STEPS:

- *Play with completing this sentence: If I could design a Unicorn Version of myself, it would look like this…. (+2 Gold Stars)*
- *Jot down a few ideas of how you might pick just 3 of those qualities/outcomes and start creating them. (+2 Gold Stars)*
- *Bonus points if you take action on one of them, remembering the 1% rule!! Wink! (+2 Gold Stars) Booyah!*

TOTAL POSSIBLE STARS FROM TODAY: 6 STARS

Day 47 — FOCUS: Let's Keep Going – Unleash Your Epic Self!

Hey there, you Fearless Focuser! It's Day 47 of our adventure, and guess what? We're making our way through the FOCUS phase. But hold on, this doesn't mean focus is out the window—it just means we're about to add the second ingredient from our Epic 3 toolkit. Exciting, right?

Before jumping into that, let's make sure we're totally clear on a few important things:

1. The "Abyss" doesn't have a bottom, so let's not get stuck staring at it. Look beyond!
2. Remember, what you focus on grows, so keep your eyes on what you want, not what's lacking. (Get that car out of Reverse and start truly going places!)
3. Focus on the feelings your accomplishments will evoke versus waiting to feel this until you see the evidence of their achievement.
4. Be your wonderful self, or heck, be a Unicorn if you can! Imagine being even more epic than you ever dreamed.
5. Your frequency shapes your reality. Your vibe speaks louder than words, so align your focus with your desired vibration and let your focus dance to the right tune.
6. Our minds weave stories by observing life on autopilot or responding as a Sovereign creator. So choose wisely.

7. Your focus shapes your view of yourself, money, and how epic you think your life can be. It all begins with how you focus and interpret things, so learn to be deliberate with your thinking.
8. Boulders fall, but it's up to you to decide what it means.
9. Life isn't just a sequence of events—it's a journey of learning, growing, and blooming.

As we move ahead, remember this: you're the storyteller of your life. What happens around you doesn't dictate your narrative. You're in control, Epic Chicks and Gents. And guess what? You don't need to build a house at the bottom of the Abyss to prove you're right for not wanting to live there. Transforming your life often boils down to making different choices and finding a different frequency, and guess how you get better at that? Practice, practice, and yep, more practice.

Speaking of practice, take a peek at the "Tinkerbell Project Blog" once again. Let's rewind to 2011—a time when my life wasn't all rainbows and butterflies – and notice how, using focus, language, and imagination; I began creating a story for myself that felt much better than the story that focused entirely on the concept of *struggle*:

Hello dear beautiful world and hello dear beautiful friends! Today, the clouds just couldn't be any more perfect, and the weather absolutely sings to my soul! The Canine Tenors are out in the backyard singing to the squirrels, singing to the neighbors, and just generally singing to life and to anyone else who will listen!

Oh yes, there were problems to solve, and ok ... SOME aggravations ... some mysteries that are still elusive, and yes, GOSH it was hard to work when it feels so much like true "make-your-heart-dance" SPRING!

Yet....I can SEE the progress all around me....!

Yes, believing IS seeing, and (in spite of my "old mind's" attempt to keep me in check...wink!) my new beliefs seem to be creating things that definitely resemble a light at the end of the tunnel!

Ok, ok.... I KNOW that we have sometimes been told that in order to be effective and to properly "deal" with reality, we have to "get to the bottom" of the issue....roll up our sleeves..." dig deep"...dissect those tender spots and really wrestle those demons to the ground...... (and this was said to a child who found the Roadrunner and the Three Stooges too violent....no wonder, the very thought of that had me hyperventilating, but I did try......!)

Yes, I tried to follow the directions on the package called "life" and I trained my brain to go over and over and over AND OVER those irritating, unfulfilling, "knock me to my knees and leave me crying" moments....

I kept thinking that if I looked at the problem from enough angles, I would somehow (magically?) wake up one day and be purged of the pain that had left me breathless and angry or hurt....

Well, my dear darling friends, as I awoke one day to find myself in a relationship filled with terror, anger, and addiction, I decided that (respectfully) this approach of trying to relive these moments in hopes of finding the missing link just wasn't working....

Yes, living through them once was quite enough... I was at the point where my anxiety was at such a level that I couldn't even drive on the highway. My stress was already so high that just the addition of basic "highway sensitivity" tossed me into an anxiety attack. I was shocked to find myself in that position, but there I was....

Yes, I did try to undo the effects of my scenario by "putting on a happy face" and pretending that all was well, but those results were equally ineffective.

My brain knew how I truly felt, and it wasn't warm and fuzzy.... Any affirmations that I made only made my attempts at feeling that fuzziness seems like sandpaper. My brain just rolled its eyes and told me that we weren't quite "there" yet....!

So, how to undo the stalemate?

I began to play....yes, play......I discovered a book called "Ask and It is Given" (by Jerry and Esther Hicks) that literally fell on the floor at my feet as I was walking through a different section of the bookstore. And as the saying goes, "And the rest is history..."

Learning to play wasn't easy because I had bought into the idea that play is the opposite of work.

I assure you it is not –wink– and for me, play can be infinitely more PRODUCTIVE than work.

At the risk of being cliche, I can't help but quote James Matthew Barrie from Peter Pan (after all this IS the Tinkerbell Project....wink again...): ***"It is not real work unless you would rather be doing something else."***

Allow me to add my own Tinkerbell wisdom to the quote and to say, "....so if you love what you do, then you will never work a day in your life...."

Yes, I began to use deliberate play...." mind games" that my mind would accept because I called them "games." I would imagine and envision great outcomes....great dreams....great loving conversations, and great feelings....

I began to play to identify the feelings I wanted to feel...the essence of what I was wishing for.... I spent more mind time at the "top" of my game than at the "bottom of it all." (Because—as Esther Hicks/Abraham has said— THERE IS NO BOTTOM.....) And if it's "play," what can be the harm in it? It certainly felt better than the infinite repeat of angst and drama....

Guess what.....things began to change....."for no logical reason." my "luck" seemed to be improving.... I could feel a big huge sigh, and I began to rewire my inner machine, and I began the process of learning to empower myself—versus my habit of just "dealing with" whatever came my way....

Part of the "play" was to find joy in my day ... in my work...in my chores...even in the most crotchety, complaining and thorn in my side folks who happened to come my way....

After all, was I really obligated to play by the rules....? Rules that said that conditions had to be a certain way for me to be "entitled" to be happy....? This rule was built upon the idea of cause and effect. It implied that happiness was the effect that we could only permit ourselves to feel if there was an obvious cause.

Hmmmm......this would also mean that until there was a recognized cause for such joy, we were not "entitled to be happy" -- now THAT was an interesting concept....

Yes, it became apparent that it was time to start breaking a few of these "rules" that tended to leave me feeling like a victim...(can you feel me smile....nothing wrong with a Cheshire cat in the middle of a Peter Pan story....)

So the story continues for several years....it started with baby steps until my entire world and my entire perception of my world began to shift....

Yes, I have become a bit of a rebel. I DO identify what I don't like, but I don't program it into my viewing favorites.

These days, I play the game of how many times can I get to the TOP OF IT....(forget the bottom of it....).

How many new ideas can I sift from the challenge.... Where's the hidden brainstorm in that particular problem? And how many wonderful "mundane" things can I actually feel GRATEFUL for?

And in the process, how many times during the day can I remember to stop and simply BASK IN THIS PROCESS??

We are alive, and we are living in a super exciting time on this planet! Our fellow humans are brimming with wonderful ideas and innovations.

AS ARE WE!

There are opportunities that our ancestors never dreamed of. We have more freedom to learn and to choose and to pass joyous knowledge on to our children. We are living in a world where there is more encouragement to truly share our uniqueness. We are the pioneers in a new unfolding....

Sooooo....as I wind down this particular day, I send out my smiles and my very best wishes, and I say:

Let's reinvent the rules...!

Let's dump the game of "What's wrong with this picture?" and replace it with our revised version of "What's RIGHT with this picture!"...

Let's tuck those troubles into bed and thank them for the great ideas they spawned, but let's rise to the top and then soar and soar and soar......

Time to leave our cocoons and "rise" to the occasion!

Have a blissful evening, dear friends!! What a great time it is to be alive....Onwards and (yes) UPWARD!!!!

Alright, back to you, superstar. You're parked next to a shiny new ride, fueled up and ready to roll. Baggage is tucked away, GPS set, and you're steering towards your dreams. What's the next stop on this wild journey? This glorious life-long vacation? What kind of epic experience are you about to create? Today's all about the magic of your choices.

Be epic. Be the Unicorn. But epic doesn't have to mean complex. Keep it simple. Explore. Iterate and keep reinventing! You've got this!! Booyah!!

TODAY'S ACTION STEPS:

- *Today, review the important things relating to Focus we listed above. (+2 Gold Stars)*
- *Note which of these you are now more regularly incorporating into your daily life. Which still needs attention and practice? (+2 Gold Stars)*
- *Bonus points if you remember that you are in your inner game gym! Six-pack abs don't happen overnight, but with consistency and dedication, shifts start happening. So, what's your plan to keep tightening the Focus muscles that still need attention? (+2 Gold Stars) Booyah!*

TOTAL POSSIBLE STARS FROM TODAY: 6 STARS

Day 48: FOCUS: Creating a Focus-Centric Lifestyle™- Energizing Your Epic Journey!

WOO HOO!! Can you believe it? It's Day 48 of our exhilarating 100 Days of Epic Adventure! You've been charging ahead and conquering a whole array of new, exciting challenges. I think that it's fair to say that you have victoriously crushed your missions as we dove into "#1" of The Epic 3: FOCUS.

Pause for a moment, and let's bask in your brilliance! You've begun transitioning from merely grasping the *concept* of focus to *embodying its life-altering principles.* The journey isn't always the perfect wave, and that's okay. There are days when you'll feel like you're surfing on a tidal wave of focus mastery, and there might be days when you're stretching the limits of your own potential.

Remember, the objective is to create your focus-centric lifestyle. That will be a new approach to your life, so *be willing to give it time.*

Whatever you're feeling, keep going! Let this journey remind you— patience is the Super Shero's steadfast ally. As you dive into the Art of Maintaining Laser-Sharp Focus (!), anticipate the occasional rogue wave on your path to greater things. It will happen, BUT press on. With your unwavering commitment to your mission, you're bound to discover that there are silver linings in those moments. An EPIC Surfer learns to interact with waves, big or small, and use them to create the outcome she is looking for!!!

So before we move onto Epic #2, let's take time for a quick refresher on how to create that Focus-Centric Lifestyle™:

1. **Spotlight on Your Focus:** *Delve into the art of intentionally identifying your focus points. Elevate your awareness, capturing the nuances of where your attention drifts.*
2. **Flip the Script:** *Practice the powerful transformation of shifting your focus from the absence to the abundance. Magnify the presence of what you desire and watch the magic unfold.*
3. **Thought Shield Mastery:** *Equip yourself with the ultimate thought antivirus. Become the sovereign ruler of your emotional and energetic state by carefully curating your thoughts.*
4. **The Joyous State Equation:** *Relish in the bliss of joyous, empowered states. Think of the Tinkerbell Project blogs and embrace how these euphoric moments become the secret sauce to unleashing extraordinary outcomes in every facet of your life.*

Your Focus-Centric Lifestyle™ should be an extension and expression of YOU! It's the ultimate quest to discover the EPIC WHO™. So what will that look like? How will the story unfold?

In a world where conflict and chaos paint our world in hues of despair, remember—you possess the unique ability to craft your vibrant canvas. Yes, we're aware of the storms the strife, but peek beyond the surface, and you'll witness whispers of something epic just waiting to be set free…That one story that you dare to share, that one story that you dare to hold true might just be the one story that someone else needs to hear.

Is today the day that *you* start creating your style of the "Tinkerbell Project Blog?" Here's my version, so use this as the inspiration to sit down today and start YOURS! I *know* you have a story that someone out there is yearning to hear:

Hello, my dear, wonderful friends!…Isn't it an amazingly perfect time to be alive?

I know…I know…there are those whose jaws would drop just to hear that I could possibly THINK such a thing–much less be willing to make that sort of statement….

The prevalent headlines have gone to great lengths to make sure that I know that this planet is "overwhelmingly" infested with illness, murder, deceit, hopelessness, crime, and even (God forbid) celebrity bad hair days...

So, based on the headlines, the question really should be, why on Earth am I even still here willing to wake up each day to such a hopeless environment??! Wink!

Yes, but....take a look around...ok, so there IS illness...there IS violence....there IS poverty...and yes, perhaps there truly are those of us who have magnificently awful "bad hair days,"...and yet....those sneaky hints of "amazing-ness" abound...

...Diseases are being cured...impactful forums for peace and awareness are being established...

And the technology...we now have computers that can quickly and easily connect each of us to the other so that we can not only observe our unique differences, but we can marvel at our similarities...

As I read the post by fellow blogger Good Morning C-Town, I thought, "Yes, how perfect that we all now have the chance to read these words from each others' hearts and to see that maybe we are not all so different ...maybe we are evolving in absolutely the perfect direction...

Maybe the days when we interacted on this planet as strangers are now fading...maybe we are entering a new phase where we embrace the beauty of our gorgeous globe and interact as friends and extended family...maybe just maybe this is the dawning of the perfect moment to be alive....!"

Yes, even in this tension-filled world, there are still people in the grocery store that will give you a smile for no particular reason..

It's even worth acknowledging our ability to emerge from the storms within...we often find the ability to overcome the impossible, even in the most dire of times...

Progress begins with the desire to question and we are all super-charged with questions.... If there were no questions, there would be no desire to create.

Can you feel it....?! The rumbling of creation....

So what if we don't yet have a "perfect" planet (although maybe in its flaws lie its "perfection" because it DOES evoke amazing inspiration)...

Do we really want it all to be "done" so there is no reason for evolution?

Isn't it exciting to see our planet grow and blossom? Isn't it phenomenal to see the new ideas that we each hatch on a daily basis?

Isn't it humbling to know that, yes, you DO make a difference... you are part of this masterpiece...the world basks in each contribution you make...each new phenomenon that you inspire...

Walk through this day as the grand creator that you are...and know that the world is honored that you are here.

There is NO ONE—absolutely NO ONE like you...And there is no moment like the present to revel in all that it means to be ALIVE!

It's time to take that moment to pinch yourself and do the full "tail in the air/ I learned this from my dog" happy dance!

We are artists of the Universe, and we are here to create! Behold the masterpiece of our day!

COWABUNGA, WORLD....HERE WE COME!

So yes, it's time to step into the second phase of our journey together. It's time to warmly acknowledge that perfection in our world is a fleeting muse. BUT now we know that within its very imperfections lies a unique kind of perfection—an inspiration that ignites innovation. Every step you take shapes our cosmic masterpiece. Can you feel the world's applause, honoring your presence and the kaleidoscope of brilliance you bring? There's no one like you, and the universe revels in your existence.

As you move through this day, wear your creator's crown proudly. Dance with exuberance, tail in the air, like the enchanting pup that taught us to celebrate life's simplest joys.

Cue the cosmic confetti, you Epic champion! It's time for that joy-infused dance of yours, celebrating the masterpiece you're crafting with every heartbeat.

The stage is yours, the spotlight is beaming, and your story, perfectly imperfect, unfolds with every conscious breath. Embrace it boldly, for you are weaving a tapestry of wonder—one stitch, one focus-enhancing habit at a time. The journey is yours, the canvas is boundless, and the symphony of life plays on.

Stay tuned for Day 49 as we elevate the canvas of your epic saga. Until then, dance, create, and shine on! Let's give one final Booyah as we close out the first act of this show. You're on your way to mastering Epic #1 – the FOCUS-Centric Lifestyle! Now, onto Epic #2 – LANGUAGE!

TODAY'S ACTION STEPS:

- *Write down and share your three biggest wins from this Mastery of Focus element. (+2 Gold Stars)*
- *Write down what will be your next "finish line" in the next 14 days. What do you want to continue building, and where would you like to be in two weeks? What would you like to be feeling? (+2 Gold Stars)*

- *Bonus points if you hold yourself accountable by sharing this with our team: team@gritmindsetacademy.com . We want to cheer you on and support you! (+2 Gold Stars) Booyah!*

TOTAL POSSIBLE STARS FROM TODAY: 6 STARS

#2 OF THE EPIC 3: LANGUAGE

Time to do a little chicken dance because you have now made it to the second of the Epics in The EPIC 3: Language!

Think about it – Our words are "symptoms" or indicators of what we believe to be TRUTH. They reflect how we feel that we are experiencing our lives and how we interpret what we see in the world.

Our language is an important clue that points to what we are focusing on. AND IF WHAT WE FOCUS ON EXPANDS, HOW IMPORTANT DO YOU THINK THOSE CLUES (OUR WORDS) ARE?

Ah-ha! What if I were to tell you that there's really no such thing as saying, "I didn't really mean it that way" because…Your words are "symptoms" of what your mind believes to be TRUTH. So if your thoughts are "thinking you, " you could EASILY solidify a belief that does not serve you. Can you see how subtle and yet important this is?

Do you know how easily your mind can be "programmed" by words that deplete you? Remember, you are the programmer of your thoughts. Choosing words deliberately and changing our word choice when those words de-energize or deflate us can profoundly affect our focus – and therefore on our thoughts, which influence our state, our emotions, and ultimately upon, our actions.

What do our actions create?

That's right: RESULTS. So if you're unhappy with your results, it might not be the fault of what's happening TO you, but rather WITHIN you… Time to reprogram that code!… Wink!

If you just let out a huge "stress sigh" right now, don't reach for that bowl of Ben & Jerry's just yet…Because, during this 100 Days of Epic, we've already started turning around that cruise ship and getting you headed in the direction YOU desire. So let's keep building that momentum and fortifying your EPIC 3.

(Yes, that just might be the sound of a flock of Epichickens squawking their Booyahs in delight at your progress…it's ok for you to be feeling mighty about now…) Onto #2!

Now that you are becoming more aware of your FOCUS's role in creating a day (and a life) that resonates epically let's explore how LANGUAGE can amplify the positive effects of a deliberate focus. Let's become alert to the impact our word selection can have on our inner narrative and our communication with others, as well.

In fact, let's EXPAND our mission beyond what we targeted in the FOCUS section so that our new objective looks more like this:

- **Focus Illumination:** Learn the art of using words to intentionally identify what you ARE focusing on versus what you THINK you are focusing on. Look deeply at the words you are choosing so that they become clues to uncover where your attention truly is being drawn.
- **Flip to Abundance:** Once you have identified where you are focusing, engage in the practice of using word selection to transform your focus from scarcity to plenty, from "it's missing" to "it's present." Use new language choices to magnify the evidence of the presence of your desires. This is what will trigger new results. At times, it can even feel like new things are transpiring as if by magic. Discover how shifting your language influences the amount of time you spend in joyous, empowered states.
- **Mastery of Mind Armor:** Equip yourself with the ultimate thought defense. Select words that "virus protect" your thoughts, becoming sovereign over your emotional and energetic state. Feel the impact of your language on your internal joy and externally improved outcomes.
- **Equation for Joyful States:** Bask in empowered joy and its potential to elevate all aspects of life. Reflect on the Tinkerbell Project Blogs, discovering the link between language, joyous states, and extraordinary outcomes.

So, with a final croon from those Epichickens, let's shake our tail feathers and dive into Day 49 in this 100 DAYS OF EPIC!

Day 49— LANGUAGE: STICKS AND STONES MAY BREAK MY BONES BUT WORDS… OH MY!

Remember that cute little verbal "comeback" we all learned as kids: "Sticks and stones may break my bones, but words will never hurt me…"? Boy, was that ever a wee bit "off"! Who knew as we defiantly blurted out to the "meanie" on the playground that there were disclaimers [!!] to this little rhyme that no one would tell us about?

In fact, it is often the *wounds from words* that we carry with us the longest – even if those words come from our inner narrative. Every word carries with it an invisible story, some sort of association or trigger often based on past experiences. By the time we've spent a decade or more on this planet, most words conjure up a memory and/or an emotion.

Even words like "love," "rich," "pamper," "help," or "pretty" bring thoughts and feelings to mind. On the surface, all seem like pretty "positive" words, don't they? So they should naturally just bring up "good" emotions, yes?

Not always.

Even for those "positive words," we often hold some emotions beneath the surface that don't make us feel good. For some, "love" is something they can't seem to find. It's a source of frustration. It's the self-fulfilling prophecy that "love hurts" or that "love is a fleeting thing." Or it doesn't come in the way they want it or think it "should" look like.

Think of author Gary Chapman's *5 Love Languages* concept. Gary explains that we each have five ways we tend to naturally express "love" – and expect it to be conveyed back to us. For some, "if you truly loved me" would mean that in order to feel loved, they would expect lots of words of affection. For these people, if their partner starts saying those words less and less (or not at all), it would signal trouble in the relationship.

Others express love primarily through acts of service. They might not verbally say things that feel "touchy-feely," but they will be the first to get the oil changed for you, do your laundry, work extra hours to provide more, etc. So imagine an "acts of service" person in a relationship with someone who believes real love shows up in words of affirmation.

The "acts of service" person might believe that "love" is an empty word. They might grumble that people quickly say, "I love you," but never truly put it into action. It always ends up being a one-way street where "I'm the one doing everything." Meanwhile, their partner has pulled back on their acts of service because, without loving phrases, they aren't feeling loved.

Can you see how even the word "love" can hold different "invisible stories" for different people? Therefore, in the first few days of our quest to align our LANGUAGE with our full-on epic-ness, let's commit to "the action" of awareness. Today, listen to the words you say to yourself and others.

When you speak to yourself, are you being your champion – or your own worst enemy? Where do your words direct your focus? How do your words make you feel? Yes, definitely take note today by writing down what you discover.

What are you hearing when you speak to or listen to others?

Are you sharing words that naturally bring out the best in them? Are you listening to their words based on a bias from your own story? How can you find more ways to deliberately "author" your story by consciously selecting your words? The alternative might just mean that your words (not YOU) start creating your story.

Today's mission is to FOCUS on becoming totally AWARE of your LANGUAGE. Because what you are aware of, you can master!

Now, let's go have some fun with this!

TODAY'S ACTION STEPS:

- *Go out today aware of the stories your words are expressing and what your words imply that you are focusing on. What inner frequency do they create? (+2 Gold Stars)*
- *When your words create a frequency that doesn't feel energizing, can you find a thought or way of expressing the moment that creates a more "in flow" frequency? (+2 Gold Stars)*
- *Bonus points if you explore the 5 Love Languages. There are plenty of videos on YouTube, or grab the book. How do you rank your own five love languages? (+2 Gold Stars)*
- *Extra Bonus: Speaking of YouTube, grab some bonus points by subscribing to our YouTube channel: @UnleashTheEpicYou . Catch our series of 1-minute power whooshes!! (+4 Gold Stars) Booyah!*

TOTAL POSSIBLE STARS FROM TODAY: 10 STARS

Day 50 – LANGUAGE: My Biggest Challenge Is…

Let's be honest.

When there is a problem to solve, we all tend to think we will improve things by talking about it… putting it under our microscope and (as we addressed on a previous day) "getting to the bottom of it."

Well, we busted that myth by establishing that there is no bottom to the madness, so what do our words have to do with shifting our focus from the presence of the problem to the presence of the solution?

Let's make this very easy:

Yes, it is very important to identify a problem – because that is also how we identify how we'd like to show up differently. HOWEVER, most of us tend to get stuck there. We poke and prod and begin every conversation with anyone who will listen with a phrase like this one:

- My biggest challenge is [blah, blah, blah…]
- The problem is that [blah, blah, blah…]
- I always seem to [get passed over no matter what I do].
- I should be [farther along than I am right now].
- I always seem to [end up struggling financially].
- I'm not [very lucky]. Things tend to [come hard for me].
- I am [a die-hard procrastinator] no matter what I try.
- It's hard to [change that]. It's just who I am.
- IT IS WHAT IT IS.

Recognize any of these phrases? You have probably heard someone *use* one of these phrases. So if we "all" say them, what's the big deal? They're true, aren't they? Well, my epic Sheros and Heroes, if this was a Star Wars movie, our beloved Yoda would appear right now because this is one of those "wise words these are" moments. Feel free to lean in and grab your lightsaber.

Let me ask you: ***when you say to someone that your biggest challenge is to find a way to feel more confident, what do you think are the most powerful words in that sentence?***

Clearly, "challenge" is a powerful word. You probably have all sorts of "invisible stories" stored up around the topic of challenge. Although there may be times when you actually love a challenge, in this context, your unseen focus has probably flipped back to memories around times that felt difficult. The association may have been compounded through the years by memory after memory of "challenges" that made you feel bad.

Maybe you remember the pain of falling off your bike many, MANY times before you learned to ride. Maybe it was struggling to finish a paper in school, only to see that the teacher graded it with a "C." Maybe it was applying for job after job and always getting the same "gone in a different direction" email while everyone else around you seemed to be getting promoted.

We have many stressful stories around "challenge," so where are you guiding your focus when you use that word? In a direction that energizes you and excites you?

Let's look at this from another perspective: when you're around someone who feels like their life is consumed by a formidable challenge, how does *their* energy feel? Like someone that you'd enjoy spending lots of time with right now? Like someone that you'd like to have on your team right now? Like someone about to find the solution to their challenge quickly and easily?

Usually not, because the state of mind of someone who is consumed by the immensity of their challenge usually isn't a state of mind that is conducive to seeing solutions. So yes, challenge is definitely a powerful word and can keep our focus away from noticing the presence of what we want – even when it's right beside us.

In this context, the word "challenge" will not create the *inner game frequency* (the electromagnetic field) that will align with the frequency of the solution you seek.

How about the word "biggest"? "My **biggest** challenge is…." Think about it…Can something be the biggest *if there is only one of them*? So yes, by selecting the word "biggest," you have now inadvertently conveyed to your subconscious that you have MANY challenges. This one just happens to be the biggest. If it's that big, it just adds to the weight that the word "challenge" was already making you feel.

Oh goodie! I don't think that I need to say more on that one…But wait! We didn't stop there, did we? We said, "*My* biggest challenge is…." We didn't say, "*The* biggest challenge is," did we? So now, by using the word "my," we have made this challenge part of who we are. Yep, it's **part of our identity.** I now identify myself as someone with two eyes, a nose, a mouth, and this big freaking challenge that accompanies me everywhere I go.

You DO take yourself with you wherever you go, so do you really want to introduce yourself to your next great opportunity with "my biggest challenge" in tow? The answer is probably no, but if this challenge is "true," how are you supposed to change that? By standing in front of a mirror saying that you're a money magnet when your mind asks if you've checked your bank account recently?

Don't get me wrong. I'm not saying that affirmations like that never work, but you can't miss the critical step. I'm talking about the step we usually miss: **finding a thought that energizes you so your mind can believe that the affirmation is possible.**

When most people try affirmations, they are doing it because "nothing else has worked." Their mind only sees the challenge, pushing back on the affirmation. But there's a different way… a *better way!* Yes, it may feel like "my biggest challenge" represents the truth. Here's where it's smart to ask, **"What am I assuming that is not necessarily true?"**

The answer? You have been assuming that the presence of this challenge is the *only version of the truth.*

In those moments, wouldn't it be also true to say one of the following:

- My biggest FOCUS right now is…
- My biggest OPPORTUNITY right now is to…
- What I'm really excited to turn around right now is…
- I love thinking about when I….
- My biggest COMMITMENT right now is…

Do those also ring true in your mind? Do those feel better than viewing the situation as "my biggest challenge"? Maybe those words even inspire a little bit of relief and hope.

So, your mission today is to be aware of the words that you are choosing and what state they create. If they don't energize you toward where you intend to go, what can you say that your mind can believe that shifts that energy/ frequency? That helps you create a state where you *can* see the possibility of opportunity, progress, and solutions.

If words are the paint on your palate, today is your day to grab your fanciest beret and start creating your masterpiece!

TODAY'S ACTION STEPS:

- *Until now (wink!), what would you have said your "biggest challenge is"?   (+1 Gold Star)*
- *Now play with shifting that around, like in the examples above. What might that sound like? (+2 Gold Stars)*
- *Bonus points if you can think of some other phrases that you have been using that sabotage you before you even get started. Write those down. (+1 Gold Star)*
- *Extra Bonus: We've created a list of 10 phrases that we hear almost everyone use that sends them down the rabbit hole. Grab your free copy and grab some extra points in the process! bit.ly/EpicWords (+2 Gold Stars) Booyah!*

TOTAL POSSIBLE STARS FROM TODAY: 6 STARS

Day 51 – LANGUAGE: That One Invisible Word

Yesterday, we played with the phrase "My biggest challenge is…" and we saw just how powerful words can be when it comes to influencing our mental state. When we select words that carry emotions that weigh us down, it impacts how we show up to face the scenario. It affects our performance, which, of course, affects our results.

However, what if I were to tell you that the most powerful of all those words we didn't even mention? And why is it so powerful? Because it typically slides right under all of our radars. That means we can sabotage ourselves all day long and never realize it. Scary!

So, what is this mystery word?

It's the word "**is**".

Say what? Sounds crazy, doesn't it? I mean, the word doesn't really "mean" anything, does it? Actually, it does. It represents what we believe to be fact – **TRUTH in all capital letters.** What we say in the present tense reflects our belief about reality – about life, about the world, about each other, and about ourselves. From our mind's perspective, these are the "non-arguables." These statements become the programming code for our inner game. They create the foundation upon which everything else is built.

Think about it: what do we say when conveying that something is beyond changing? **"It is what it is."** So if someone tells themselves repeatedly that they "never catch a break financially," do you think that they can be given an opportunity that might change their financial life and assess it objectively? Or would they tend to suspect that it will "never work"?

Do you think that someone who tells themself that they are terrible at interviews [!!] will walk into an interview sounding and acting confident? How about the person telling themselves it's "hard to lose weight"? Are they likely to adapt their lifestyle with more exercise and better eating habits, believing it will work?

We have a term for this type of thinking. It's called creating a "self-fulfilling prophecy." Yet, we still are trained to pay zero attention to our present tense statements. Imagine how different our lives might be if we were taught at a young age to deliberately choose the facts that we declare to be true.

Remember one of the big lessons from yesterday: there are typically several variations of "truth." "My biggest challenge" can be "true," but so can "my biggest commitment." One definitely helps to create a mental state that is more ripe for success and happiness.

Today, your mission is to play with the acronym **A.C.C.T.** (Remember we introduced A.C.T. in the Focus section- NOW it's time to add another "C" for CELEBRATION!)

- **A = Be Aware of Your Present Tense Statements (and How They Make You Feel)**
- **C = Celebrate When You Catch Yourself Saying Something That Feels "Negative"**
- **C = Commit to Changing It To Something That Feels More Energizing and Aligned**
- **T = Realize that Transformation is As Simple As Making A Different Choice**

What present tense statements are you currently saying about yourself that define how you see yourself? Are these present tense statements locking you into a box of perceived "limitations"? Where have you been assuming that there is only one "realistic" version of truth? Where have you been doing that at the expense of your mental state?

Today is the opportunity to start shifting things dramatically for yourself by using your words to guide your focus more clearly in a direction that can propel you further than perhaps you previously believed you could go.

It starts with "getting your I.T. together" – your inner technology and the programming code for an epic inner game. What kind of powerful present tense statements will you code today? Let's DO THIS! Booyah!

TODAY'S ACTION STEPS:

- *Today is the day to take A.C.C.T.-ion. Listen to your present tense statements and commit to making the shifts and adjustments.   (+2 Gold Star)*
- *Keep track of the phrases that keep showing up again and again. Are they based on an assumption that is not necessarily true? (+1 Gold Stars)*
- *Bonus points if you can think of some other phrases that you have been using that sabotage you before you even get started. Write those down. (+1 Gold Stars)*
- *Extra Bonus: Did you grab your list of 10 self-defeating phrases that we hear almost everyone? If not, now's the time… Hint! Grab your free copy and grab some extra points in the process! bit.ly/EpicWords If you already did, you're flying on Epic, so grab the extra stars anyway!! (+3 Gold Stars) Booyah!*

TOTAL POSSIBLE STARS FROM TODAY: 7 STARS

Day 52 – LANGUAGE: A Tension Span

Tense creates tension if you don't pay attention.

Your "I am" statements can be some of the biggest "tension-creating" statements you subject yourself to. If you listen to yourself, you'll probably notice that you make these statements over and over AND OVER again – not just to yourself but even solidifying them by stating them as Truth to others.

Notice that these "I am" statements come in some common variations:

- I'm not good at ….
- I'm always….
- One thing that you'll learn about me is…
- I never seem to be able to …
- I've tried but I still can't …
- I can never …
- I am someone who…
- I just don't …
- I tend to …
- I am bad at…
- I always mess up when …
- I am terrible at …

These are just a few of the common examples.

Here's a jolting statistic: The average 2-year-old child hears *432 negative statements per day* but only 32 positive statements each day, according to a research study at the University of Iowa. **432 vs 32!** So, is it any wonder that your mind gets programmed to believe that the negative thoughts deserve the airplay?

However, it's never too late to change that pattern. Be warned that it *does* take commitment to be successful at replacing the tendency toward negative thoughts. Just as you repeatedly heard volumes of negative statements before they became ingrained into your psyche, you must now be willing to commit to **many**, *many repetitions of more positively focused dialogue* to rewire those thinking habits. Guess whose responsibility it is to keep those positive statements flowing? Wink! Remember what we said about patience being the ally of the Shero and Hero of any Epic Story?

Yes! It is *normal* to initially feel like you've suddenly enrolled in an inner game boot camp. Adjustments can feel awkward, but remember that this change will be worth it! Don't allow yourself to say that "it's hard." (**Remember the power of the present tense statements.**) Replace that thought with one that says that it's temporarily new and unfamiliar – but you're excited to think about when it's the new normal. Woo hoo!

So today is the day to focus on starting with **AT LEAST** 20 POSITIVE PRESENT TENSE STATEMENTS you can make about yourself. Even better would be to write them down! Here are some examples to get you started (and remember that you want to find a way to make them believable):

- **I am so excited to see myself finally taking action to create the future I know I deserve.**
- **I am resourceful and tenacious, so that will carry me far.**
- **I know that some of the most successful people I admire were once in a place like where I am today.**
- **I know that "impossible things" are happening around me every day, so why not for me?**
- **I am committed to exploring a new, more rewarding path beginning today.**
- **I have faced great challenges and come out the other side, so I know I'm capable.**
- **I am a do-er, so when I'm passionate and get clarity, I make things happen.**
- **I can be unstoppable when I want to be, and I'm absolutely ready to be unstoppable about this right here, right now!**
- **I don't have to do it all in one day. I'm capable of doing lots of small steps, so I KNOW that I will get there.**
- **Now is my time!**

So, it's time to amplify your game so that you are now creating even more deliberately empowering "I am" statements. Get focused, and here's an **EPIC NINJA TIP**: once you get good at finding 50 positive things to say today, double it! Go for 100! Remember that consistency is key! Today is your first day. Don't make it your last! And yes, your "tension span" will definitely thank you!!

Booyah! You've got this!

TODAY'S ACTION STEPS:

- *Go back and look at the I AM statements you created earlier. Expand upon them until you have 20 (yes, 20) EPIC empowering I AM statements! Have fun with this! How creative can you get? How vulnerable and real can you get? (+2 Gold Stars)*
- *Now, take a look at either your physical health or your professional career. Can you create some deliberately empowering I AM declarations around those specific areas of your life? (+2 Gold Stars)*
- *Bonus points if you DO double up and come up with 100! (+2 Gold Stars) Booyah!*

TOTAL POSSIBLE STARS FROM TODAY: 6 STARS

Day 53 – LANGUAGE: Two Incredibly Impactful Words

By now, you should see why our words *matter!* They are indicators of how we view ourselves and the world, and they can also be emotional triggers. Remember that no word in your "normal vocabulary" is just a word. They all come with invisible stories that lead to associations, which then lead to specific emotions.

We create certain thoughts and feelings when we use specific words in our self-talk. Those thoughts and feelings impact the type of decisions that we make. Do you make your best decisions when you're worried? When you're afraid? How about when you're feeling confident? Or secure?

We have learned just how powerful our present tense statements can be. They can energize us or deflate us. And not simply for our performance. If you're leading a team, your present tense statements can inspire your team or make them feel that the task at hand is insurmountable. Communication – whether it be within your inner narrative or with those around you – is key.

So today is about two words that, in my humble opinion, serve as "life rafts" to get you from that deflating thought onto that "island of great potential." What are those two words that should become your best friend beginning today?

TEMPORARY and YET.

Note how inserting one of these two words into a more de-energizing statement can introduce an infusion of hope and possibility:

- I'm not making enough money >>> I'm not making enough money **yet**
- I keep getting passed over at work >>> I **temporarily** keep getting passed over at work
- I feel like crap >>> I feel like crap but I know that it's **temporary**
- I don't feel any better >>> I don't feel any better **yet**

Now note how you can make it even more impactful by adding a powerful "so…" statement that would look a bit like this:

- I'm not making enough money >>> I'm not making enough money **yet so I'm even more excited, committed and ready to do what I need to do to learn how to start changing that. I know that others have been here, and if they can learn, so can I!**

- I keep getting passed over at work >>> **I've been getting passed over for promotions at work, but I know that's temporary, so I'm more committed than ever to get coaching and mentoring to help me learn why this keeps happening and how I can change that. I KNOW that I'm capable. I just need the right guidance and training.**

- I feel like crap >>> I feel like crap, but I know it's **temporary, so this gives me even more incentive to keep going even when I don't think I feel like it. I understand that some things feel like they get harder before they get easier. I don't like feeling like crap, so I'm committed to being tenacious through this phase if needed!**

- I don't feel any better >>> I don't feel any better **yet, so this just reinforces my commitment. I'm determined not to feel this way in the future, and I know it's normal for change to be a process rather than a moment. I know many others made the commitment and kept going, and I can see how that can be me. How that WILL be me! The day will come when I look back and say, "Wow! I can't believe all of my progress!"**

Can you see how specific words can guide your expectation toward the expectation of success? In my experience, while Schuy was in the ICU and I was trying to find those more empowering thoughts, once I got to the place where my "better thoughts" gave the feeling of *knowing* that things would work out, it became truly miraculous. Things that were technically impossible became our reality. It began to look as if Life had to conform to my vision.

So today is the day to commit to staying ahead of those thoughts. No more allowing your thoughts to *think you*!

Where can you insert the words "yet" and "temporary" that can lead you toward your version of "…and so…"? This is the secret sauce, so don't mistake *language action* for *no action*. This is the foundation of **attracting the right actions** into the other aspects of your life!

Now get out there and start "language actioning!"

TODAY'S ACTION STEPS:

- *Go out into the world focused on your present tense statements – this time, ready to see where you can soften resistance by using the words "temporary" or "yet." (+1 Gold Stars)*
- *How did it feel? When did you remember? When didn't you remember? How might you get in the habit of using "temporary" and "yet"? (+1 Gold Star)*
- *Bonus points if you can think of other phrases to help soften downward-spiraling statements. Write those down. (+3 Gold Stars) Booyah!*

TOTAL POSSIBLE STARS FROM TODAY: 5 STARS

Day 54– LANGUAGE: They're Playing My Tune

Can you imagine any superheroes without a theme song? Think about it: doesn't the soundtrack often make the scene? Think about the hugely impactful videos. Is it just the words that captivate you – or is it once again the music that gives it the emotional push that makes it go viral?

Groups like U2 or Led Zeppelin have learned that just a few notes played on a single guitar can simultaneously shift thousands of people's moods and energy. No words. It's just a powerful riff, and the energy in an entire stadium goes wild.

Studies show that the limbic system in the brain, which is involved in processing emotions and controlling memory, "lights" up when our ears perceive music. The chills you feel when you hear a particularly moving piece of music may result from dopamine, a neurotransmitter that triggers sensations of pleasure and well-being.

We've talked about the language of words and its effect on humans. Now, let's talk about another form of communication and emotion creation: MUSIC.

Music *is* its own form of LANGUAGE. It connects with us emotionally in an immediate and powerful way. It can be the secret reset button when you're feeling blue. It can also throw you back to a painful memory when your day was going well. Music has power. Therefore, it's important to recognize that it, too, brings energy and focus to the equation.

Today, I will encourage you to be very aware of the **music** you select for your brain to interact with. Learn to leverage its power. In fact, let today be the day that you join ranks with the superheroes of the galaxy, like the epic Princess Leia from the movie *Star Wars*.

I once watched an interview with Carrie Fisher, the actress who immortalized that role. She talked about the moment that director Steven Spielberg unveiled the Princess Leia theme song with the statement that "everyone deserves to have their own theme song."

It struck me: oh my gosh, this is TRUE! As silly as it might sound, think about it… what if we were to believe that we were actually (wait for it) **worthy of having our own theme song?** Talk about a seal of approval. An elevated status. An "epic booyah!"

So, in the spirit of all the things epic you have yet to bestow upon this little galaxy, let's learn to use music to your advantage.

Here's one way to get started.

- **STEP 1: FIND <u>YOUR</u> THEME SONG – What will it be?**
- **STEP 2: Get in the habit of playing your theme song at least once every morning to "prime" you for your day.**
- **STEP 3: As you listen to YOUR theme song, practice repeating your most empowered "I Am" statements to yourself and allow the energizing state to build.**
- **STEP 4: Listen to your theme song prior to any important meeting or conversation while reminding yourself of what YOU bring to that table.**
- **STEP 5: Find a "day is complete/ mission accomplished" song for yourself. Play this on your commute home and/or at the end of your day. This will quickly program your mind to understand that it can decompress and savor a well-done job.**
- **BONUS: It may be super powerful to pick another song specifically for an important occasion or a critical day. Use music as the booster that it has the potential to be. Use it to celebrate. Use it to calm down. Most importantly, use it deliberately!**

So, can this focus on music really make a difference? Shouldn't we be focusing on "more important stuff?" My response would be, "Can we really focus on the more powerful stuff when we are being influenced by stuff that we don't even realize?"

Here's what I mean: When I was in my mid-20s, I realized that I was feeling anxious and depressed quite frequently. It was a restless feeling that bordered on panic. As I explored a bit more deeply, I realized that I had gotten into the habit of listening to artists who (although I adored them) were actually **reflecting** my feelings of angst – which meant that they were inadvertently amplifying those feelings.

I explored whether it would make any difference to change that up – to deliberately choose music that captured how I **would like to feel versus how I was currently feeling.** It was shocking. Perhaps this is why we can go into a movie or concert feeling stressed by the world and emerge feeling ready to dance in the aisles. Music can be THAT influential.

After that "experiment," I made what felt like a tough choice at the time. Rather than selecting music that commiserated with my pain, I began deliberately choosing things to listen to that could elevate me *beyond my pain.*

So today, add another layer to your quest for "epic." Remember that we communicate in frequency (vibration), not solely with our words. Claim your sovereignty over what triggers the emotions within your mind by deliberately exploring the impact of the "**language**" of music.

What *songs* can provide the "secret sauce" for the magic you will create today? What is the theme song that will make you feel bigger, bolder, and ready to step into the world with your unique brand of "Epic You-ness" – that irreplaceable brilliance that is so ready for all the world to see?

Find it and rock the world with the resonance of your Superpowers!

TODAY'S ACTION STEPS:

- *Pick out YOUR theme song! What will it be? Download it so that it's ready and waiting for your Epicness!   (+1 Gold Star)*
- *Today, play your theme song before significant moments like meetings, phone calls, zip line adventures... wink! Maybe even strike a Superhero pose!! (+2 Gold Stars)*
- *Bonus points if you also pick out a Victory Song!! Now, how epic is that???. (+2 Gold Stars) Booyah!*

TOTAL POSSIBLE STARS FROM TODAY: 5 STARS

Day 55 – LANGUAGE: Influences and Impact

Flashback Moment! Let's go back to Day 26, when we talked about the five people you surround yourself with. Well, guess what, Epic Ninjas? The topic is actually even deeper. What we're really talking about is IMPACT. It's the critical question: What and who are you allowing to impact you?

Yes, we talked about the people you physically choose to surround yourself with, but what about all the "noise" you inadvertently allow in? The words, the language, the endless chatter that overwhelms your mind into a state of dullness, stress, and overwhelm...?

These days, most of us inadvertently face a barrage of impactful influencers. Their words, perspectives, ideas, and opinions blare out from our phones, our technology, our radios, and our TVs. Like it or not, when we hear it frequently enough, it becomes (yes) programming – and programming that slips sneakily into our inner game.

It impacts how we view others, how we view ourselves, whether we trust, whether we doubt, whether we have hope, and whether we despair... it impacts so much of how we experience life that it is absolute foolishness not to step in and deliberately choose the access that we will give to these influences.

Here's a fun challenge for you:

If you were to create a pie chart reflecting what you hear/ listen to during your day, what would it look like? How much of the chart would be podcasts, social media, radio, TV, negotiations, business interactions, energizing conversations, depleting conversations, your mental chatter, etc.? Now, if you were to color in the parts of the pie based on whether they trigger a "feel good" inner frequency or a "debilitating" inner frequency, what would that tell you?

Nowadays, in order to be substantially impacted by someone's perspective or opinion, that doesn't necessarily mean you must be physically in the presence of these people. You don't even have to know or interact with these people personally. You just have to agree to "let them drive a few miles from the back seat."

So yes, the revised statement that accurately reflects our lives today would be that you become an average of "the five influences you *allow* to have the most impact on you." Yes, even if one of those influences is what you view on your phone.

So, the moment of truth: Who ARE you allowing to have the most influence on YOU? What influences how you see the world … how you see YOURSELF? Is it someone in your family, your social circle, or some of the voices on TikTok, Instagram, Facebook, Linkedin, or the general media dishing up content that makes you react?

With technology so dominant these days, the fact that you become the average of your five greatest influences (or influencers) can be **EPIC** – or it can be **catastrophic**. **It totally depends on who/what you give your attention (focus) to.** And, of course, what version of reality does this input motivate you to buy into?

Our minds crave clarity and direction. In other words, **GUIDANCE**. *If WE don't provide that, our minds look elsewhere. Yes, even when someone else's "certainty" leads us in a direction that turns out to be a destructive one.*

When we live in a world where "fear sells," where the way to "stand out" for many influencers is through "shock and awe," is it any wonder that we can feel so exposed and fragile? When we hand over our autonomous thinking to someone else, is it a surprise to discover that we no longer know who we are – much less what it is we want to evolve into?

Today, your mission is to take back ownership of your *most precious resource – your mind, your identity.* No more squatters in this glorious castle. No more hitchhikers in the back seat. No more bad code. No more hackers holding your potential genius for ransom. No more waiting for the outer world to change and to award you the jackpot.

Beginning today, YOU get to deliberately **choose the influences** that spend time priming your brain. Doing this is so simple:

- **Use today to find five podcasts and five influencers who will elevate and energize you!**
- **Feeling stuck? Find a coach or a mentor to help you break through your "boulders" and pull back the curtain on those blind spots. Confused about the difference**

between a mentor and a coach? No problem! On the coaching page of my website, www.gritmindsetacademy.com/coaching, you'll find a quick download that explains the differences between the various styles of mentoring and coaching.
- **Set a reminder on your phone once, twice, or three times a day to listen to a motivational talk on YouTube. Even if it's a 1 minute short! Shameless promo: yes, I do have a Youtube channel at https://bit.ly/GRITTube**
- **Instead of watching reality TV or "killing time" (scary concept), find great documentaries that remind you of the success and possibilities that surround you each and every day.**
- **Find a community like our Society of Epic Chicks or an event like our LIVE YOUR DESTINY Breakthrough Experience where you can meet other "joy-rriors" and positively focused people like yourself. Curious? Check out www.aboutepicchicks.com**

Today's EPIC OPPORTUNITY is to reclaim your sovereignty over **the Five Influences** on your mind. As you deliberately select who to give access to your mind, get in the habit of asking yourself:

- Do they align with your future vision of yourself?
- Do they energize and inspire you?
- Do they nurture you?
- Help you grow?
- Champion you?

Remember, you are the **Master of your masterpiece,** so making sure that you are choosing your influences *deliberately* will transform a life filled with potholes into one that feels **EPIC!**

TODAY'S ACTION STEPS:

- *Create a quick pie chart of what you listen to and hear during a typical day (see above). (+2 Gold Stars)*
- *Now rank each pie chart slice by giving it a color based on whether it triggers a "feel good" inner frequency or a "debilitating" inner frequency. (+1 Gold Star)*
- *Choose your five deliberate influences based on the bullet list above! (+2 Gold Stars)*
- *Program some positive listening reminders into your day/week. (+1 Gold Star)*
- *Bonus points if you write down and/or post the five criteria for positive influences listed above somewhere in your home or office. Be sure to post them in a visible location. (+2 Gold Stars) Booyah!*

TOTAL POSSIBLE STARS FROM TODAY: 8 STARS

Day 56 – LANGUAGE: The "But" Hole

Yes: the "But" hole.

This is a nasty one – and I'm not talking about the crazy person during your morning commute who just cut you off in traffic. I'm talking about the *one word* that often, almost single-handedly, can keep you STUCK! Yes, that darling little word "**but.**"

Let's be honest: how many times during the day do you say something like:

> "I would love to work out more, *but* I just don't have time."

> "I know I'd make a great manager, *but* they'd never consider me."

> "I really want to do something I love, *but* I just don't see how I'd make money."

These statements are like placing an order at your favorite restaurant and changing it five times after ordering. You keep going back and forth (and back and forth and back and forth…) between items – as you can imagine, your server absolutely LOVES this! However, not only does this behavior turn you into the talk of the wait staff for the evening, but it also **takes forever for your meal to arrive finally.**

Why? **Because you keep changing your mind about what you want to *be on your plate*….** Do I want to focus on consuming the "presence of fried chicken" or the "lack of the presence of fried chicken– i.e., the salmon"? You must stay clearly focused on what you want or go hungry. And the word "but" does not lead to clarity. It leads to confusion, and a confused mind does not take action.

Here's what I mean. Let's go back to Example #1:

> *"I would love to work out more, but I just don't have time."*

Look at the first part of this sentence:

> *"I would love to work out more…"*

Pretty good, right? This part of the sentence sets you up to focus on the feeling of what you want. It gets you to the energetic **frequency** of what you want. These words align with the emotions and feelings you want the experience to create. This frequency invites you to imagine how proud you will feel of yourself as you exercise more consistently, how satisfying it will feel to start noticing the difference in the way that you look and feel, how great it will feel when others start commenting on your new energy level and overall healthy demeanor, etc.

HOWEVER, the moment that you say the word "but," all of that potential momentum **comes** *screeching to a halt.* You basically just told your mind, "Don't go there. That's not possible…" So, guess what programming code you just imprinted onto your subconscious? Yep, the **lack**. The dominant focus is:

> "I just don't have time."

Remember- what we focus on expands.

Do you really want to create more inability to prioritize time to do what you want or to make money doing something you enjoy? Do you want to teach your mind to believe these things are *unrealistic*?

This downward spiral of Lack is what we call "the BUT hole." Because think about it: that one little word *rarely* points to a focus where things you desire are born.

So how do we change that?

Let's go back to our three Defining Questions, which we'll explore in more depth on Day 62:

- What can I control?
- What can my mind believe?
- What am I assuming that is not necessarily true?

In this case, you CAN learn to control the words that you choose. So… (no pressure) *from this moment forward*, you will **start catching yourself when you use the word "but."** Instead of the word "but," **substitute the word "so."**

What can your mind believe, and what have you been assuming that is not necessarily so? Clearly, you have assumed that what follows after the "but" is the only version of the truth. Start asking yourself if that's accurate. When you choose to use the word "so," what can become the "new truth?" A truth that your mind can also believe?

How about this:

> "I would love to work out more, *so I'm going to get creative and figure out a way to make that happen. My husband wants to work out more. Maybe we can even work out together?"*

> "I know that I'd make a great manager, *so I'm going to see if I can get some coaching on how to get better at my interview and communication skills. If I continue improving, I feel confident I can nail the next opening ."*

> "I really want to do something that I love, *so I will invest in finding out how other people do it. There must be coaches and mentors who can help me. I'm willing to do what it*

takes if it means being happier and more fulfilled and less exhausted at the end of the day."

Can you see how this sets your focus on a "solution-oriented" path? Rather than focusing on the boulders in your way, the word "so" draws your focus to what lies beyond the boulder. Make sense?

So your mission today is to stay far away from the "But Hole" and set yourself up for EPIC success by deliberately choosing to use the word "so"!

TODAY'S ACTION STEPS:

- *Listen to your words today and make a note of every time you either speak or think of the word "but." (+2 Gold Stars)*
- *When you notice yourself using "but," see how you can shift it to "so." make a note of how that new sentence feels in your emotional frequency. Can you feel the difference in inner game frequency?! (+2 Gold Stars)*
- *Bonus points if you continue to make a note of your "buts" so that you can master your ability to replace the majority of them with the word "so"! (+2 Gold Stars) Booyah!*

TOTAL POSSIBLE STARS FROM TODAY: 6 STARS

Day 57 – LANGUAGE: May the Force Be With You

Remember the iconic scene from The Empire Strikes Back when Yoda imparts wisdom to Luke Skywalker, saying, "Do or do not. There is no try?"

It was a powerful scene with a profound message. Yet, how often do we shield ourselves from potential failure by saying, "I'm going to try to _____?" As we've explored the "epic" journey, we've discovered it's all about unwavering commitment. It's about clarity, focus, and unapologetically going for it. When we consistently show up as the most epic version of ourselves, we become a *force* to be reckoned with!

Today, we will focus on another word you might be using without realizing that it steals your power and saps your momentum. Yes, the word "try." Purging the word "try" from your vocabulary helps you not only set up the expectation for success but also begins to build both your self-trust and confidence.

The word "try" often leaves an escape hatch for "not doing." It gives us permission to renegotiate our commitment based on fleeting emotions. This emotional sway can lead to a lack of trust in our ability to follow through. And when trust wavers, confidence takes a hit.

This doesn't just apply to our self-talk but also extends to our conversations with others.

For instance, imagine you're managing a team and need a 20% increase in revenue. Compare these two statements:

- *We need to try to bring in 20% more revenue by the end of the month, so I need each of you to make those calls and set up those sales conversations. Come on, people. Let's try and get those numbers up!*

Versus:

- *Here's where we are in revenue right now. This is an exceptional team, and I believe that each and every one of you in this room can definitely generate an additional 20% – maybe even more – by the end of the month. So let's see what you can do. Go set up those sales conversations and make those calls. We'll regroup in a couple of weeks, and I do not doubt that we'll see some pretty exciting numbers the next time we meet.*

Which of the two generates the expectation of probable success and, therefore, the most forward momentum?

Even when delivering constructive criticism, the word "try" can inadvertently set up your listener with an expectation of missing their mark. Have a look at these two. Which do you think would set up Jennifer for the most success?

- *Jennifer, I need you to try to be more strategic with your decisions. I can't promote you until I see that you can manage your team more effectively and get better results.*

Versus:
- *Jennifer, let's talk about what can be possible for you in the future. I believe that you have the potential to go far in this company. The next step toward seeing you achieve that is for you to now learn how to focus even more strategically as you guide your team. That will boost your team's results, and as you start consistently inspiring those results, you'll demonstrate that you're ready for that next level of leadership.*

Or even in times when you need to correct a team member's performance, deliberate choice of language can be pivotal:

- *Scott, we need to talk about your performance. It seems to be slipping in the past few months, and some of your team members have mentioned that you've missed some important goals and deadlines. We don't want to have to let you go but to avoid that, we will need to see a sincere effort on your part in the coming weeks to **try** to improve your performance and results.*

Versus:
- Scott, let's talk about your recent performance. You've been with our company for several years, and there's no question that we want to see you be successful. I'll be candid: your numbers are not where they should be, and I want to help you turn that around. Let's go over what you feel is working and what's not working so that you **can commit to** making some changes that will get rid of some of the obstacles that may be at play here. We both want to see you succeed, so if there are other factors I should know about, please be candid so we can work together on setting up a strategy to improve things. Otherwise, let's set up some targets and time frames when we can take another look and ensure that you're seeing the progress that I believe you're capable of. Can I count on you to **commit to** investing in some of these changes?

[Notice there are also no "buts" in this statement.]

To be fair, there will be times when you (or the person you are communicating with) need a jolt. In those cases, your use of words such as "but" or "try" should be intentional and serve a very deliberate purpose:

- *I will not tolerate that type of behavior, so if you continue to use that type of language with me, I will have no other option **but** to leave.*
- *I'm not so much concerned with whether you succeed or not. I just want to see that you are at least **trying**.*
- *I have looked at the possibilities from lots of different angles. I know that it's a risk, but it's something that I'm willing to go ahead and **try**.*

Notice that in these last two sentences, the word "try" is used synonymously with the concept of "starting." The momentum around the word "try" in that context is one where it focuses forward. It focuses on starting versus stopping or slowing. Contrast that to the momentum around the comment "I will try," and you'll see that the frequencies feel different. The underlying energy under that statement feels like trying to drive your car with the parking brake on.

When the momentum feels like it is starting, it's more energizing. When you say, "I will try," it feels like you already expect some level of likely defeat. There are shades of impossibility built into that phrase. Can you feel that?

To sum it all up, your mission today is to keep your radar tuned to the words "but" and "try." Note the impact of specific words (and the invisible stories that you associate with these words) on your energy and expectations.

When you use the word "try" with either yourself or others, make sure that you are doing it deliberately and that you find supporting language that communicates without a doubt that you expect to ultimately see success.

Begin to view words and phrases from the CEO's or Sovereign's perspective of the epic resource we call your mind. Get more deliberate and strategic with your choice of words. What language will help the EPIC YOU to flourish and flow?

Your mission is to continue building your language into a tool that sets you (and others) up for EPIC success. Make more empowering language choices. Focus on becoming a more deliberate communicator and watch what happens!

TODAY'S ACTION STEPS:

- *Go out into your Universe with your lightsaber poised to obliterate the world of "try"! How many "tries" can you identify? How many can you rephrase? (+2 Gold Stars)*
- *At the end of the day, check in to see how well you did. When did you most often catch yourself using the word "try"? Was it a specific topic? How might you shift that going forward? (+1 Gold Stars)*
- *Bonus points if you can identify a false assumption that your use of the word "try" is pointing to. How can you improve upon that assumption? What can you commit to start doing? (+2 Gold Stars) Booyah!*

TOTAL POSSIBLE STARS FROM TODAY: 5 STARS

Day 58 – LANGUAGE: The Intention Exercise

Until you've experienced the power of setting intentions, the concept can seem a bit superfluous and, for some, even like a woo-woo waste of time.

Yet, if you are willing to **commit** to getting into the habit of building your "intention-setting muscle," you will start seeing some remarkable coincidences [!], which then ultimately lead to a string of results that can only be traced back to this new habit.

Here's the secret, though:

Remember that our minds must be able to believe that something is possible. If you've never experienced the power of setting intentions, your mind may still find it hard to believe that setting intentions will impact an outcome. Therefore, if you set an intention that is too specific at first, your mind will inadvertently focus on the gap between where you are and what you are setting as an intention. Even though your words express the intention, what will you get more of if your mind is focused on the gap?

Evidence of the gap! Then (boom) you believe you have proof that setting an intention is just a bogus action!

Instead, start by warming up that muscle with a more general intention such as one of these:

- I intend to see a great outcome to this – *whatever is truly the highest and best...*
- I intend for anything that can go well *to go even better...*
- This conversation is going to go well, *and we are all going to be happy with the outcome...*
- This process *is going to flow smoothly for me and I'm going to like the outcome...*
- I intend to wake up *refreshed and energized and ready for a day that will surprise and delight me...*

Today, your mission is to begin playing with the habit of setting more deliberate intentions throughout your day and as you crawl into bed. Again, think from the perspective of the Sovereign or CEO of your BE-ing. Play with scenarios that are both big and small.

Waking up in the morning? Set an intention that you will have a *remarkable day, whatever that ends up looking like today.* Heading to the grocery store? Set an intention that *everything will flow perfectly so that I have an easy trip right from the moment I pull into the parking lot.* Crawling into bed? Set the intention that *things are always working out for me, and tomorrow will be yet another example of epic things showing up for me.*

If you're new to setting intentions, today is your day to start this new habit. If you've been setting intentions for a while, use today to encourage yourself to go even bigger. How can you set intentions that help you expand and show up as that even more EPIC expression of the WHO you are destined to BE?

Oh, by the way, speaking of words, note that I refer to this as a **habit, not a "one-off."** Hint… "just saying"…. Are you willing to commit to building up YOUR power of Intention? The benefits **will** surprise you!

TODAY'S ACTION STEPS:

- *Create a morning intention to set the tone for your day. (+1 Gold Star)*
- *Create an intention to be available in situations that start feeling stressful. Memorize that intention declaration. (+2 Gold Stars)*
- *Bonus points if you repeat empowering intentions throughout your day and journal what you discovered. (+2 Gold Stars) Booyah!*

TOTAL POSSIBLE STARS FROM TODAY: 5 STARS

Day 59 –LANGUAGE: The Writing is On the Wall

Have you ever written a grocery list or a "to-do" list?

Why do we do that? Because we want those items to stay top of mind. We want to make it easier to remind our minds what to focus on – and to ensure that we **take action**. Writing things down reinforces our intention and gives us a certain amount of repetition – a combination that I have found sets us up for success.

Writing things down also can really be an asset for those of us who tend to be visual learners. Words and phrases pointing to our next target can be posted in visible locations for our mind (including our subconscious) to constantly acknowledge and see.

Reinforce and repeat.
Reinforce and repeat.
Reinforce and repeat.
Reinforce and repeat.
Reinforce and repeat.
Reinforce and repeat.

Today, we will add visual cues and reminders to our arsenal of EPIC.

Your mission is to START by **writing down seven of your biggest intentions for the week**. Write three on a piece of paper (the bigger, the better, and feel free to embellish, doodle, and decorate). Post each of these in prominent locations around your house. If you feel inspired, write each of those three intentions down multiple times and post them in even more locations around your house.

For the other four intentions, you'll **use your phone reminders.** Ask Siri or Alexa to remind you weekly of these things as follows**:**

First additional intention – Reminder for 9:30 a.m. on Mondays and 3:06 p.m. on Thursdays.
Second intention – Reminders for Tuesday at 11:32 a.m., 2:22 p.m., and 6:03 p.m.
Third intention – Reminders for Monday at 4:18 p.m. and Wednesday at 10:52 a.m.
Fourth intention – Reminders for Wednesday at 3:36 p.m., Friday at 8:08 a.m. and 5:23 p.m.

Here's the **epic part:**

- **Commit to taking at least ONE relevant action each day that supports at least one of your intentions.**
- **Commit to making this action *non-negotiable*. You will not go to sleep unless that one action (even if it's a small action) has been taken.**

The fringe benefit here (aside from moving you closer to those powerful intentions) is that you are also building your trust in yourself and, therefore, your confidence. BOOYAH!

So start building that writing habit and get creative by figuring out bolstering ways to use apps and technology to support you!

TODAY'S ACTION STEPS:

- *Create your written intentions per our juicy instructions above. Get creative. Doodle. Add stickers, bling, photos – whatever inspires you. Remember, you are not just going through the motions. You are creating "energy + motion" (EMOTION). (+2 Gold Stars)*
- *Create your phone reminders for your intentions. Plan out the language so that it helps you focus on the presence of what you desire from this intention! (+1 Gold Star)*
- *Bonus points if you start taking consistent action on these intentions! Look at them! Savor them until you feel the EMOTION percolating! (+2 Gold Stars) Booyah!*

TOTAL POSSIBLE STARS FROM TODAY: 5 STARS

Day 60 –LANGUAGE: The Words of Acknowledgement Game

When's the last time that you surprised someone with a card of appreciation "just because"? Have you shot a quick text or email to a co-worker to thank them for their help?

My son and oldest daughter are both married and have kids. My son, wife, daughter, and husband are all so good with their kids. Today, I took 30 seconds to text each of them and share how wonderful it is to see them as parents. And you know what? It was a definite dopamine hit **for me,** as it was for them. By their responses, clearly, my random text meant so much to them.

The video game industry has shown us how powerfully dopamine can impact us, but what if this "Words of Acknowledgment Game" can have an even deeper impact?

Meet what I fondly call your "Ras-matazz" – the field of positive psychology calls it your Reticular Activating System or RAS.

This is the part of your mind that serves the function of what is valuable input for you – and what to filter out. It lords over your focus and shines the spotlight on things that align with it.

In action, it can look like this: you *clearly* identify wanting to buy a new car. You're considering a red car. Suddenly, you not only see red cars on your drive to work, but you also start noticing the red cars in the movie you're watching. You see an article about red cars. And just like that, the world is now overrun with red cars, even though you don't remember noticing any of them just days earlier.

This can also work against you if you're not careful. Let's say you're starting your day by watering the plant next to your computer. The phone rings. You answer it without noticing that the plant has started leaking water onto the table under your laptop. Suddenly, you see water all over your table, and you rescue your computer, hopefully, before it is damaged. You tell the person on the phone that "it's going to be one of those days."

As you hang up the phone, you notice that now you're running late for a meeting. You scroll through your emails, trying to find the address, but now the email seems to have disappeared. When you find it, you bolt toward the door, tripping over the cat and dropping your keys. As you get to the car, you realize that you left your phone on the table when you reached down to grab the keys that fell when you tripped over your cat.

In other words, your ever-loyal "Ras-matazz" has helped prove what a genius you are because clearly, you wanted to focus on evidence that confirmed that "it's going to be one of those days." And it sure is turning out that way.

So, how can this be valuable regarding language – and specifically to the underlying magnetic frequency that your language creates? (**Remember that the frequency communicates the programming code.**)

When you commit to playing the "Words of Acknowledgment Game," you subtly instruct your mind (your RAS) to look for things **that please you.**

Then, guess what happens?

The more you look for things that please you and the more great things you find to complement and acknowledge, the more your RAS gets the message that **you want to see/experience more things that make you feel good.**

So today, it's time to get this "Ras-matazz" on your team. How many ways can you find to surprise and delight others with your words of acknowledgment – and reap your benefit to boot?

Pick up some note cards or even post-its – and start playing!! BOOYAH!

TODAY'S ACTION STEPS:

- *Reach out with a quick verbal hug and/or words of acknowledgment to 3-5 people. Savor the pleasure of giving someone a boost! (+2 Gold Stars)*
- *Feed your RAZ by finding five things to compliment today. Train your mind that the things that please you make you come most alive! (+2 Gold Stars)*
- *Bonus points if you commit to weaning yourself away from statements like "It's going to be one of those days." What do you think the RAZ puts on its radar when you say that? More proof of the "bad day." (+1 Gold Stars) Booyah!*

TOTAL POSSIBLE STARS FROM TODAY: 5 STARS

Day 61 – LANGUAGE: Unveiling Your Blind Spots- Illuminate the Path to Your Epic

Woo hoo! Day 61! By now, you are seeing why the old approach of relying on the external world to provide happiness is a wild goose chase. Surrendering the hamster wheel of your mind to autopilot threatens to turn you into emotional roadkill, steering you right into the path of your own worst enemy. (Wink… ok, bad pun!! But you get the point!)

In this journey towards your fullest potential, it's high time to roll up your sleeves and muster the courage to revamp the patterns ingrained over the decades. It demands identifying the cobwebbed corners where you've held yourself back. It's about yanking away the curtain to face head-on those limiting beliefs—those "baby elephant collars" we identified on Day 45.

How do we do that? Fortunately, an enlightening insight emerges as we dive a little deeper into the realm of language. Here's the scoop:

When I was first introduced to the intricacies of the inner game, the notion of "limiting beliefs" constantly baffled me. Seriously, how does one eliminate something lurking in the blind spot?

Yet, I have discovered that these "limiting beliefs" are symptoms of a larger issue that I call "blindspot thinking™" that leaves behind footprints! Just like the childhood game of "hot and cold," these verbal clues triggered my emotional barometer to kick in. When I strayed from focusing on the presence of what I wanted, the "getting colder" signal buzzed, bringing along less-than-warm-and-fuzzy feelings.

What caught my attention was that these warning bells always followed my "doom-focused phrases" hinting at struggles or setbacks:

- "It's going to be hard to…"
- "The problem is that…"
- "I've already tried that…"
- "I already know that…"
- "That won't work…"
- "I'm just someone who…"
- "That's just the way that I'm wired…"
- "There's no use in even trying…"

You see the pattern, right? My language was a breadcrumb trail. My skewed representation of "fact" was unintentionally drawing me into the realm of impossibility.

Sure, there are instances where due diligence reveals a "non-lit" light bulb. However, let's be real—often, we assume if one or two bulbs aren't shining, none will. That's another perfect example of where we succumb to blind spot thinking™ tucked within our "not necessarily true" assumptions.

So, your task for today is to catch your limiting beliefs red-handed. Tune in to phrases echoing those above and lock into your emotional frequency. Picture it as a personal hot-and-cold game. Ask yourself if your statements steer you toward empowering beliefs, exciting energy, and the scent of your target on the horizon.

Or are you venturing into cooler territory? Does the air bear the weight of impossibility, struggle, and despair?

Here's where the epic ninja magic gets serious: When the chill creeps in, recognize that your language can recalibrate your focus—this very focus that wields your power. Remember Day 50? We rebooted our expectations by simply shifting "my biggest challenge" into "my biggest commitment." By changing one word, success suddenly felt not only possible – but *imminent*.

Now it's your turn. How do you use your language to hit the reset button? How can new words blow through your blind spots? Take a leap and explore how you, too, might be able to rephrase the familiar questions that have been deflating you. Until now, that is – because we're here to rewrite the bad code that stands between you and maximum forward momentum.

Sometimes, shaking off the shackles of blind spot thinking is as simple as replacing "what if I can't" with "what if I CAN"?

Epic leaders, chicks, and gents learn that sticking around in your blind spot is optional. Today, you're behind the wheel, and it's your time to commit to being the explorer ready to venture into the arena of "what if I CAN???"

As you slide into that fancy vehicle and tap the gas pedal, perhaps now is the moment to set the GPS for your next destination: "WhatIfICanVille." Picture yourself cruising out of your driveway, windows down, basking in this remarkable expedition called Life while your theme song plays on the radio. When you halt at a red light (inevitable, right?), whip out your trusty phone and set a reminder that sporadically pops up with the words "What if I CAN???"... Oh, wait, the light just turned green! Off I go! Who else is game for this journey?... Just saying… wink!!

Feel the energy, catch those blind spots, and remember, the path to your Epic is paved with Power Phrases that will illuminate your way. Keep steering toward WhatIfICanVille—adventure awaits!

TODAY'S ACTION STEPS:

- *Based on the above phrases, are there one or two ideas or even changes you've wanted to pursue that have been stopped in their tracks by the "what if I can't" thoughts swirling in your head? Write those down. (+1 Gold Star)*
- *Now play with writing beneath those "WHAT IF I CAN"? If "failure" was not an option or (remember Sarah Blakely and Thomas Edison) if you knew that all failures would lead to something even more awesome, what might you start doing and exploring today? Write that down. (+2 Gold Stars)*
- *Bonus points if you can think of some other phrases that you have been using that sabotage you before you even get started. Write those down. (+2 Gold Stars)*
- *Extra Bonus: Remember that we've created a list of 10 phrases that we hear almost everyone use that sends them down the rabbit hole. If you haven't already, grab your free copy and some extra points in the process! bit.ly/EpicWords If you've already downloaded these, you are ROCKING THIS, so grab the extra points anyway!! (+2 Gold Stars) Booyah!*

TOTAL POSSIBLE STARS FROM TODAY: 7 STARS

Day 62 — LANGUAGE: Unveiling the 3 Defining Questions — Question #1

Ah, human curiosity! It's the driving force behind our ever-questioning minds, isn't it? Even as children, some of our first expressions of language are in the form of questions as we saturate those around us with a barrage of "why, why, why, why, why…?"

For the past 61 days, we've come to grasp the profound influence that our questions hold. The way we frame them, the words we choose, what they cause us to focus on, and what they make that focus mean—they all wield the power to shape our responses.

In moments when we're feeling stuck, it's often because we're not posing the right questions or perhaps not phrasing them effectively. But that's where our journey takes a leap today.

Yesterday, we began understanding how shifting from "what if I can't" to "what if I can" helps reshape our outlook. Today, let's dive even deeper. Let's tap into an even greater potential: the art of learning to craft superior questions.

One of the most pivotal revelations during these 100 days is recognizing that despite what you might previously have believed, **you do have significant influence – if you know how to access and implement it.** Realize you do possess the capability to steer the ship that's perhaps felt adrift. As you integrate this fresh approach, change will ripple through.

The shift will unfold not just within you but also in the world surrounding you. The more you embrace your role as the master of your mind's domain, the swifter these changes will materialize.

We might not command every facet outwardly, but never forget your inner game is yours to rule! So, let's keep fortifying those mental muscles and display unwavering dedication and ownership.

Yes, my dear, bid adieu to old, aimless habits. Embrace the game-changer attitude: by adopting behaviors that seat you as Sovereign, you elevate yourself to the CEO of your existence. So why settle for limited when limitless is within reach?

Envision yourself back at the wheel, steering your emotions and thoughts strategically, embodying a true leader. Even professionally or in the context of your family, to lead others authentically—even your offspring—you must first master self-leadership.

Now, we'll notch it up by giving you access to 3 questions that will change how you interact with and experience the world when you embrace them. In my experience, these are the three questions to hold close to when making an important decision or facing unpredictability and crisis.

I call this the realm of the 3 Defining Questions—a "triad of inquiries" that guided me during Schuyler's time in the stormy waters of the ICU. These three questions have elevated hundreds of my professional clients to remarkable heights. Today, let's delve into the first of the three questions, knowing that more juicy revelations await.

Question 1: "What can I control?"

Ah, the hurdle that often trips us up! Fess up; how often have you invited stress into your life as you "strained to restrain" the unmanageable? What this first question inspires us to do instead is to perhaps pivot a bit by focusing on what lies within our grasp.

Are you feeling stuck in some aspect of your life right now? Pause and ponder—might you be trying to control something that is not your business? Are you trying to fix something from the past when your talents are better applied to creating something bold and beautiful for the future?

Really think about it: *so much remains under your influence that has been hiding in plain sight!* Now's the opportunity to shift your focus to the sphere you DO hold sway over and discover the tremendous power that comes with this type of course correction. When I received that life-altering call about my daughter's accident, I couldn't rewrite the past or dictate her condition, but I could command my thoughts and commit to playing my inner game to win!

So, what's within your grasp right now? Pledge to transform intention into action, fueled by the growing momentum within your inner game! Remember, fellow adventurers of the EPIC, you're the architect of your fate—let your inner game chart the course to your leading edge!

Tomorrow, we'll dive into the second of the 3 Defining Questions, poised and ready to reshape your journey toward EPIC grandeur. Until then, rock on and keep shining bright!

Let's go out there, dazzle the world with our "ninja joy-rrior" questions and rev up this day with a dose of unyielding positivity! Who's ready to be ready? There's a glorious life out there waiting to be explored. You can't control the road's potholes, but you can shift the gears to navigate beyond them!

TODAY'S ACTION STEPS:

- *Today's another Awareness Day! Commit to responding, not reacting, to the things happening in the world around you. Focus on controlling what you CAN control. (+3 Gold Stars)*
- *Grab a sheet of paper. We'll add two more questions to it before we're done. Today, write on that paper: The 3 Defining Questions, #1 What can I control? (+1 Gold Star)*
- *Bonus points if you check in at the end of the day and journal your discoveries. Were you trying to "fix" things or "argue" things beyond your control? Or were you able to remember to take a breath and respond based on what you CAN control (even if it's only your thoughts that you can control)? (+3 Gold Stars) Booyah!*

TOTAL POSSIBLE STARS FROM TODAY: 7 STARS

Day 63 – LANGUAGE: The 3 Defining Questions – Question #2

In the vast Universe of life, some would say that the greatest distance is the 12 inches between your brain and your heart. How often have you sought solutions to problems, heard something that "made sense intellectually," but struggled to put it into action? Your heart and emotions couldn't fully internalize it to bring about real change, right?

Let's talk about the classic saying, "Fake it until you make it." Personally, I find that to be a slippery slope...

Years ago, as a single mom juggling the unbudgeted expenses of raising three kids, affirmations intrigued me. I was encouraged to repeat, "I am a money magnet. I am a money magnet." I understood the concept, but my skeptical mind kept whispering, "Money magnet... really? Have you looked at your bank account recently…?"

Instead of aligning my focus with the abundance and financial flow I desired, my mind's disbelief caused these affirmations to accentuate the gap between where I was and where I wanted to be. Remember: what you focus on expands. The more I practiced hopeful affirmations while living my mind's reality of "clearly not having enough," the more I focused on the lack rather than the presence of abundance. Why? Because the thoughts that my mind was thinking prevented me from being able to make that giant leap.

If I truly was going to experience abundance and see financial relief, my mind needed to buy into the possibility that such prosperity could occur – that success was inevitable. When I was deluged in bills, my mind just couldn't believe that it was possibility.

Don't get me wrong; affirmations can work wonders when your mind truly believes in their potential. But for most of us, it's not an instant switch from doubt to complete belief. So, instead of the "fake it until you make it" or the "affirmation approach," I discovered a powerful alternative: asking the right question.

This brings us to

Question 2: "What CAN my mind believe?"

When I was on that plane, headed to be with my daughter as she fought for her life, I knew I had to find a way for my mind to believe in the possibility of a miracle or a positive outcome. At first, it seemed nearly impossible, but I started asking myself some new questions. This is so important that I'll say it again: *I started asking myself some **new** questions* – because we typically keep asking the same questions repeatedly, hoping for a different answer.

Asking new questions or the same question in a new way is critical. So, on that plane, I began searching for a question whose answer would lead me to a place where my mind *could* believe that a miracle for my daughter might be possible.

So I asked myself, "Had anyone ever achieved what everyone said was impossible? The answer was a resounding yes! I was literally flying in a plane, once thought impossible."

Then I pondered if anyone, at any point, had experienced a miracle. Again, the answer was undeniable—miracles have happened throughout history, even inspiring Hollywood's real-life-based movies.

With these questions and answers, I inched my way from despair to hope and, eventually, to a sense of knowing, a belief that things would be "fine," whatever that new "fine" might be. And, oddly enough, Life began to align with my vision. Miracles happened, and my daughter survived the unsurvivable.

No, I'm not saying my mind alone saved my daughter, but tapping into the power of believing made a profound difference. It felt like a different kind of magic—some might call it Faith – a certain energy/ frequency that unleashed possibilities beyond what seemed imaginable.

So, going forward, as you strive for transformation, do the work to help your mind believe that your dreams aren't just possible—they're inevitable. Today, take a moment to ask yourself: What can YOUR mind believe right now?

Your epic journey is filled with potential, and the power of your mind is the key to unlocking the extraordinary EPIC YOU that is waiting patiently to be unleashed!

TODAY'S ACTION STEPS:

- *What can your mind believe? As you encounter moments during your day when your mind tells you that you can't, are there some better questions that you can ask so that your mind shifts to believing that you can? (+3 Gold Stars)*
- *Grab your sheet of paper from yesterday. We'll add one more question to it tomorrow. Today, write on that paper: #2 What can my mind believe? (+1 Gold Star)*
- *Bonus points if you check in at the end of the day and journal your discoveries. Were you asking some better questions? This is a skill, so practice because the better your questions, the better your results! (+3 Gold Stars) Booyah!*

TOTAL POSSIBLE STARS FROM TODAY: 7 STARS

Day 64 — LANGUAGE: Completing the 3 Defining Questions – Question #3

Now for perhaps the most powerful question: Question 3!

Can you guess what that question might be? Let's start with a few phrases that perhaps you have heard once or twice:

"It is what it is."

"That's just the way things are."

"I'm just being realistic."

These types of phrases can be the chains that keep us hopelessly attached to the hamster wheel. They subtly discourage us from questioning; however, questioning is good. You just have to know which questions propel you and which will paralyze you. The quality of our lives *directly corresponds* to the quality of the questions we ask. So, if we're staying stuck on questions that deflate us, we're allowing our own worst enemy to win.

So, with an emphatic drum roll, let's unveil the one question that is the key to freeing yourself from the repercussions of sloppy thinking. Meet Question #3 of the 3 Defining Questions:

Question 3: "What am I assuming that is not necessarily true?"

Let's rewind to my experience on the plane when Schuy's life hung in the balance. Remember when I said that medical history and precedent had dictated that survival was virtually impossible if you could see a patient's brain following an injury? Logically, Schuyler's wounds were "realistically" unsurvivable.

If there was ever a moment to believe in an inevitable tragedy, it was then. There seemed to be zero reason for hope. However, I honed in on that critical question: "What might I be assuming that is not necessarily true?"

Considering my other thoughts—acknowledging that impossible things do happen and miracles occur often enough—I realized that I was assuming the worst simply because medical precedent dictated so. But had other miraculous cases faced any less dismal precedents? Absolutely not! That's what made them so miraculous. So, if one miracle could occur, why not this miracle? And isn't there "always a first time?"

With my thoughts framed that way, my mind *could* believe that a miracle was possible. I did not need to automatically *assume* that our story would follow the path of typical medical precedent.

Acting on those new beliefs, I took my thoughts one step further. The Law of Att'r'action's training and the principles of the inner game all indicated that to access the force behind these Truths, I must continue to find thoughts that would get me to a place that felt like a sense of "knowing." Almost like that "déjà vu" feeling. To do that, I asked myself how I would act and feel if I *knew* a miracle *would* happen. How would that "knowing" impact my being and actions?

That question became my turbo-charge, fueling a potent inner game – because when we act as if what we want *has already occurred or that it's a "done deal," life often seems to conform to that vision.*

If you feel that this sounds a bit airy, fairy, I would tell you this: sometimes we have to be open to a bit of the "woo woo" to get to the "woo hoo." Courage is often what you're willing **to do** in your *inner game,* not simply how you act in your *outer game.*

Take a moment to soak this in because I know this can feel like a stretch. It certainly did for me, but boy, am I glad I dared to take that leap. **I will also mention that the doctors who began calling us the "miracle family" still believe this leap made the difference.** Apparently, it's not uncommon for the patients who show up with the strongest inner game to give themselves a tangible edge. Unfortunately, a strong inner game is not easy to learn from scratch when you're in the middle of a crisis. Perhaps this is why Jackson Memorial invited me to be their keynote speaker on the topic of the inner game just a few years later.

So…as you step into the world today, I encourage you to take a close look and question the assumptions you hold as TRUTH. Are they limiting, keeping you small, or making you feel insignificant? What if those assumptions are *false*? If you are feeling stuck in a rut, afraid to make changes that you know you need to make, it's entirely possible—even probable– that some of your "truths" are the things that have been holding you back.

Today, seize the opportunity to claim *your* miracle. Find your "I'm Possible." By asking better questions by rooting out your assumptions, you'll realize that your "limits" are merely the beginning of bold new horizons!

Time to polish up your mastery of the 3 Defining Questions! Look out, Epic Future! Here you come!! Booyah!

TODAY'S ACTION STEPS:

- *Does my story bring one of your stories to mind? Where have you been assuming things about yourself, your career, and your life that simply may not be true? Think about it and write it down. (+2 Gold Stars)*
- *Grab your sheet of paper from yesterday. This will be our final question on this paper. Today, write on that paper: #3 What have I been assuming that is not necessarily true? Now hang it somewhere in your home or office where you'll see it easily. And yes, feel free to decorate it! Make it yours!! (+1 Gold Star)*
- *Bonus points if you start making some changes based on your realization that some of your beliefs have just been assumptions – and these assumptions are not the only version of Truth! (+2 Gold Stars) Booyah!*
- *EXTRA BONUS: Share your biggest AHA so far by emailing us at team@gritmindsetacademy.com . Who knows? There might be a special reward in it for you… just saying!!! (+3 Gold Stars) Booyah!*

TOTAL POSSIBLE STARS FROM TODAY: 8 STARS

Day 65 – LANGUAGE: The Epic WHO

Yesterday, we busted through even more myths inside the "upside-down world" of "blind spot thinking." We discovered how powerful the right questions can be in our quest to find the language and focus that transform us into a force to be reckoned with.

Yes, we have established that we are a curious, questioning species by nature. So, would it surprise you if today's mission is to look at one of the other questions that has been responsible for sidelining some of our big dreams?

Let's start with the story of the man in the one-wall prison.

He struggles endlessly to bend the bars covering the window to free himself from his prison. Because he is so focused on the bars on the one wall, he does not notice that no other walls are surrounding him. If he simply looks to his right or left, he would see that his freedom easily awaits him.

So let's spend today looking away from the bars on our window and seeing what sort of wonderful things lie to the left and right, shall we? On this day, the "bars on the windows" are the questions that take us in the direction of the word **"how"**:

- How do I make more money?
- How do I get rid of all of this stress?
- How do I find the relationship of my dreams?

When we have something epic that we want to achieve when we crawl into bed at night and dare to ask ourselves "what if," we often derail ourselves immediately by asking how. If we don't immediately have that answer, we often *assume* that our desired achievement just cannot be achieved.

Well, guess what?

When we start with the question "how," we overlook the most important "ask" of them all: THE #EPIC WHO ™!

- Who has already done this or something similar? (And what are their stories?)
- Who can I model or seek as a mentor?
- Who can teach or coach me?
- Who do I need to be to achieve this?
- Who am I right now, and what do I have that is already working in my favor? And where am I getting in my way?
- Who do I need in my corner or on my team? Who should I bring on board and/or brainstorm with?
- Who is qualified and experienced enough to advise me?
- Are their communities or networks that would benefit me?

Once we have focused on the #EPIC WHO ™ questions, those responses can more clearly point us toward the "how" solutions.

They can help us ask other "solution-focused" questions:

- Do I need to ramp up my inner game? Change perspectives or change what I'm focusing on?
- Would I get better results if I let go of certain things?
- Should I examine the ways that I spend my time?
- Would I benefit from looking at how I talk to myself or others?
- Do I need to recalibrate how I show up in my day?
- Do I need to ask new questions? Take a deeper look at what I'm assuming.
- Do I need to grow, learn, or gain skills to transform these dreams into real destiny?

Guess what? Focusing on THE #EPIC WHO versus the how makes it much easier to gain momentum, bust through the fear, obliterate the self-doubt, and identify a strategy that can achieve things that previously might have seemed impossible.

So here's your next level opportunity: where would the areas in your life benefit from combining the Defining 3 Questions with some of these THE #EPIC WHO questions? Can you see the turbo-charge potential here? Let today be the day when you give yourself permission to dream. As you dream, resist the old habit of bogging yourself down with "how" when you could lift yourself up with "who"?

This is going to be an #EPIC time for you! It all begins with knowing THE #EPIC WHO™!

TODAY'S ACTION STEPS:

- *Identify one idea or objective that you have toyed with in the past that you have shelved because you didn't know how you would achieve it. (+2 Gold Stars)*
- *Now start brainstorming WHO might be able to guide you, instruct you, mentor you, coach you – even accomplish some of the steps for you or with you. (+1 Gold Star)*
- *Bonus points if you check in at the end of the day and journal your discoveries. Were you asking some better questions? This is a skill, so practice because the better your questions, the better your results! (+3 Gold Stars) Booyah!*

TOTAL POSSIBLE STARS FROM TODAY: 6 STARS

Day 66 – LANGUAGE: Goal Diggers

It's Day 66, and hopefully, you now have some new dreams percolating! That gives us the perfect opportunity to circle back to a word we also touched upon on Day 21: the concept of GOALS. So now that we are really beginning to fully appreciate the invisible stories attached to specific words let's be sure that we're not destroying the potential joy within our dreams by labeling them "goals"!

Yep, you heard me right: our fixation with goals can be the very thing that kills any momentum that might be building within our dreams! You might remember, whether it's my Society of Epic Chicks, ladies or my C-suite leadership clients, they all know that I believe that we have one goal and one goal only:

… To be taking our last breath saying, "Oh my gosh, that was freaking EPIC! I hope I get to do this again sometime!"

Everything else is a target, an opportunity, an objective, or an invitation to iterate!

Because when you think about it, *what is the "invisible story" attached to the word "goal"?*

When you set a goal, you inadvertently throw yourself in the car's back seat and become like the child obsessed with "Are we there yet?" You wake up in the morning, and one of the first realizations is that you have not yet achieved that goal, so you start your day off *from the position of failure!* How's that for uninspiring?

On the other hand, if you can think of those big dreams in the context of targets, objectives, and opportunities, you open yourself up to more flow and your highest frequency. You also open yourself up to the possibility of *exceeding* the objective *without allowing the outcome of this one pursuit to define you.*

So you see, once again, your choice of words encourages you to prepare for success or difficulty. It's a recalibration toward the process versus strictly toward the outcome that can enhance your joy, energy level, and effectiveness along the path.

So today, hit that reboot button on the topic of goals even more emphatically. Allow those dreams to go big without allowing them to define your self-worth. They should feel like a playground, not a prison – even when that prison has only one wall. Write down a few objectives you would like to "play" with. Get into the "giddy fun mode" of exploration and discovery.

Feeling ninja? Now, play with mapping out your systems and strategies because remember – targets are only as good as the systems you have in place to get there.

Today, you ARE looking like that force to be reckoned with! Check out those EPIC new objectives and possibilities!

Ready, set, GO! Let's do this!

TODAY'S ACTION STEPS:

- *Identify 3-5 objectives you intend to focus on this week. Are there some possibilities that you are ready to explore? Can you agree to adopt some light bulb thinking – meaning that you learn and iterate whether it lights up or not? Now that's NINJA! (+2 Gold Stars)*
- *Now start looking at these objectives. Begin strategizing what your first "lightbulb" experiment will be. What will you try first? (+2 Gold Stars)*
- *Bonus points if you check in at the end of the day and journal your discoveries. What worked? What didn't work? What will you adjust on your next light bulb? (+3 Gold Stars) Booyah!*

TOTAL POSSIBLE STARS FROM TODAY: 7 STARS

Day 67 – LANGUAGE: All Work and No Play Makes Jack a Dull Boy.

I confess I am definitely NOT a scary movie type of chick! So when my mom and I ventured to the SHINING at a theater in New York City, I found it terrifying! (To say the least!)

So why am I quoting a movie that was responsible for my decade-long fear of beautiful mountain resorts? Because, dear Chicks and Gents, "all work and no play makes Jack a dull boy" is a statement that rings true.

Most of us have gotten so busy that we feel "guilty" for taking time to do something others might judge as "play."

Well, here's the thing. In fact, here are TWO THINGS:

1) We have established that words DO have power because they carry with them the invisible stories of past associations. There was a time when "play" meant dopamine. Play meant joy. Therefore, when we actually DO allow ourselves to "play," we happen to convince ourselves to do things that, if this was considered work, we might say would be intolerable. Take downhill skiing or mountain biking, for example. Both require high-risk tolerance and the ability to regulate stress. The focus must be unerring, and there's no quitting halfway down the mountain. Even sports such as golf or flag football put you face-to-face with competition. There is a strong possibility that you will lose and possibly be humiliated in the process. Yet, in all these cases, you usually *return to play another day. Why? Because your mind has categorized this as play!*

2) Study after study supports that even adults benefit greatly from play. Psych Central https://psychcentral.com/blog/the-importance-of-play-for-adults#benefits says that the benefits range from health advantages to stress management to increased creativity, joy, and optimism. Of course, play is a phenomenal way to refresh and hit the reset button. It's a great way to clear your emotional frequency when it's stuck on low and the perfect way to reboot an overwhelmed mind.

So what's the message here?

Knowing what we now know about the influence of word selection on our behavior and beliefs, these are two powerful calls to action:

- **Explore ways that you can substitute the word "play" in circumstances where you had previously been using the word "work"** or in scenarios that might tend to dip into emotional stress. Especially in circumstances where you tend to think that something will be a "struggle immediately," see how you can replace the concept of work/hard with the concept of adventure/ exploration/play. For example:
    - Let's *play* with this idea. We might get the breakthrough that we've been looking for.

- Here's your *home play* this week…Focus on being aware of any patterns that make you get in your way. Have fun with it, and congratulate yourself as you start seeing things.
- I hear what you're saying. May I play with that? I think that there might be a counterpoint to consider…
- I know that this approach is unfamiliar, so I'm going to invite you to play with it and let me know what you discover…
- You've given me a lot to play with here, so I'm excited to see where this leads…

- **Start envisioning "play" as an integral component of your optimal performance system.** I even recommend that you go as far as making it non-negotiable. And, yes, allow times when it can be as silly as possible. My Society of Epic Chicks, for example, has found that the day can feel substantially brighter when you squeeze a rubber chicken or two. Even after my keynotes, we often add a "gamification" element – the science of learning through play. You'd be amazed to witness the level of enthusiasm a sales team can achieve when they see their VP donning a pair of tin foil ears and channeling Yoda's persona for the camera!

Your mission in today's quest for epic-ness is to banish the mandatory focus on work [!!] and embrace the power of PLAY!! How can you make whatever you are doing today more fun and energizing?

TODAY'S ACTION STEPS:

- *How can you integrate the concept of play into your day so that those things that felt like drudgery or a chore (or even "The Shining" scary!) don't seem so bad anymore? Can you even find ways to make them feel like a game?   (+3 Gold Stars)*
- *What can you plan into the next five days that has a play element to it and recharges you in the process?   (+3 Gold Stars)*
- *Bonus points if you take action on incorporating the concept of more play into your life. Notice the shifts you see in your day when you "authorize" your mind to indulge in play. (+3 Gold Stars) Booyah!*

TOTAL POSSIBLE STARS FROM TODAY: 9 STARS

Day 68 – LANGUAGE: The Day of Four Phrases

Let's continue the concept of "play" by focusing on a game that will help you build your "word selection muscle" while increasing your ability to focus at the same time deliberately.

The Game? It's called the Day of Four Phrases.

One of my favorite neuroscientists is the great Dr. Joe Dispenza. As I mentioned, I spent decades studying a wide array of inner game principles and genres ranging from the works of ancient philosophers to martial arts to the fascinating work of Abraham Hicks in the niche of Law of Attraction – and far too many to mention in between.

What I love about Dr. Joe Dispenza's work is that he takes many of the concepts that were written off as "woo woo" for decades (if not centuries) and grounds them in scientific fact.

In one of his interviews, he mentioned training your mind to be more present and deliberate by embracing four daily intentions or phrases. It triggered an idea – a "what if?" You see, I also highly admire the work of RTT® (Rapid Transformation Therapy) founder therapist Marisa Peers. She has some wonderful insights and concepts around language and, specifically, our inner narrative's role in all aspects of our lives. I began pondering how I could create a practice that would incorporate her philosophies with what I also know about language and combine that all into an adaptation of Dr. Joe Dispenza's exercise.

What I came up with is a practice that reinforces these four daily phrases with "epic-inducing language." The target: slowly but consistently redefining how we see ourselves by setting momentum-building intentions.

Examples:

- Success isn't just possible – it's inevitable, and this is what it looks like "in progress"!
- Everything always works out for me in rewarding and sometimes mysterious ways!
- Things are moving at a fast pace, so fortunately, I'm someone who loves a good whiTheind!
- I wonder how the world will surprise and delight me today.
- I'm a world-class leader, so I thrive on this!

The mission is to select four phrases for the day or the week and focus on keeping those phrases front and center. Craft phrases that trigger a frequency of excitement, moment, and positive expectation.

Keep a chart that tracks all the times you recite one of these phrases, and literally reward yourself with gold stars or emoji stickers. Remember the value of a dopamine hit, and start racking up your points! The more days you sustain this ritual, the more you become the sovereign of your mind.

Can you see the trend here? We're busting through the "it's hard" bias by turning our efforts into play. No more allowing your words to define your destiny haphazardly! Words have power, so use their power to enhance your own! REMEMBER!!! You are the AUTHOR! When life pushes back, go for the dopamine!

Now, that's **definitely** worthy of a **Booyah!**

TODAY'S ACTION STEPS:

- *Identify and imprint your four phrases on your mind's radar.   (+2 Gold Stars)*
- *Now keep reminding yourself to keep those phrases top of mind throughout your day. (+2 Gold Stars)*
- *Bonus points if you check in at the end of the day and journal your discoveries. How did those four phrases impact your day? (+3 Gold Stars) Booyah!*

TOTAL POSSIBLE STARS FROM TODAY: 7 STARS

Day 69 – LANGUAGE: The Flight of the Introvert

Ok, let's admit it. There are some categorizations that in modern society are rarely (if ever) a compliment. So, while we are crafting words and phrases that empower us, let's call out a few labels we have been attaching to ourselves that almost always keep us feeling like we don't really fit in [!!].

Labels are words, and words have power, right?

So, "riddle me this, Batman…"

Let's look at the labels "realistic" versus "unrealistic." How beaming with pride, do you feel if someone calls you "unrealistic"? It's shame-inducing, yes? In fact, don't you find yourself going to great lengths to ensure that even the biggest haters on the street see that you are behaving "realistically"? After all, doesn't "realistically" imply "responsibly"?

Think about the irony: we're encouraged to "think outside the box," but then we're criticized for being "unrealistic" if we stray too far by "coloring outside of the lines." How the heck can we get it right if we follow that script?

Yet, I ask… were the Wright Brothers, rocket scientists, or even AI programmers thinking "realistically"? Once again, how do we define realistically? Were these innovators grounded in science? Yes, but it was a form of science that had to dance beyond the boundaries of "impossibility."

So it was this ability to think differently that catapulted them to their version of Epic!

Then there's that wonderful categorization of "introvert"...

Now, now…hold on a sec! Before your brilliant mind chimes in with a "but I truly am an introvert," let me clarify what I'm really getting at—the subtle nuances and overtones behind that label. Let's look at the invisible story attached to that word.

Virtually always when a client explains to me that they are an introvert, even if they are "fine" with being an introvert, there is a hint of a sheepish apology or implied flaw lurking beneath the words.

Rarely would you compliment someone by saying, "You are such an introvert!"

Now, this doesn't mean that the qualities of an introvert aren't freaking epic. It simply means that socially, we have packaged the word "introvert" into something most people wouldn't want advertised on their resumé.

This can leave us feeling slightly "less than" and "imperfect" if we have bought into the belief and "definition" that *we are an introvert.*

Here's a real-life example: I had a client named Jonathan who came to me because he felt he was terrible in interviews. Even when he knew he had the right qualifications for the job, he would freeze up, starting with the first "tell us about yourself" question.

Try as he might to imitate the ideal interview responses he viewed online, he just couldn't seem to get it right. I'll be honest: he was pretty awful when he first started sharing his typical replies to the interview questions with me.

But here's the thing: it wasn't because *he* was awful. It was because he was trying to be someone *who he was not. He was trying to fit into a generic mold.*

Here's one of the biggest messages of the entire book:

- *FITTING IN IS NOT A SUPERPOWER.*
- *BEING GENERIC IS NOT A SUPERPOWER.*
- *SHOWING UP AS SOMEONE THAT YOU ARE NOT IS NOT A SUPERPOWER.*
- *YOU'RE SUPERPOWER IS BEING YOU.*

For Jonathan, the breakthrough came when we got to the "biggest failure" question. I asked him if he had ever been bullied. He said, "Of course! Lots of times." As we dove into that story, it led to a metaphor from one of the *Star Trek* episodes, which led to this statement:

"I'll admit it, I'm a geek. One of the big reasons why I'm in the field that I'm in is because I love being around other geeks. I love our conversations and being able to geek out on technology and all this stuff."

As he shared this, he lit up so much that it was infectious. He went from being boring and unremarkable to being a standout. And yes, he suddenly realized that being a geek was his superpower.

Then, when we dove into the "3 Biggest Strengths" question, he shared how his team viewed him as their secret weapon because he could go into a meeting and hardly be noticed. He would be the one who would sit there and observe. That was his stealth mission. By the end of the meeting, he would have extracted critical information that would become invaluable for the team. That quality easily allowed us to craft a great story into his interview response. "My team has nicknamed me after the superhero, The Invisible Man. They call me their secret weapon in meetings because I'm known for my exceptional ability to observe and remember details." Sounds much more epic, yes?

Now, who's willing to define themselves simply as an introvert?

This is where I draw your focus back to the third of our "epic questions": **"What am I assuming that might not necessarily be true?"**

Could you assume that labels like "introvert" are the only "authentic" way to explain your qualities? Have you been suffocating your true superpowers by trying to fit in? Do you really need to confine your unique brilliance into that box – especially when looking in that mirror and judging yourself?

Even if you align with some of the qualities embodied by a label like an introvert, rather than allowing the common perceptions around the word define you, how about trying something like this for size:

I revel in my solo time and use my solitude to energize me. That means I can walk into a room without being the center of attention. I'm a thinker, an observer, a ponderer. I love listening and watching what is going on in a room. I may not say much, but it will be epic when I do say something, and people will want to listen…

How does that feel?

More empowering?

So here's your mission today: **Look at the words you have been using to define yourself and commit to freeing yourself from the "baby elephant collars" within your self-image.** You are emerging as the adult elephant and are using your AWARENESS to "real eyes" that you have other choices. Use that same awareness and ask yourself, "Can some of the qualities I may have been trying to hide reveal themselves as *my superpowers?*"

Unless your current labels and terminology inspire you, retire them – and then find new terminology that helps you feel your unique brilliance and go bold!

Remember that you are on a quest to unleash your most epic self and be willing to **see yourself in your true, perfectly imperfect brilliance.**

You've GOT THIS! So get out those red markers. Rewrite those descriptives in your story and bask in the superpowers of that Shero/Hero version of yourself that you've always been destined to BE!

TODAY'S ACTION STEPS:

- *What labels have you been using to describe yourself that could be more empowering and energizing? What labels don't create the image of someone heading toward epic? Are you using those labels consistently in the present tense? Remember that it acts like programming code. Identify 1-3 labels you have been using that could be powered up and improved. (+2 Gold Stars)*
- *Now, start using the examples above to begin playing with reworking those labels. It's ok if you first hit a light bulb that doesn't light up. Keep iterating until it starts to create those inner frequency tingles that make you feel good! (+2 Gold Stars)*
- *Bonus points if you begin using this iterated way of describing yourself when you describe yourself to others! No apologies or disclaimers! You're too epic for that! (+2 Gold Stars) Booyah!*

TOTAL POSSIBLE STARS FROM TODAY: 6 STARS

Day 70 – LANGUAGE: Will You Supersize It?

As we venture even more deeply into the impact of communication, specifically our words, you should see that our choice of words and phrases can be like the quality of fuel we put into our engines. They can propel us great distances or leave us feeling stuck at the side of the road. So why do we just toss our words around as if they have no impact?

We have common phrases that we repeat on autopilot and wonder why we start feeling like every day is the same.

"How are you?"

"I'm fine."

How many times in our lifetime do we say that? So often that we are using it again to make our point! It's an "autopilot-inducing" phrase, so I will play with you today and invite you to stop doing that. In fact, your mission today is to experience the wild and wonderful world of "Language Lived Largely."

Today, when you are asked by the cashier in line at the grocery store, "How are you?" your mission is to respond with, "I'm fabulous." Play this game even when you need to find a phrase to change your state or frequency. For example, you arrive at the bus stop just as the bus pulls away. Or you turn your car onto the roadway just in time to have to stop for a train.

Instead of saying your customary "gosh darn" (or something like that…wink!), today you're going to surprise yourself and the world by putting on your best Jim Carrey face and saying, "That's freaking awesome!"

Today, **go out into the world as someone who sees the world with a sense of humor**, who uses their words to go BIG and to make themselves (and others) giggle and laugh. Explore the neverending repertoire of juicy modifiers!!! Step out of your car into a "deliciously energizing summer day." Instead of wondering if others will think that you are foolish if you express your joy and delight, *just* find ways to express your joy and delight. As Nike says, JUST DO IT!

Supersize your aliveness by infusing your conversations with words that trigger positive emotions. At first, it might feel oddly vulnerable, but do it anyway because, my dear, you don't need to earn the right to live each moment fully.

Today, create the new habit of selecting words that deliberately uplift and recharge you! Even the occasional goofy word like… you guessed it, BOOYAH!!

TODAY'S ACTION STEPS:

- *Your mission today is to go out into the world and explore how you can express yourself more freely! Take some chances! Go big! Go Bold!! (+2 Gold Stars)*
- *Now start applying this to your inner narrative! Play with choosing more words that uplift and inspire you. And remember to celebrate when you catch yourself in an old language pattern. You wouldn't have caught that just days ago, so definitely celebrate – and then change it!! (+2 Gold Stars)*
- *Bonus points if you write down how it felt at the end of the day. It might feel a wee bit unfamiliar at first so encourage yourself to keep going. How are others responding? How did it feel to start saying more supportive things to YOU? (+2 Gold Stars) Booyah!*

TOTAL POSSIBLE STARS FROM TODAY: 6 STARS

Day 71-LANGUAGE: From Flaw to F-O-cused Possibility

Picture this: You're strolling through an enchanting garden, mesmerized by the beauty surrounding you. Each flower and leaf seems to dance in harmony, and you can't help but feel a sense of peace and wonder. In this moment, your focus is drawn to the exquisite flow of nature, not searching for imperfections but basking in the magic of its existence.

Now, imagine applying the same approach to your own life. Too often, we fixate on flaws, scrutinizing every perceived misstep and stumble. (Remember reading about this on Day 9? As you may have noticed, these concepts easily play well together!) It's easy to get trapped in a cycle of self-criticism, feeling stuck and disheartened. But what if we now enlist our language on an even deeper level to help shift our focus from finding flaws to discovering the flow?

Here's the secret: Flow is all about aligning with your unique rhythm, embracing your strengths, and fostering a focus on possibilities. It's like playing the "what's RIGHT with this picture" game instead of the "what's wrong with this picture" game. Instead of dwelling on past mistakes, consider them stepping stones on your journey to growth. **Embrace the wisdom they offer and let go of self-judgment!**

The path to finding your flow begins with self-awareness. Observe your thoughts and feelings *without judgment,* just like a curious observer in that beautiful garden. Listen to your words. What clues are they exposing? Identify patterns hindering your progress and recognize moments when you feel most alive and empowered! Think of what we have already learned. What are your present tense statements, and how do they make you feel? What is the story that you repeat to yourself and others over and over again?

As you cultivate self-awareness, the *next step is to amplify your strengths*. Acknowledge your abilities, talents, and passions that set you apart. Embrace the true belief that your unique gifts can lead you to extraordinary accomplishments.

When we focus on flow, we shift from dwelling on limitations to exploring possibilities. Every challenge becomes an opportunity for growth and learning. Instead of being discouraged by setbacks, we view them as chances to refine our approach and uncover new avenues. Our words need to align with that. That calls for awareness.

Flow is also about mindset. Nurture a deliberately optimistic outlook and envision your desired outcomes. Visualize success, envisioning yourself confidently navigating through life's twists and turns. *Your thoughts shape your reality, so choose to see potential and abundance.*

One powerful technique is to set intentions aligned with your flow. Clarify your goals, and stay open to unexpected opportunities as you pursue them. Sometimes, the most extraordinary paths unfold from seemingly small and simple decisions.

Remember, *perfection isn't the objective.* Embrace the journey, and in doing so, you'll tap into your flow state more frequently. **Celebrate progress,** no matter how small, and trust that you are growing and evolving with each step.

It's about shifting one little letter in your vocabulary. That one little letter can be the big game changer in your EPIC YOU story!

So, let's use our words and dialogue to reframe our focus from finding flaws to exploring the possibilities of flow. Embrace the enchanting dance of life, and as you do, you'll discover the true essence of your extraordinary potential. Welcome the flow, and watch your world transform!

In the world of EPIC LANGUAGE MASTERY, even one tiny letter can make a life-changing impact! Let's step out into the world shifting more "A's" to "O's"!

TODAY'S ACTION STEPS:

- *Your mission today is to focus on sustaining the inner frequency of FLOW. What thoughts can you think? What shifts can you make? How can you find more beauty in*

today's Life Garden? Keep track of the times you feel like you are in flow today. (+2 Gold Stars)
- *At the end of the day, it's time to reflect on your notes. How much of the day did you maintain your flow? What were you doing differently in those moments from the moments when you dipped into Flaw? (+2 Gold Stars)*
- *Bonus points if you create a strategy for yourself that helps you increase the amount of time that you operate from Flow. Can you steadily spend less and less time in Flaw? Who do you need to show up being in order to make that shift? (+2 Gold Stars) Booyah!*

TOTAL POSSIBLE STARS FROM TODAY: 6 STARS

Day 72 – LANGUAGE: Owning Your EPIC Story – An Odyssey of Empowering Possibilities

Welcome to Day 72! By now, you're probably noticing more words and phrases you choose just out of habit. Some of them probably haven't helped you step out into the world feeling your best, have they? Now, it's time to realize that we create our life story when we put all those phrases together. We get to choose whether that story is created intentionally or by the whims of a life lived on autopilot.

You probably now appreciate how much the story you *believe* impacts how you *experience* your life. If you believe your story is one of constant growth and success, you will expect to thrive. If you are always telling yourself and others a story that focuses on things constantly going wrong, don't be surprised if that's what keeps showing up. Make sense?

We've learned that words create thoughts that trigger emotions, and they will influence our decisions. Our decisions lead to our actions, and our actions typically determine our results. Therefore, we're seeing why it is important to become more deliberate with our words – especially if we want to experience our lives epically.

So, today is a day to pause and reflect on what we have learned about mastery of Focus and the Language you use to tell your story. You are the author of this tale- you CHOOSE the words! Will the amazing things you hope to achieve be portrayed as destiny or fantasy?

In the grand theater of life, you are the playwright crafting a narrative that is uniquely yours. Your story is not defined solely by the events that have unfolded in the past; it's a blank page waiting for the bold keystrokes of possibility and empowerment. Today, right now, is the perfect day to *significantly (and permanently)* commit to shifting your focus from dwelling on "what's wrong with this story" to discovering "what's EPIC about YOUR story?"

You may still sometimes get entangled in the web of self-doubt and self-criticism. That's a normal part of the learning curve. It's not unusual in the beginning to replay the scenes of our past, scrutinizing our actions and decisions and lamenting the twists and turns we could have avoided. But let me share a truth: Your story is not meant to be a tale of perfection but a grand epic of growth and resilience.

Remember: Owning your story is not about fixing the past; it's about taking ownership of the present and creating a powerful future. It's recognizing that every scene in this adventure, even those marked with obstacles and setbacks, has served as a valuable lesson in your own blockbuster movie. It's about acknowledging the strength you've gained, the wisdom you've acquired, and the courage that resides within you.

Think about it – what if your life is indeed a shero's / hero's journey? You are the protagonist, embarking on a quest filled with challenges, allies, and triumphs. You possess the power to shift the narrative and amplify the potential within you.

I invite you to seize this opportunity to approach your future with a pen in hand. The blank pages of possibility await. Let go of the beliefs that have stopped you in the past. Be aware of each moment, acknowledging the growth it has brought and the wisdom it has bestowed. Give yourself permission to release the shackles of self-doubt and embrace your unique strengths and gifts instead. Commit to owning your EPIC story, and starting right now, step boldly into the next chapter armed with your growing mastery of Focus and Language, knowing you have the resilience to face whatever comes your way. Your story is an EPIC adventure waiting to unfold.

What words will YOU choose to create a tale that you love telling?

TODAY'S ACTION STEPS:

- *Your mission today is to return to the epic story you are crafting. Now that you know even more about applying the strategies of Focus and Language, write down where you see yourself in a year. (+3 Gold Stars)*
- *Go back and compare it to the earlier versions. Are you more focused on the presence of what you want versus the lack of the presence? Do your word choices resonate with possibility and expectation? (+2 Gold Stars)*
- *Bonus points if you can write an additional draft that goes even BIGGER. Are you willing to imagine a story that might be "wrong"? Hint: Was Edison's light bulb that didn't light up "wrong," or did it lead him to an even better version that he had started imagining? (+2 Gold Stars) Booyah!*

TOTAL POSSIBLE STARS FROM TODAY: 7 STARS

Day 73 – LANGUAGE: The Magic of "Being" - Unveiling the Secret Sauce

We have been focusing on using our deliberately crafted language to write our own Shero's/Hero's Epic Story! So what better way to learn how to write a compelling story than from one of the masters himself: William Shakespeare. He was known to have written comedies and tragedies because stories can be written either way, can't they? Perhaps one of the most famous of his quotes was this:

"To BE or not to BE, that is the question." Ah! The mighty words of Shakespeare.

Notice that this wise observer of the human spirit did not say, "To DO or not to DO." So why are we tellers-of-our-own-story still so distracted by the *doing*? Why do we believe that our stories are all about what we do???

In the quest for success and achievement, we often get caught up in the whirlwind of *doing*. We meticulously plan our actions, strategize our next moves, and tirelessly work towards our "goals" (wink). But in the flurry of doing, we often inadvertently overlook the essence of *being*.

Who we show up *being* is shaped entirely by the words that we repeat over and over again– words that we believe describe and define us. Words that we believe will help us to be more understood. Words that show that we fit in – or perhaps that we don't.

So, as you continue to write your future story more deliberately, it's really, *really* important to consider the following: **What words are you going to use to define yourself – because it is those words that will influence how you approach your own story and how you interact with the world.**

I have seen it over and over again. *When clients get clear on who they intend to show up being, that becomes the secret sauce that unlocks unparalleled twists of fate – things that can even appear as if by magic in their lives.*

Consider this: Have you ever noticed how two people can execute the same task, but the results vary drastically? It's because the catalyst for epic results is not the action itself *but the energy, intention, and mindset– in other words, the inner game – with which it's carried out.*

The key to unlocking a destiny that excites you lies in your ability to become the sovereign of your focus. It's your words that fuel this focus and that make you come even more alive. And yes, your words create your understanding of who you need to BE. They are the lights on the runway that allow you to step into the embodiment of your highest self, the version of you that radiates confidence, resilience, and unwavering determination.

Let *doing* be the vehicle that propels you forward, but let *being* become the compass that guides your path. It's not enough to know *where you are*. Those who consistently create epic things personally and professionally clearly understand *who they are*. When you align your actions with your authentic self, this is where I have seen the magic begin to unfold. This is where I see clients become a magnet for opportunities, a beacon of inspiration to others, and a force to be reckoned with.

I've seen dream jobs "come out of nowhere" (many, MANY times). I've seen "the right people" suddenly show up. I've seen all sorts of "coincidences" rain down not only on my clients but also consistently in my own life when the focus shifts to *Being*.

Prioritize "being" over "doing." Commit to showing up as the best version of yourself in every moment. Cultivate the qualities and traits that empower you to embrace challenges with courage and navigate adversity with grace.

It's a subtle shift, but it can profoundly impact your results. **Instead of chasing external validation, seek inner alignment. Instead of focusing solely on achieving external goals, nurture your internal growth.**

When you consciously choose who you will show up being, the "impossible" often becomes the "new normal." Your actions become infused with purpose, passion, and intention. You'll discover that the missing piece was never about doing more; it was about *being* more.

So, as you embark on your journey toward success, remember that *being* is the foundation upon which your greatness is built. Embrace the power of *being* and watch as the world responds to your newfound sense of self. When *doing* comes into harmony with *being*, an endless variety of notes suddenly gain the potential to create a symphony of success that resonates far beyond your wildest dreams.

Yes, welcome to the ranks of the great storytellers of all time! And dear William, I think we'll choose "**to be**." Thanks for the insightful question!

Epic Chicks and Gents, your EPIC MISSION today is all about the BE-ing!

TODAY'S ACTION STEPS:

- *Your mission today is to look back at the revised story of your life. Can you use what you have learned to recraft how you have defined yourself, including the actual words you have been using to describe yourself? (+2 Gold Stars)*
- *Now, let's take it a bit further and write words or a paragraph describing who you intend to be as you move into the future. (+2 Gold Stars)*
- *Bonus points if you weave that into a declaration/ intention and refer to it as you start your next few days. Can you be bold enough to share this revised version of yourself with others? (+3 Gold Stars) Booyah!*

TOTAL POSSIBLE STARS FROM TODAY: 7 STARS

Day 74 – LANGUAGE: The Power of Appreciation Over Apology

We know you ARE the SuperShero/Hero in this epic story. So the question is, do you, as the SuperShero/Hero step out into the world in the boldness of appreciation or the timidness of apology? Seriously, think about it.

What if you were to count how many times during the day you say, "I'm sorry"? Would it be more than 10? More than 50?

In the tapestry of human language, two words hold extraordinary influence: "Sorry" and "Thank You." We've been exploring how our use of words can shape our interactions with others and our perception of ourselves. Many of us have become accustomed to apologizing constantly. In fact, we often mistake our apology for politeness, as if we carry an inherent belief that we are a nuisance and a bother to those around us. We apologize for things beyond our control, and we even feel shame when asking for help when others would be happy to assist us.

But what if we were to unravel the significance that lies within the choice between "Sorry" and "Thank You"? Imagine how our lives would blossom if we embraced appreciation as our guiding principle instead of perpetually apologizing.

Let's face it; when we apologize for existing, we unwittingly define ourselves as unworthy or "not enough." It's time to break free from this limiting narrative and start fostering a culture of self-worth within ourselves and our interactions. Shifting from "Sorry" to "Thank You" is transformative. It's a paradigm shift that leads to a more empowered and joyful life.

Consider the difference between apologizing for making someone wait and expressing gratitude for their patience. Instead of saying, "I'm sorry for keeping you waiting," say, "Thank you for waiting." *This small but profound change conveys respect for the other person's time while honoring their understanding.*

Similarly, when seeking help or support, trade the apology for appreciation. Instead of feeling shame for needing assistance, say, "Thank you for helping." Embrace the notion that seeking help is an act of courage and vulnerability. Gratitude replaces self-deprecation, fostering an environment of compassion and camaraderie.

Apologies can create distance, while appreciation fosters connection. When we choose to say, "Thank You for being flexible with your schedule," we acknowledge the other person's willingness to accommodate, deepening the bond between us.

Now, let's consider the magic that unfolds when we practice acknowledgment towards ourselves. Replace self-criticism with self-appreciation. Rather than apologizing for perceived flaws or difficulties, say, "I *have* a pretty freaking epic story, and I always seem to get through the challenges. I have a lot to look forward to, and I have a lot to feel proud of. It hasn't always been easy, but I did it anyway. " Embrace self-love and acceptance. This is necessary if you want to see your confidence and self-esteem soar.

Are you cringing right now because the idea of appreciating yourself feels a bit vain? Don't worry. You are *definitely* not alone.

It may not come as a shock that during my LIVE YOUR DESTINY Breakthrough Experience, one of the most formidable exercises for my Epic Chicks is, ironically, speaking about the beauty they see in themselves! Giving ourselves credit is not something that most of us are trained to do, especially speaking it OUT LOUD for others to hear! Nevertheless, mustering the courage to acknowledge your epicness is the first step towards emanating resonance in your surroundings, creating a life you love – and possibly even positively impacting the world. Translation? **Do you want to wake up loving your life? It begins with learning the language that allows you to love YOU.**

Here's the thing: The impact of choosing words of appreciation over apologies is not confined to our social interactions. It ripples through every aspect of our lives, including our relationship with ourselves and the universe. *Appreciation and self-acknowledgment open doors to abundance, attracting positivity and synchronicities that align with our highest good.*

Today, your mission is simple: Swap out unnecessary apologies with heartfelt expressions of thanks. Nurture a culture of appreciation within your mind and heart, and witness how your world transforms. Watch as your relationships deepen, your self-esteem soars and your journey becomes filled with moments of awe and wonder.

So, let's fill the pages of our future story with language that expresses appreciation and empowerment. Let "Thank You" be the foundation of your interactions, and let acknowledgment paint your world in hues of contentment and fulfillment. Choose the words that elevate your soul and create a symphony of positivity around you. The hidden potential of this subtle shift is waiting to weave its spell, and all it takes is the courage to say, "Thank You."

TODAY'S ACTION STEPS:

- *Your mission today is to focus on your "I'm Sorry" phrases and your "Thank You's". Make a note of how often you are using them. (+2 Gold Stars)*
- *What did you discover? When do you tend to apologize? When do you opt for "thank you"? Do people get offended if you say "thank you" rather than "I'm sorry?" What is your takeaway from today? (+2 Gold Stars)*
- *Bonus points if you can start shifting that habit and banishing all those superfluous apologies from your language! (+2 Gold Stars) Booyah!*

TOTAL POSSIBLE STARS FROM TODAY: 6 STARS

Day 75 – LANGUAGE: Embrace Your Superpowers –Shifting from Comparison to How Can I Grow

How often have you read about someone's monumental accomplishment on Facebook or LinkedIn? That incredible promotion? That "perfect life"? How many times have you felt just a wee bit envious?

In our daily lives, we often find ourselves trapped in the comparison game, using words and language that can chip away at our self-esteem and act as programming code for our self-consciousness. Whether we compare ourselves to others or label one struggle as our "biggest problem," we inadvertently set ourselves up for feeling disempowered. It's like defining ourselves as something less than what we need to be, what we believe we should be, or what we want to be.

But what if we flip the script and embrace our superpowers? Instead of viewing areas of growth as weaknesses overshadowing our strengths, we can get excited about the potential to grow and develop further. When we acknowledge our superpowers and recognize areas of opportunity, we liberate ourselves from the shackles of "judginess."

So, now that we are here creating empowered stories, let's shift our vocabulary. No more strengths and weaknesses. Instead, let's adopt superpowers and opportunities to grow. This simple change in language can create a profound shift in how we perceive ourselves and others. By recognizing our superpowers, we can be proud of what we bring to the table, and by acknowledging our plethora of options, we allow ourselves and others the space to improve and evolve.

Let today be the day we break free from comparisons and self-criticisms. Instead, let's revel in our uniqueness and potential to learn and progress. Embrace your superpowers, and don't be afraid to explore the possibilities that lie ahead. Remember, every superhero has room to develop their abilities, and every hero's journey is filled with exciting opportunities to cultivate.

As you enter your day, make a conscious effort to catch yourself when you slip into the comparison trap. *Replace "strengths and weaknesses" with "superpowers and opportunities to grow."* By doing so, you'll elevate your self-esteem and create a culture of empowerment and support for those around you. Let's celebrate the superhero within us all and unlock our true potential together. Today, go out and embody your superpowers, and watch how the world responds in kind.

So, how many exciting ways can you still grow and gather others along the way today?

TODAY'S ACTION STEPS:

- *Your mission today is to focus on where you have been creating stress by obsessing over comparisons. Being ambitious is fine, but lose the temptation to compare yourself*

with the world. Stay aware and make note of when those comparisons creep in today. (+2 Gold Stars)
- *At the end of the day, it's time to reflect on your notes. How much of the day did you dodge the comparison trap? What were you doing differently in those moments from when you started comparing? Did comparing yourself to others make you feel your best? (+3 Gold Stars)*
- *Bonus points if you create cue phrases to shake you out of comparison when you notice yourself doing it. Commit to releasing yourself more and more so that you can focus maximum energy on all the ways YOU are thriving, expanding, and growing! (+2 Gold Stars)*

TOTAL POSSIBLE STARS FROM TODAY: 7 STARS

Day 76 – LANGUAGE: Embracing Work/Life Harmony

What *is* your story? Take a moment to see how it has shifted from when we started 76 days ago. Is it still cluttered with "must do's" and "I'm so busy's"? I can't tell you how frequently I have heard this [and confession… how often I have thought this to myself…]:

"I am always so busy! I just can't seem to find the time to actually enjoy life!"

If you're like the majority of my clients, you may find yourself uttering this recurring theme – the desire to find a career that allows for more time and resources so that you can live a truly epic life! However, pursuing this vision often leads to an approach where you're devoting so much time and energy to "making a living" that you neglect the day-to-day opportunities for joy and fulfillment that makes you feel truly alive!

This relentless pursuit can leave you feeling drained. If you follow the traditional path, you may even lose sight of your authentic self and forget about all of the wonderful things that make you YOU.

But here's the Epic Ninja part of this day: it's not as much about *what you are doing as what you are TELLING YOURSELF that you are doing.*

I know that's a tough one to get your head around, so bear with me. I'll explain.

Remember my client Leanne, who loved horses? Until we helped her create more harmony in her life by creating her Personal Empowerment System™ tracker AND *until she became conscious of the story that her own mind was creating,* her words expressed a belief that the lifestyle she desired was impossible. Even worse, her focus was stuck on observing only the evidence of reasons to be upset.

If her words are convincing her that what she wants cannot be achieved and what she IS living is making her stressed, what do you think are the odds of her feeling satisfied – much less happy? Probably close to zero, right?

Unfortunately, though, even the word itself, "balance," sets us up for that kind of defeatist thinking. It implies that we should be achieving a mix between work "and life" that is 50/50 – which then insinuates that if we don't have that, we're missing out. Even the words "work" contrasted to "life" sounds like when we're working, we're not capable of feeling fully alive. Work is programmed to be a nuisance and a bother.

Can you see the set-up for defeat and frustration in these words?

However, let's go back to Leanne. What if instead of telling herself she can't find work/life balance, she told herself this:

I'm someone who strives for excellence, and I love seeing when I complete something, knowing how well it's been done. This means when I'm at work, I really immerse myself. I dive in. What I'm looking for isn't balance – it's actually harmony. This means I have found a way so that once a month, I replenish myself by taking a 3-day weekend. I totally hit the reboot button, thinking only about my gorgeous environment and my horses. This allows me to really go deep when I'm at work, knowing that I can look forward (guilt-free) to this special time with my amazing horses.

Which version of her life do you think would make her feel better? Is there a more energizing version of *your* story? Of course, you don't have to be that elaborate (wink!), but you get the picture, yes?

Will there be moments that feel like "work"? Absolutely. The misstep comes when we begin to equate our entire professional life with the feeling of toil. It is up to us to focus on our professional life as if it has the potential to enrich parts of our soul that our personal lives don't uncover. It is up to us to insist on focusing in a way that allows us to discover more ways to influence, impact, and expand *thanks to* our professional "aliveness."

So here's the transformative idea I want to share with you: You're not looking for balance. You're looking for a **flowing sense of harmony.** *True success is no longer defined by work/life balance but by this state of work/passion harmony.* Unlike balance, which suggests a precarious equilibrium, harmony offers a rich tapestry of notes that can come together beautifully, allowing for rest and rejuvenation moments.

When we commit to finding our state of epic flow, when we create life stories that express more fulfillment and play, our work stops being such a grind. It can even become part of the overall symphony of your joy. When our words and stories don't turn work into our adversary, our careers and professions can nourish our growth, fuel our connections, and even empower us to make meaningful contributions to the world.

Discovering this harmony is an ongoing process. There's nothing "wrong" when it involves continuously iterating and honing our professional pursuits until we find work that brings us genuine joy. In the meantime, we must cherish the joy in everything we do. We must seize the opportunity to find moments of delight even at the job that is definitely not the "end game."

This was a lesson that I discovered immediately after college. After having spent years at prep school and then in college, there I was working as a server on the opening team of Manhattan's elite Gotham Bar And Grill. Back "in the day," that meant that I was an aspiring actress— i.e., a "wait-ress." Always waiting…HOPING… that one of the high-profile agents or celebs would "discover" me. Wink!

Shockingly, that never happened — but I discovered something about team, leadership and work in general that has stuck with me to this day. The lesson is this:

The work is the work. The pace is the pace. The customers are who they are. So I am the variable. I get to choose whether I make it stressful, frustrating, and overwhelming — or whether I find the fun in the challenge. Will I love it or hate it?

In the "hate it" category were the things like the occasional customer who chose to be condescending and rude, the new kitchen team that couldn't seem to get its rhythm right, seeing my entire section seated at the same time… if you've ever waited tables, you know what I'm talking about.

However, in the "exhilarating column" was this: how freaking awesome to meet all of these new, interesting people… could I turn this into a game of EPIC organization so that I brought out all of the drinks at the same time, greeted each new table within one minute of when they were seated, had my Specials of the Day Monologue down to a science, and do it all so that I gained momentum as the night went on?!

Yes, what I learned is we can let the "bad days" or "bad aspects" of our jobs define us if we care to tell the story that way. Or, we can choose to find ways to tap into our growing mastery of Language and construct a more exhilarating tale around work so that we can outsmart the"bad" and insert the "fun."

A challenge can be unfair and impossible — or it can be a gamified personal quest (Move over Frodo…).

When you build your inner game muscles to your specifications, it's amazing how many of the things that used to annoy you suddenly become stimulating and fun… And who knows? You might even find that you actually love more and more of what you do…?

As we recalibrate and reboot our lives to find work that brings fulfillment and a sense of contribution, we discover that lasting success is more than just making a living. It is about allowing the potential harmony in life to teach us how to truly live. And as is probably evident by now, in "our dictionary," Epic is synonymous with finding ways to feel fully alive.

So, dream big and set audacious targets. Create strategies that lean into the concept of life harmony, and never tell a story that puts your "coming aliveness" on hold. Instead of falling into monotonous routines, let's embark on "imagi-cations" – explorations that transport us into new worlds of possibility even in the middle of a work day where not everything is going "right".

Perhaps, open yourself to being willing to embrace each day with the wonder of a crazy wannabe actress at a high-end NYC restaurant, ready to explore and discover the extraordinary in the ordinary rush of customers on any given Saturday night.

Now, *that's* a story that will be delicious to tell!

TODAY'S ACTION STEPS:

- *Brainstorm a new version of your professional day-to-day life story that revolves around creating harmony versus stressing over constant "balance." Can you create a version more like Leanne's new story? (+2 Gold Stars)*
- *Create a checklist of five ways to gamify your professional day. Yes, feel free to model it on my waitressing days! (+2 Gold Star)*
- *Bonus points if you implement your new story and gamification tricks TODAY! (+3 Gold Stars) Booyah!*

TOTAL POSSIBLE STARS FROM TODAY: 7 STARS

Day 77 – LANGUAGE: Embracing the Dazzling Brilliance Within

Look at you! We are just over three-quarters of the way through our journey, so who's feeling the urge to break into the Chicken Dance? Crank up the music, and let's go! As we move into Day 77 of these 100 Days of Epic, let's pause to reflect on the first two elements of THE EPIC 3: FOCUS and LANGUAGE.

By now, you should be beginning to see how your ability to master your focus and your language can impact how you experience your life, especially your sense of reality. Think about it: this means that, contrary to what you might have felt earlier, you *do have more power than you might have realized. It's becoming clear that how you assess your life experience is a choice dramatically influenced by what you are focusing on, what you are making that focus means, and what words you use to describe that focus.*

So, if the choice is up to you, why not choose to focus on things that propel you forward whenever possible? Don't *assume* that even during a crisis, you can't choose to focus on things that empower you.

A case in point is this entry from my *SKY IS THE LIMIT* book, which shares my actual FB posts when the boulder crushed Schuy. If I had focused on the horror of the situation or the doom-filled medical precedent, I would have felt powerless and hopeless.

You can see from the following that I chose to take a different approach based on all I knew about the inner game:

"Today, let's celebrate the boundless energy that resides within each of us, creating a vibrant and powerful 'city of lights'! We are not alone in this journey; we are part of a community of brilliance, each light integral to the completeness of the cityscape."

"Life presents us with challenges, moments when we feel overwhelmed like the powerful waves of the ocean. Yet, even in those moments, our individual light is not alone. We are surrounded by a network of captivating lights, ever powerful and brilliant."

"We may face tragedies, uncertainties, and doubts, but remember, we do shine! Out of the darkness can emerge a profound beauty that takes our breath away."

"As human beings, we are rich beyond words, with the freedom to be one radiant light or dazzle as part of a collective brilliance. I encourage you to light up the sky today as you have never done before, unleashing your brilliance and daring any shooting star to shine brighter."

Yes, these uplifting words were written in 2016 during the first weeks after the boulder fell when many believed my daughter would not survive. The odds were slim, yet she defied those odds thanks to a great medical team coupled with the power of inner strength and determination.

Here's what I want you to take away from all of this:
- Life is filled with "impossibilities" that can become "I'm Possibilities" when we have a powerful inner game.
- Miracles and transformations are not far-fetched notions; *they happen every day.*
- The key to achieving things that may initially seem impossible is to believe in them – and to believe that we *can* create an ENTIRE "Epic Life Makeover" if we're willing to simply make some critical changes to our approach.
- All significant transformations in your life begin by being willing to do the work on your inner game and on your level of commitment to mastering all three elements of The Epic 3, even in those moments when life seems to be pushing back.

If you face formidable boulders, feeling scared and alone, consider this: Life is an exquisite dance partner, capable of inspiring sublime surprises and delights when we least expect it. The road may be challenging, but we don't have to journey alone.

These days, Schuy is still working toward doing many of the daily things that most of us take for granted. Yes, for now, at least, her life still requires a wheelchair. However, as I find ways to savor life with my incredible daughter, I marvel at the blessings that have emerged despite the obstacles. Life may not always follow the path we anticipate, but therein lies its beauty. We adapt, we grow, and we find new versions of ourselves.

If you are struggling today, seek those tiny specks of brilliance, those glimmers of hope. Believe in them, for they are worth holding onto. You have the strength to persevere to keep going. The lights of this beautiful Life Cityscape shine all the more brightly because of your radiant brilliance!

Now, onto the final mastery in The Epic 3!

TODAY'S ACTION STEPS:

- *Look back at your biggest takeaways regarding the significance of FOCUS and LANGUAGE. What are your top three AHA moments, and how will you begin incorporating what you have learned into your daily life? (+4 Gold Stars)*
- *Write a checklist for 1) What will you start doing now? 2) What will you stop doing now? and 3) What will you focus on doing differently? (+4 Gold Stars)*
- *Bonus points if you post this in a location where you can refer to it regularly and use it as a loving reminder, like lights on your runway! (+4 Gold Stars) Booyah!*

TOTAL POSSIBLE STARS FROM TODAY: 12 STARS

THE THIRD MASTERY – #3 OF THE EPIC 3 – IMAGINATION: The Power of Envisioning and Igniting the Force Within

Wow, Epic Chicks and Gents! You've come so far on this journey of mastery. You've learned to harness the power of your focus and discovered the immense influence of language on your life. Now, it's time to unveil the final layer of this transformative process – the enchanting realm of imagination.

Remember when we were children, and our imaginations knew no bounds? We would play for hours, creating fantastical worlds and transforming everyday objects into magical treasures. But as we grew older, the world seemed to tell us to leave our imagination behind and face "reality."

Yet, there's one area where we were still encouraged to use our imagination freely – to envision reasons to worry, doubt ourselves, and fear. Forget about waiting for the other shoe to drop – as adults; it often feels like we're waiting for an entire shoe store to come crashing down upon us. Even with the boldest dreams, their fears and self-doubt can make everything tumble.

Today, we continue the quest to reclaim our imagination as the powerful resource it truly is. Like our version of Star War's "The Force," we'll focus on diffusing the stories of the imagination that keep us feeling disconnected and small as we embark on mastering the art of Envisioning. Our imagination is the catalyst for creation, and neuroscience proves that what we can envision, our minds can manifest.

On the other hand, fear is often just a fictional tale spun by our minds about something that may never come to pass. It halts our progress, leaving us stuck in place. However, when we strengthen our imagination muscle to envision possibilities, we ignite forward motion like never before. It's the innovator's edge, the ability to ask "what if" and venture into the realm of limitless potential.

In these next days, we'll guide you in tapping into this transformative aspect of yourself. Your imagination, combined with your mastery of focus and language, will become the booster fuel propelling you toward your biggest dreams. This is the opportunity to finally put a name to that elusive piece in the puzzle that seemed to be missing.

This is your invitation to reclaim your sovereignty over your mind and wield your imagination like a powerful magic wand – the lightsaber of your inner Jedi. Let the force guide you toward your desired future. With patience and determination, you'll be able to watch as things that previously felt impossible begin to unfold in your reality.

As you prioritize the power of envisioning, you'll begin to dismantle the barriers fear once erected. Instead, you'll pave the way for progress, growth, and a life filled with the extraordinary.

So, let's begin the thrilling next phase of our adventure into Epic: our journey into Imagination, where possibilities know no bounds. Use this new ability to iterate the life you desire and deserve. Your epic transformation awaits, and your imagination will be the key that unlocks its full potential.

Our next episode awaits!! The quest into the captivating world of ENVISIONING begins! But first, let's begin by understanding the power of the "dark side" of the force. Fear and self-doubt can maintain such a hold on us that we end up living a life that is truly not lived.

Day 78 – IMAGINATION: Your Success Code – Getting Your IT (Inner Technology) Together

Learning to harness the power of your imagination allows you to wire your "Inner Technology" for greater levels of success. I playfully call this "getting your I.T. together." This practice demands that you learn to ask questions that require your imagination to stretch beyond the place where your beliefs typically stop you.

These should be questions that demand you go deep, even pondering some ideas that may feel strange and unachievable.

When Schuyler was in high school, years before the boulder, she came home one day bubbling over with excitement because Africa's first female president had spoken at her school. I had not heard of this incredible woman, but as Schuy shared some of her wisdom with me, I knew that I had to find out more. As I dove into her story, I discovered one of her quotes that remains one of my favorite quotes to this day:

"If your dreams do not scare you, they are not big enough." Ellen Johnson Sirleaf, *This Child Will Be Great: Memoir of a Remarkable Life by Africa's First Woman President*

Part of the secret of building a strong Success Code for yourself is being willing to dream beyond your "how" – meaning that you need to resist the temptation to limit your dreams to only what you believe is "realistically" achievable.

So, what do some of the questions look like that can help you find your Success Code?

Let's start with these 17 QUESTIONS in this order:

1. What do I believe that SUCCESS looks like for me?
2. Why do I believe that SUCCESS for me would look like that?
3. Why do I believe that I would feel SUCCESSFUL when SUCCESS looks like that?
4. For what purpose do I desire this SUCCESS?
5. And if I achieve that PURPOSE, what do I believe that I would feel that is different from what I am feeling now?
6. Why specifically do I want to FEEL THAT?
7. And why specifically do I think that this would POSITIVELY IMPACT my life?
8. What problem would this SUCCESS solve in my life?
9. What would be the COST if I do not pursue this SUCCESS?
10. If this SUCCESS turned out to be just the BEGINNING of even more EPIC SUCCESS, what might that EVEN BIGGER LEVEL OF SUCCESS look like?
11. If SUCCESS turned out to be something completely different that would still feel like SUCCESS, what might that look like?
12. If SUCCESS turned out to be something so remarkable that it surpassed my wildest dreams and tapped into something that I never thought could be possible, what might that end up looking like?
13. If my SUCCESS could positively impact others or even the world, what might that look like?
14. How might the strengths that I have developed, thanks to my greatest struggles, CONTRIBUTE to my ability to achieve SUCCESS?
15. WHO do I need to start showing up BEING in order to set myself up for that type of success?
16. What do I need to START doing, STOP doing, or DO DIFFERENTLY in order to turbo-charge my SUCCESS MOMENTUM?
17. What is the first step that I will take today?

Today, take a moment to write down your responses to those 17 questions, and you will be on your way to creating the programming code of a new, even more impactful level of success. When you start feeling overwhelmed or unclear about your path forward, return to these 17 questions. You'll find that these help your own "I.T. department" to recalibrate, reboot, and restart so that your programming code is ready to run the version of you that is as EPIC as it is unstoppable!

Here's to your uniquely wonderful imagination and that EPIC Future that is ready to unfold!!

TODAY'S ACTION STEPS:

- *Take some time to answer the above Success Code Questions. (+4 Gold Stars)*
- *Write down anything you learned about how you have been viewing success. Is it really the things you want or the belief that these things will allow you to experience feelings that equate to success? Have you been playing too small? Mistaking success for a flawed version of perfection? Be willing to look deeply at your current Success Code. Where can you improve your IT? (+3 Gold Star)*
- *Bonus points if you start implementing your most significant observations from this exercise beginning TODAY!. (+3 Gold Stars) Booyah!*

TOTAL POSSIBLE STARS FROM TODAY: 10 STARS

Day 79 – IMAGINATION: Rewriting the Narrative – From Failure to Empowerment

As we are working on the process of recalibrating our fear, we are rebooting our definition of failure EVEN FURTHER. Previously, we saw that "failure" is merely one perspective, and it's a perspective that is totally subjective. This interpretation of data pushes you to quit – or, in many cases, to decide not even to get started.

You've also seen how important our language and focus can be when making choices. How we see the world definitely impacts our decisions. So, as we focus on things that occur in our lives, if we allow our imaginations to "imagine the worst," do you think we are set up to make great decisions?

Probably not. The best decisions aren't typically made when you're in the grip of fear, suspicion, self-doubt, distrust, or worry. The repercussions of your decisions can be life-impacting.

Do you know that when I was 14 years old, I gave up my big dream of becoming a ballet dancer just because my ballet teacher didn't cast me in the leading role? Being passed over for something I wanted so badly and thought I had earned crushed me. Decades later, in my 50s, I discovered I didn't lose the starring role because I hadn't been a gifted dancer. It was simply because my parents were going through a divorce, and while the finances were being sorted out, they hadn't paid my ballet teacher's bill.

The irony here is that not only did this completely change the trajectory of my life, but I used it as "proof" that I should never again trust that little voice that told me, "Yes, you can." After all, who wants to be set up for failure and pain? Right??

Chances are, you've been there.

You are definitely not alone. It's surprising how many of my clients overlook this powerful culprit that keeps them stuck: the haunting fear of repeating past failures. Especially the failures that seemed so formidable from the perspective of a child.

Unraveling and conquering the fear of repeating past pain isn't easy, even for my most positively focused clients, even with my help. There's no quick fix, and that's alright because lasting change requires patience and perseverance.

Yet, once we overcome this fear, a remarkable transformation occurs — we emerge with an entirely revitalized way of looking at ourselves. We start seeing the beginning glimmers of renewed self-trust and enthusiasm. So how do we achieve this? How do we start chipping away at that fear?

First and foremost, it demands determination and a willingness to delve into vulnerability in pursuit of something you have perhaps deeply (and often secretly) long yearned for.

A starting point I often suggest is writing two letters.

The first letter should be from your Epic Future Self to your current self. Imagine that this future version of you has achieved everything you have wished for – and then some. What advice and encouragement might she want to share? Don't mistake this for being one of those "everything happens for a reason" letters. Think of it more as an opportunity for your Future Self to assure you that the pain and frustrations are part of the "recipe." You're halfway through your *Lord of the Rings,* so keep walking. As you write the letter, remember that right now, you are simply a younger version of this Future You. All the success and joy that you see will soon be yours.

Now write the letter from your Future Self to the younger version (or versions) of you. From the perspective of your Epic Future Self, begin by congratulating each earlier version of yourself for navigating the original set of circumstances, even if you didn't get the desired outcome. And even if you have been feeling ashamed of the results that you got.

Remind your past Self that trying isn't a failure; it's a chance to learn. Acknowledge the fears and affirm that your Future Self has heard them. Assure your younger Self that your Future Self has used these fears to help them adequately prepare so it's safe to release these fears and move forward.

As you imagine what your Future Self might say in these letters, invite your Future Self to share its vision of "mission accomplished" — how you'll feel, how others will perceive you, and the myriad of benefits you can envision.

Remember to acknowledge that the many "wins" of tomorrow will exist thanks to the pain, lessons, and sacrifices of yesterday and today! It might have been excruciating, but you weathered the storms. You "did it anyway," so allow your Future Self to acknowledge that your struggles will not have been in vain.

With the letters in hand, it's time to prove that you can trust yourself as you step out into the world and face new possibilities. Begin with small successes. Perhaps dine alone at a restaurant, try a new sport like pickleball, explore a new recipe, volunteer at a food bank, attend a meetup, or embark on an online class — reveling in each newfound version of who you can show up as. This journey entails building on your core, embracing vulnerability, and celebrating even the smallest successes.

Today is the day to EMBRACE CHANGE! In fact, see what it can feel like actually to savor it! See what it feels like to redefine yourself as someone deserving of trust and respect. Someone who has everything you need in order to excel in unfamiliar terrain. Give yourself the Shero's/Hero's welcome that is long overdue. And realize that you don't need that stress and self-criticism to "protect you."

You are a beautiful work in progress. If you haven't seen the success you crave, look in the mirror and tell yourself, "Dear/dude, it's because the game isn't over yet! And I love how I'm playing it!"

This is your life, your playground, so seize the opportunity to go outside and get a little sweaty. Let's revel in the adventure of life and cherish even those "scary," delightfully unfamiliar moments! Often, in those moments when we need to be our most resourceful, we innovate and grow. It's also those moments that make the game so fun (and exhilarating) to play!

TODAY'S ACTION STEPS:

- *Write your letter from your Epic Future Self to your current You. What would your Future Self say to congratulate, comfort you, inspire you, encourage you, acknowledge you… Imagine what that incredibly happy and successful version of you might want to communicate to you from the future. Remember, you are just the younger version of this amazing soul! (+3 Gold Stars)*
- *Now imagine the letter that your confident and happy Future You would write to the younger version(s) of you. What words of gratitude or wisdom might it share with your 8-year-old self, your 16-year-old self, your 22-year-old self? Would they want to communicate that any struggles or heartache would prove to have been worth it? Would the Future You tell your younger selves that they've done well and that your older self can take it from here? What would this letter say? (+3 Gold Star)*

- *Bonus points if you seal these letters and put them where you keep important documents. Set a reminder on your phone to open them and reread them in a year! (+2 Gold Stars) Booyah!*

TOTAL POSSIBLE STARS FROM TODAY: 8 STARS

Day 80 – IMAGINATION: Failure Feeds Your Superpowers

Can you tell that I firmly believe that NO ONE should allow Fear to hijack their EPIC? I'm so adamant about this that I crafted my entire two-and-a-half-day LIVE YOUR DESTINY BREAKTHROUGH EXPERIENCE around it.

And, as the women in my Society of Epic Chicks can tell you, it *is possible* to start overcoming some of your most stubborn fears in as little as three days! But you do have to be willing to shake up your current habits and beliefs a bit. You must be willing to look into the darkest crannies of your blind spots. You have to not only *think* without limits, but you must be willing to step forward into the face of your fears and create a space where your ability to imagine success is greater than your ability to imagine reasons to fear.

And you have to be open to considering some new possibilities… especially when it comes to some people's biggest fear, the fear of FAILURE.

What if I were to suggest that failures actually *feed your superpowers?*

You heard me right. As you look at the playbook of success for some of our culture's most epically successful people, you always see a common theme: Never have they gotten to where they are (and sustained it) without those moments that seemed unbelievably low. In fact, many of them *credit* the tough times for their ability to rise to future heights. Because this pattern is so prevalent, I would suggest that failure is actually *the* secret ingredient to epic success. The evidence overwhelmingly suggests that throughout history, the greatest inventors, athletes, and celebrities faced numerous failures on their journey to greatness.

We've talked about many of them earlier in the book, but are you aware of these others?

One very famous example is Sarah Blakely, creator of the multi-billion dollar success- Spanx. She shares the story that every evening at the dinner table, her dad used to ask her brother and her what they had failed at today. He didn't ask this question as a criticism. He wanted to normalize the value of exploring ideas so that Sarah and her brother would learn to get creative, course correct, and grow constantly regardless of the initial outcome. Sarah's dad instilled in them the understanding that iteration (and therefore "failure") is a critical component of success.

Therefore, when Sarah was launching her Spanx product, she braved going directly to Neiman Marcus rather than following the "customary channels" in retail, where the practice was not to approach them first. You "had" to wait until Neiman Marcus approached you. Clearly, Sarah's ability to think beyond the limitations of possible failure allowed her to achieve a level of success that others had not.

Another classic example of imagining beyond the possibility of failure is the story of the "accidental math genius" George Dantzig. As the story goes, Dantzig was studying statistics at UC Berkley's graduate program. He arrived late for classes one day and noticed there were two problems on the blackboard. He assumed they had been assigned for homework, so not wanting to fail at his homework, I copied them down. As he started working on them, he noticed they were "a little harder than usual." Not to be defeated, he ultimately turned in his "assignment" to the professor and went on with college life.

Six weeks later, his statistics professor was banging on his door, excitedly telling him that he had just written an introduction to "one of your papers." He was anxious for Dantzig to read it so the professor could send it out for publication. Dantzig apparently had no idea what his professor was talking about until the man explained that the two problems on the blackboards were famously unsolved statistical problems — not homework at all.

By imagining beyond his fears and beyond what might initially have seemed possible, Dantzig became yet another example of how fear of failure can point you in the direction of your superpowers.

The trend is the same for companies, high-level professionals, and entrepreneurs.

Here's another famous example: the story of Blockbuster and Netflix. When Netflix was early in its business growth, it approached Blockbuster about joining forces. Netflix was looking for an investment of $50 million to help it scale. Blockbuster, which had thousands of stores at the time, was less than excited and turned them down. Initially, it was a devastating rejection for the young company. Today, however, Netflix has grown into a multi-billion dollar company. And Blockbuster? Their last remaining store finally closed. Netflix learned to iterate and grow. Blockbuster clearly did not. One innovated beyond its fear of failure. The other was brought down by their fear of change.

What does this tell us?

Failure serves as a guide, pointing us toward the path of success. It teaches us valuable lessons and provides essential feedback that helps us improve and grow. Embracing failure as a *natural part of the road to success* allows us to persist and develop the grit necessary to reach monumental achievements.

As you power up your Epic 3, I encourage you to lovingly retire that 'ole friend – that concept of failure. What if instead of categorizing your world into columns of successes and failures, you step forward, looking at victories and opportunities to iterate/grow?

What if you were to realize these moments that don't immediately result in the "W" are the moments that offer you clues of even bigger, more innovative possibilities? So, the next time you encounter something you might have called "failure" on your journey, remember that it's not the end.

Remember the Sarah Blakelys, the George Dantzigs, and the Netflix. Trust the GPS and know this is all part of your Epic Success Story.

Those temporary "pushbacks" are stepping stones toward new, even more delicious frontiers, leading you closer to a potential so brilliant and remarkable you might not even have considered it before. Embrace the so-called "failure," learn from it, and let it fuel your determination to reach that epic destiny.

TODAY'S ACTION STEPS:

- *What is one action you have been afraid of taking because you are afraid that if you try it, you'll not succeed? (+2 Gold Stars)*
- *Write out three variations of the story where not only might it go right, but it could go EVEN BETTER!! (+3 Gold Stars)*
- *Bonus points if you now take action. How can you begin going for that big "impossibility" and busting through some of those fears? (+3 Gold Stars) Booyah!*

TOTAL POSSIBLE STARS FROM TODAY: 8 STARS

Day 81- IMAGINATION: Fear- Your Light Bulb Moment and the Dark Corners of Shame

When your passion for something is big enough, it can override the fear. And "epic" is when your desire to overcome the "impossible" is greater than your desire to give in.

If you have ever stopped yourself from trying something because you thought, "What if I fail? What if I'm wrong? What if I look foolish?" trust me – you are not alone.

However, let's get even more tangible. Let's take a look at another potential gift that "failure" can offer: the gift of ITERATION.

Looking back over the millions of years that humankind has existed on this planet, our consistent superpower has been the ability to iterate and adapt. This is probably the most overlooked and under-appreciated skill that we possess. This agility has ensured our species' continued existence amid chaos, uncertainty, and disruption. This ability, combined with our capacity to innovate and imagine, has led us to create many of the modern "miracles" that surround us every day.

Throughout time, the process for advancement has always been the same. We are presented with data that suggests an obstacle or problem. We process its clues and implications. We adapt. Through this process, humanity has discovered everything from fire and the wheel to rocket ships and AI.

So, based on millions of years of successfully adapting to change, when you are presented with the need to iterate, that's setting you up to progress forward – not evidence that you have stalled or slipped backward.

So today's the day to declare your LIGHT BULB MOMENT. It's time to free yourself from the chains of panic that most of us feel when we encounter one of those obstacles or problems. Especially when we encounter that perceived failure multiple times!

Think about it: the light bulb! Can you imagine our lives without it? Do you know what the most powerful ingredient in that invention was?

I say that it was Thomas Edison's willingness to "fail" — time and time and time again.
Yes, Thomas Edison continues to go down in history as one of the most epic inventors (and iterators) of all times — and yet, he invented many products that were considered total flops: the automatic vote counter, the electric pen, the tinfoil phonograph and many more.

Probably one of the most awe-inspiring aspects of Edison's "greatest success" is how he endured so many failed attempts before successfully creating the functioning light bulb. Versions of the story vary between 1,000 and 10,000 "failed" attempts, but either way, how many of us would have the tenacity to believe something is possible when we've just experienced "failed attempt #68"(much less "failure #999)?

So if you are chiding yourself for even just a couple of things not going well, take a breath and note that there are at least three messages here:

- If you want to ultimately find your own "light bulb moment," you have to be willing to be Thomas Edison and boldly commit to discovering the 999 ways NOT to create a light bulb. Even when it doesn't "work," you're still making progress. This iteration process has led to millions of success stories, so why not believe that this call to innovate and imagine will evolve into YOURS? Know that when your LIGHT BULB MOMENT DOES light up, it will brighten up the world in ways that you may never yet have seen.

- The second lesson here? It's the power of the imagination. Unguided, our imagination is adept at creating stories that elicit fear or worry. These stories can seem incredibly real and quickly immobilize us. They can even subtly redefine who we believe ourselves and our world to be. However, when you take ownership of your imagination when you guide it, participate in its creation, and focus it on something "epic," you tap into the kind of "magic" that transforms impossibilities into the next "new normal."
- Pushback is not a threat. It is an opportunity to achieve things that are sometimes bigger than we previously imagined. Resilience and the ability to adapt are wired into your DNA as a human being. Maybe not literally, but certainly as proven over time. It is part of the flame that burns within you, part of your desire to choose the life you want to live and to be willing to challenge yourself to go live it!

Learning to embrace the boulders that fall among us and learning to see them as opportunities to improve versus evidence of a downfall is the key to creating your level of "epic unstoppability." And don't you deserve that? You most definitely DO!!

Your mission today is to approach your next big objective as if part of the formula is to blaze through at least five attempts. In other words, GET STARTED — even if, at first, you get a few wires crossed! Every bulb that tells you "what not to do" gets you that much closer to experiencing the sweet victory of your LIGHT BULB MOMENT!

Claim your million-year-old superpower! Make today a day to iterate versus deciding to stop! Booyah!

TODAY'S ACTION STEPS:

- *Step out into your day now, observing everything that transpires through the lens of resilience and iteration. If the ability to adapt and imagine is your superpower, how would you respond to any data that suggests the need for change? (+2 Gold Stars)*
- *At the end of the day, look back at your day. Did you remember to shift your perspective? How did it feel? What did you learn and observe? (+3 Gold Stars)*
- *Bonus points if you now look at some of the fears you may have had around failure. Can you tap into your natural problem-solving ability and iterate your way to the new "I'm possibility"? Can you envision yourself celebrating your next Light Bulb Moment? (+3 Gold Stars) Booyah!*

TOTAL POSSIBLE STARS FROM TODAY: 8 STARS

Day 82 – IMAGINATION: Fear Lives In Your Comfort Zone

"Fear is not real. The only place that fear can exist is in our thoughts of the future. It's just a product of our imagination causing us to fear things that do not at present and may not ever exist. That is near insanity, Qatar. Do not misunderstand me, danger is very real but fear is a choice. We are all telling ourselves a story and that day mine changed."

This has become one of my favorite quotes about fear, and it is spoken by Will Smith's character to his son, Qatar, in the movie *After Earth*.

First, stepping outside your comfort zone can be intimidating, but it's vital to personal growth, confidence, and success. Yet, we often mistake this feeling of unfamiliarity for danger. It's not like tigers or bears are chasing us. In fact, it may not even be that we know exactly what we're afraid of or what these fears look like. Sometimes, we can't even identify them.

Part of the reason that fear can grip us so strongly is its ability to disguise itself. The roots of its power over us often stay in the shadows of our blind spot. Whether it's fear of success, fear of failure, or even the fear of being judged by both ourselves and others, we have been trained to think of those thoughts as warnings of impending danger, pain, and suffering. We think of them as some big adversary lying in wait for us, which could destroy all hope of having access to the epic life we dream of living.

But as we pull back the curtain, don't we start to realize that *fear lives in the very comfort zone that we are so afraid of leaving? Are we mistaking the "comfort zone" for the "familiar zone"?*

That's a question that may take a moment to digest. So today, begin the recalibration by asking yourself if the things you fear are truly sources of danger. What are you choosing to focus on, and what are you making that focus mean? What story are you allowing your imagination to create? What version of your life story are you agreeing to tolerate? The clue is in the language within your story. How are you currently describing that epic story of the hero/shero we know as YOU?

Unless you find yourself having jumped out of a plane without a parachute, I will encourage you to challenge yourself to take a second look at what is just a fear "story" and what is real danger. Embrace the unfamiliar and make it your new familiar. Seek new experiences. Take a different route to your regular destination, try a thrilling activity like ziplining, or try venturing out to a transformational event to bust through fears and self-doubt.

During our Live Your Destiny Breakthrough Experience, the powerhouse women at the event face a challenge that their minds beg them not to attempt (if you wish to know what it is…you will have to come and find out for yourself! (wink!)) Trust me, they are terrified because every cell in their body is telling them that they are facing real danger. The freedom from their mind's reign of terror comes when they overrule this fear and execute the challenge despite the emotions they are feeling. From that moment forward, they step out into the world as a version of themselves that many had spent an entire lifetime searching for.

Because here's the secret: when you conquer activities that your mind initially deems impossible, you build trust in yourself. It doesn't have to be a spectacular feat. It can be as simple as making a call you have been afraid to make. This newfound self-trust allows you to tackle other challenges with greater confidence. By deliberately straying from routine and embracing the unfamiliar, you open yourself to endless possibilities.

Remember, every achievement starts with a step outside your familiar zone. After all, what you are seeking is not currently part of your *familiar experience,* is it? And honestly, how comfortable have you really been feeling in your "comfort zone"?

Yes, maybe that story that feels like fear has just been a story of new familiarity begging to be explored.

So, today's mission is to push yourself beyond the place where your beliefs have been stopping you. Pull back the curtain on those out-of-date fears and create a new destiny where possibility is everywhere. Epic often arrives disguised as the impossible – and as the "scary"!

TODAY'S ACTION STEPS:

- *Write 3-7 things you know you fear. (+2 Gold Stars)*
- *Rank them on a scale of 1-10, measuring how much fear you feel when you think about them. Now, rank each of them relative to how much of a "clear and present danger" they actually create. Are they actually on par with the danger of falling out of a plane with no parachute or being trapped in a burning building? (+3 Gold Stars)*
- *Bonus points if you can now begin exploring how you might start telling a new story that focuses on triumph versus tragedy around each fear. What can you come up with? (+3 Gold Stars) Booyah!*

TOTAL POSSIBLE STARS FROM TODAY: 8 STARS

Day 83 – IMAGINATION: Fear Loves Confusion

When we feel fear, our instinct tends to be to go, go, go! You may have heard the acronym for fear: "Forget Everything And Run"! (Tony Robbins says it a wee bit differently, and you can "imagine" what his version is…)

But running to "take action" before you have a clear plan for that action and a clear understanding of why you are choosing to take that action can lead to chaos or worse. However, there are also times when the fear is so intense that the "action" you choose to take is "no action."

Is that necessarily the "safer option?"

Confusion can be a crippling force that breeds fear and keeps us from taking action – or causes us to act impulsively. When we're uncertain about our direction and purpose, fear can paralyze or sabotage us very, very quickly. The key to breaking free from this cycle is understanding where we are and who we are.

The path forward becomes more apparent when we gain clarity about our objectives and values. Understanding ourselves and our passions enables us to make decisions aligned with our authentic selves. From this place of clarity, the next steps become obvious.

So, how do we become crystal clear?

I'll share this with you: before I work on systems or strategies with any of my clients, I insist we hit the pause button to allow time for the critical "identification" piece. We need to know not only "where they are" and the circumstances they find themselves in. We need to ensure we can clearly identify "who" they are right now.

Let's face it. It's not uncommon to get really excited about something at one time in your life, only to discover that after you've done it for a while, continuing to do it might feel like torture. That's because you are constantly evolving.

It's also not unusual to have other people tell us what we "should be" doing. It's true that sometimes others can see things in us that we don't see, but if that "someone" is not an expert, that observation often comes tainted with their fears and biases.

Before my high achievers are given the green light to decide that next big step, we make sure that they see themselves as they truly are – right here, right now… yes, today!

We look at everything from their passions to their "must-haves." Would you believe that when we're examining their passions and skills, even my top leaders often identify less than ten? With a deeper guided dive, that number usually expands to at least twenty, if not 30.

So, super important is to remember that clarity is your power. *Clarity is one of the antidotes to fear.*

As you embark on your next journey and before you make your next big decision, remember to ask yourself that super important question: ***not just "how" but "who."*** Who are you *really*? Have you changed? How have you grown? Can you acknowledge your growing strengths, and can you make peace (versus criticize) the aspects of you that are not in your genius zone?

Now, ask yourself who you need to be to achieve your dreams. Who can support you on this path? Remember, epic achievements are rarely solo endeavors. Surround yourself with a supportive team. Get clear and draw strength from each one of the Epic 3 Masteries (Focus, Language, and the Power of Imagination).

You can eliminate confusion and fear by getting clear on your path and being true to yourself. With a focused vision, you'll be empowered to take bold and purposeful actions on your way to that most epic, most unstoppable – and fearless – version of the Future YOU!

Today, take time to begin strategizing about the path ahead by first **writing down your passions, skills, experiences, must-haves, and "nice ifs."** Get really familiar with the feeling of seeing your EPIC WHO from the *perspective of your strengths*. Be willing to embrace all that you already *do* bring to the table. Commit to looking at this more empowered version of yourself at least once daily for 30 days. Stay true to this practice, and you will see that those "intimidating things" are not so far out of reach after all!

TODAY'S ACTION STEPS:

- *Make a list of your passions, skills, experiences, must-haves, and "nice ifs." Rather than a list, we like to put these visually on a Mindmap. This helps our mind really grasp the immensity of what we already bring to the table. (+4 Gold Stars)*
- *Now go back and see if you can expand that list. If you wrote down five things you're passionate about, can you expand it to 15? Can you include concepts you're passionate about (honesty, innovation, personal growth, lifting up others who cannot help themselves, etc.)? How about things that you love doing but you haven't done since you were a child? Things that you still want to have the chance to do? Try to hit at least 15 items in each category. (+2 Gold Stars)*
- *Bonus points if you read your finished map or list it aloud as if it's a story... I'm [Your Name}, and this is my Epic You Story. Do this for 30 days, and it will start rewiring how you see yourself. (+2 Gold Stars) Booyah!*

TOTAL POSSIBLE STARS FROM TODAY: 8 STARS

Day 84 – IMAGINATION: The De-Stuckifier – Conquering Fear with Confident Action

As we continue our mission of busting through our fears, you probably notice one dominant theme: *Fear is the enemy of empowered clarity.* Because clarity leads to confidence. Therefore, one critical objective of the envisioning process is clarity. For you, that might mean deciding what to do next. "Should I or shouldn't I?" "Door #1 or Door #2?" Life is filled with important choices. So how do you know what to choose?

Have you ever finished your "pros and cons" list feeling even more torn and confused than before you started? Believe it or not, one of the emotions that often hides in the margins of your pros and cons list is fear.

Let's face it: fear can convince us that standing still is the safest option. It tells us to wait, to be cautious, and to avoid taking decisive action. But here's the truth: **There is no "standing still" in life. Every choice, whether taking action or not, is an action.**

The challenge lies in assessing how our decisions will impact our lives. Fear often clouds our judgment, making the future seem unpredictable and unfamiliar. We must develop *"intu-ention" – the synergy between intuition and focused intention to overcome this.* That can assist us in clearly envisioning who we want to be, what we want to achieve, and how we want to impact the world. With a strong, clear vision of the future, we gain the confidence to recognize the best path forward as we take appropriate action.

Transformation happens when we shift from the "nowhere" to the "now here." It doesn't always require complex efforts; it demands confidence.

Remember: Confidence doesn't mean having all the answers; it means declaring yourself as the captain of your ship, steering towards a clear, purposeful destination. Of course, being ready to iterate as needed.

To build confidence and bust through the fear that shows up as indecisiveness, here are four incredibly revealing questions you should immediately ask yourself when feeling torn. These are part of my *De-Stuckifier Formula*, which is the clarifying process that my clients swear by when they have an important decision to make:

- How will taking this step positively impact my life/outcome?
- How will not taking this step positively impact my life/outcome?
- How will taking this step negatively impact my life/outcome?
- How will not taking this step negatively impact my life/outcome?

Whenever possible, literally write your responses on a piece of paper. Now for the "epically ninja" part:

Once you've written all your responses in each column, grab four colored markers. I use green, purple, red and black. Now, go back and revisit each column. For the first two columns, circle the answers based on two criteria *without overanalyzing*:

- Circle a response in green if this is a strong positive. If this would be an outcome that would really feel great to you and/or if you know it's important *to you.*
- Circle a response in purple if this benefit is moderately positive or if you're not sure you can count on this being an actual outcome. It also gets a purple if you could probably figure out how to get the same outcome from the action in column one.

Now go to your last two columns, the negative impacts, and do the same thing with the red and black markers:

- Circle a response in red if it's a strong negative. Even if you think that it's "silly" for this to feel like a strong negative, circle it. Don't forget about the negatives that are inner

game negatives, such as "I'll feel like I took the easy way out" or "I'll face a lot more stress."
- Circle a response in black if it feels only moderately negative or you're unsure if this outcome would occur. Also, circle a response in black if you can adjust to overcome this negative, if you might still see this outcome from the other action, and/or if you can figure out a workaround for this issue.

Remember to choose colors based on your first reaction. Don't justify or, again, overanalyze.

Once you've finished the circling process, assess the circles and let them guide you. Typically, they point very clearly toward an action – even if the revelation is "Oh wow! I can actually have BOTH!"

With newfound confidence, acknowledge fear's caution, release it, and take control. Fear becomes a positive tool when it inspires positive action.

Use the De-Stuckifier as your ally, bolstering your confidence to face the unknown. Now you have identified your next finish line, it's time to step powerfully into action, knowing you are the captain of your destiny.

REMEMBER: You can't miss the boat because you ARE the boat. So, set your course and sail, Captain!

Today, address your fears and commit to taking inspired action. Envision and embrace the epic journey ahead. Make this day the day you conquer fear with confident action and propel yourself towards infinite possibility.

TODAY'S ACTION STEPS:

- *Is there a decision you are trying to make or a fork in the road leaving you stuck? Maybe you are trying to decide between two opportunities. Maybe you're wondering if it's time to make a change. Maybe you're simply wondering if I should do this first or that first? Pick a target and run it through the first part of the De-Stuckifier. Create your four columns and then "brain dump" your responses without pausing to weigh them or pass judgment. (+4 Gold Stars)*
- *Now go back into each column and finish your De-Stuckifier by using the markers like I described above. Don't overthink it. Just make the decision: is this positive a green or a purple? Is this negative a red or a black? Don't choose the "right" answer. Qualify it by how important it feels to YOU. (+3 Gold Stars)*
- *Bonus points if you take a look at your completed project. What is it telling you and what will you do next based on this new information? Great! Now go do it! (+3 Gold Stars) Booyah!*

TOTAL POSSIBLE STARS FROM TODAY: 10 STARS

Day 85 – IMAGINATION: Commit and Refuse to Renegotiate

We've "ninja-ed" our way to new processes that amplify our confidence and clarity. We know how to make clear decisions. But how many of you have decided to do something differently – only to find yourself falling back into old habits just days later? Maybe you talk yourself out of going to the gym because it's rainy outside, and "I don't feel like it?" Maybe you lose steam applying for a new job because "there's so much housework to be done."

Before you know it, you've paid hundreds of dollars for a gym membership you never use. The house is clean, but you're facing year 5 of a job you started hating back in year 2.

If you're blushing right now, don't beat yourself up too badly because I always see this! (And dare I confess to having done this!) Client after client will tell me that they tend to procrastinate or give up when they've just started.

This is another sign that you're working with a poor imagination, not simply a self-discipline muscle that has gone MIA when needed. Being able to stick to your commitments is an essential ingredient in creating results that feel epic. However, in all fairness, this is not just a switch that you can flip. It requires repetition and, yes, patience.

There *is* a learning curve – or let's call it a "growing curve." When you have spent most of your life allowing your emotions and "autopilot patterns" to rule supreme, it doesn't change in a day, a week, or even a month. Yet you *are beginning to* build new inner game muscles and see evidence of change.

You are coming from a place where you're not even aware the reason that "I'm not good at following through with what I start" is because you're allowing your feelings to dominate and rule. This is called the place of "unconscious incompetence."

As you become aware that you need to learn to override your emotions, you'll start working on strategies for building your commitment skills. Initially, you'll probably allow your emotions to sneak in and derail you, but at least now you'll see that you are allowing this, and you'll keep trying. This is called being "consciously incompetent". In other words, you know you have some changes and improvements to make.

This can be the toughest part of the quest because your mind will tell you you're not up to this task. Some people quit here, but not you, Epic Chicks and Gents. You've come this far, so you WILL keep going.

When you persist in making changes, you'll start to catch yourself just before your "feelings" sink the ship. If it's pouring rain outside, you pull up a high-intensity training on YouTube instead of curling up with Netflix. The commitment was about getting movement, not where or how you got that movement. You start finding more and more ways to get creative and stick to your commitments. This phase is called being "consciously competent." You're improving, but it definitely takes focus and effort.

Eventually, getting exercise and movement becomes second nature to you. Your emotions no longer override those good intentions, and you have a new routine you can be proud of. People start noticing and saying, "How did you do it?" This is when you become "unconsciously competent." You do these great habits without putting much thought into them.

So here's the Epic Ninja Tip in all of this: *to help you break through the resistance phase and get to those new routines and habits, tap into the power of your imagination.*

Here's what I mean. Let's break this down:

1. Why do we not follow through? Because we believe that we don't *feel* like doing it. Therefore, if we can start to *feel like doing it,* won't that inspire us to do it?
So, how do we start *feeling like doing it?*
2. We tap into our new mastery of The Epic 3…First, we shift our focus to *imagining/ envisioning the presence of what we do want.* That means we create a powerful story that starts to trigger the *feelings* we ultimately want. This becomes the set point for our inner game thermostat. As we move forward, I'll teach you the envisioning technique we use here at G.R.I.T. Mindset Academy.
3. We start associating *those* feelings with who we are – and, therefore, with the type of actions that we do and do not take. Ex: the person who truly has given up drinking doesn't say, "I'm not drinking today." They say, "I don't drink."
4. We reinforce our *imagination* and "which we now see ourselves as being" with language that supports that – maybe even a victory song that makes us feel as if we already *have that triumph, that we ARE this version of ourselves – we ARE the victor, do-er of inspired action.*
5. Now that we have become the sovereign of our focus, our language, and our imagination, we now DO what our feelings used to prevent us from doing. *And when our actions change, so do our results.*

What you can envision, you can (and will) achieve.

Commitment is a powerful force on your journey to epic-ness. Once you decide on your next step, commit to it fully. Refuse to give yourself an "out" or renegotiate your goals. Fear and self-doubt can easily creep in when you allow room for doubt.

Today, stay dedicated to your path and be persistent, even when faced with challenges. Realize that the road to success is rarely a straight line; it's filled with twists and turns. Remember the "1% to Victory" rule! If something isn't working, seek guidance, get creative, and adjust your approach, but don't give up on your dreams or your promises to yourself.

Imperfect action will take you further than perfect contemplation. Don't wait for the perfect moment; seize the opportunities that present themselves. Commit to your objectives and take consistent steps toward them. Your unwavering commitment will propel you to achieve things others believe impossible.

BE the sovereign of your inner game and watch this new empowered version of you transform your dreams into your "non-negotiable" reality. Who's ready to "BOOYAH"??

TODAY'S ACTION STEPS:

- *Identify one thing you know would significantly impact your results if you can consistently do it. Is there a new habit or approach that you've been putting off? Is there a change or a perspective that would create an important shift for you? (+2 Gold Stars)*
- *Great! Now, take a moment (write it down if you can) to imagine what it would feel like to have this already embedded into your lifestyle. How would that look? How would you feel? What would others say and notice about you? (+3 Gold Stars)*
- *Bonus points if you now create a commitment plan. What agreement with yourself can you make during those times when you don't feel like following through? Will you agree to at least do it for 10 minutes? If you committed to going to the gym and worked late, can you agree to eat a little lighter and hop on your bike at home? Maybe even get your heart rate up by dancing like a silly fool or find a high-intensity workout on YouTube? Can you bolster your commitment using vision board-type photos, inspiring Post-It note messages, or even just hanging up your skinny jeans as an incentive to keep going? Today is all about imagining your way to the commitment that leads to success! (+3 Gold Stars) Booyah!*

TOTAL POSSIBLE STARS FROM TODAY: 8 STARS

Day 86 – IMAGINATION: The 1% Consistency: Embracing the Journey of Epic

Today, we're less than 16 days away from the 100 Days of Epic finish line! Things are getting real. Your fear is on the run. Your commitment is on the rise, so let's be honest – when you think of that big epic future, does it sometimes feel like you're trying to imagine how to get to the top of Mount Everest in a single bound? Before you know it, there are your buddies Fear and Doubt hopping into your backpack.

If you're like most of us, you just got busted!

From the perspective of standing there at the bottom of the mountain, we just can't imagine that there can be an easy path. Ironically, our modern obsession with seeking the easiest path has led us to introduce unnecessary difficulty into our lives. We've got our perception of what's "easy" all tangled and in many cases, just plain wrong.

One crucial lesson I've learned from the boulder that unexpectedly crashed into our lives is that epicness is not born from ease. Instead, it flourishes in the realm of 1% consistency. Remember the 1% target? Today, we show you how it can turbo-charge your results when you apply the same rule to consistency!

But wait? Am I implying that you only need to be consistent 1% of the time? Wink! Not by a long shot. What I mean is that you don't have to consistently strive to maintain peak performance. That will eventually burn you out, and it's not sustainable.

Optimal performance is different from peak performance, and it's far more strategic. It leans into the rule that strategic action applied consistently will give you far better results than spurts of peak performance that you can't sustain.

I remember a particularly challenging climb up the Canadian Rockies that I did when I was not quite 20 years old. Carrying a heavy 70-pound backpack through steep inclines for hours was physically and mentally demanding. Many times, my mind protested, complaining about the fatigue, the seemingly endless journey, and the unhappiness of it all. In those moments, I had to force myself to focus on the next step, then one step more, and another. My only solace could be found in the beauty of the path, the trees, and the surrounding forest.

Eventually, the moment arrived when we emerged above the tree line. It seemed to come out of nowhere. One moment, we were surrounded by trees. Two steps later, we were on top of the world. As I looked around, I saw that we were so high up! The view was simply breathtaking! I marveled at how far we had come, even though throughout the climb, my mind had doubted that we were making "any" progress.

As you pursue whatever epic things you decide to pursue today, as you begin to allow yourself to envision, resist the urge to feel impatient. Avoid the "this won't be enough-ness" syndrome. Gently redirect your thoughts toward the next tiny step – 1% of the effort. Think strategic versus speed or volume. Embrace the concept of consistency and repeat it diligently. Like the slow and steady climb up the mountains, the commitment to those incremental steps leads us to the extraordinary.

Yes. On this journey, you will encounter boulders – obstacles that may seem insurmountable. But remember, our boulder experience taught me a valuable truth: these boulders do not always show up to break us; they break the barriers holding us back.

So, keep walking, keep stepping, and trust that the tree line with its awe-inspiring view might be just around the corner. As you persistently move forward, you'll discover that epicness is not found at the end of an effortless road but in the persistence of the human spirit.

In pursuing your unique version of epicness, find solace in the beauty of the journey, even when it feels tough. Embrace the growth and transformation that arise from consistently taking one step at a time. Whether you're taking those steps in your beat-up Nikes, your ballet shoes, flip-flops, or your fanciest stiletto heels (or dress shoes, gents…), you're still stepping.

Remember, it's not about rushing to the summit but cherishing each moment along the ascent.

As you navigate the obstacles that cross your path, know that these too, have a purpose. Allow them to clear the way for your true potential to shine. You are capable of so much more than you can imagine. Stay resilient, maintain your 1% consistency, and unlock the panoramic vistas that await you at the summit of your epic life.

Today, let go of the allure of ease and embrace the power of persistence. Envision the glory of this journey, knowing that your consistent strategic effort will lead you to extraordinary heights. The view from above the tree line will be well worth it, and your epic story will be one of inspiration and triumph.

Keep stepping, and let your epic journey unfold before you.

TODAY'S ACTION STEPS:

- *Is there an area of your life that hasn't progressed "fast enough"? Write down a list of 3-5 small strategic moves that you can make that can move you 1% closer to the (next) finish line. (+3 Gold Stars)*
- *Take action on these strategic moves. Make completing them a priority today. (+3 Gold Stars)*
- *Bonus points if you now assess: what worked? What didn't work? Where do I now iterate? Should I hold the course or adjust? Do I need some sort of help or guidance? (Remember, sometimes we don't know what we don't know, and trying to figure it out on our own by trial and error can be more costly in both time and money than finding a mentor or coach to point us toward the North Star – versus just another shiny object! Now act accordingly. (+3 Gold Stars) Booyah!*

TOTAL POSSIBLE STARS FROM TODAY: 9 STARS

Day 87 – IMAGINATION: Fear has a Physiology, So Breathe

We've talked a lot about the connection between your fears and your inner game, but isn't it true that when you are worrying or afraid, your entire body joins the party? Ever felt like you were so afraid that you could barely breathe?

That's not uncommon because our bodies and minds are very, VERY connected. That is why our **"dis-ease"** can often ultimately reflect itself in tangible disease. Prolonged negative stress is proven to be dangerous for our bodies.

So yes, fear can feel overwhelming, but understanding its physiology can be a game-changer. Studies show that fear and exhilaration share similar physical symptoms. The crucial difference lies in how we interpret these feelings and, according to multiple studies, whether we are remembering to breathe.

When we have labeled certain physiological sensations as symptoms of fear, we hold our breath. We tell ourselves that we're feeling exhilaration, and we breathe. So what does that tell you?

When you're feeling fear creeping in, *first take a moment to breathe*. Breathing helps regulate your nervous system and keeps you centered. Next, before you label what you're feeling as fear, *try asking yourself this question: "What if I'm mistaken? What if what I'm experiencing right now is the rush of exhilaration?"*

Play with that possibility. Embrace the excitement and anticipation of stepping out of your comfort zone. When you've done that, maybe take it even one step further… Ask yourself *how you would be feeling if you actually loved these kinds of experiences.* Could you have defined yourself all wrong, and could you be someone who finds these moments exciting and stimulating? Who would you show up being?

Maybe instead of slumping over and acting as if you're trying to disappear, you stand up taller. You throw your shoulders back. You stare at this moment eye to eye and feel a surge of anticipation and excitement. Who knows? You might even show up at that moment "owning your stage" – maybe a bit like Mick Jagger!

It's no secret that Mick Jagger adores the physical symptoms he claims to experience while waiting to go on stage. Hearing the roar of the crowd, and feeling the energy beyond the lights, Mick describes the feeling as orgasmic. He loves feeling his sweaty palms and the pounding of his heart as every fiber in his body focuses adrenalin on delivering a performance that will thrill the crowd. He literally misses it when he's not on tour.

Barbara Streisand, on the other hand, also experiences these same symptoms. However, throughout her entire career, her mind has interpreted this feeling as sheer terror.

These two epic performers experienced the same physical sensations. The only difference was their interpretation of what these sensations meant. These interpretations were just stories in their imagination. For Barbara, her imagination fed her a story that represented danger. For Mick, his imagination created a story that indicated inevitable pleasure.

You can see how our stories even impact our physical experiences. Not to mention our actions, which then impact our outcome. Mick Jagger continues to be known for his iconic stage performances. Barbara Streisand turned her attention away from live performances. She has made millions by writing over 100 songs and directing more than five movies.

By understanding the physiology of fear and realizing that your imagination's specific stories often trigger your physiology, you have the potential to regain your sovereignty over your emotions. Can you explore the possibility of reframing these feelings as exhilaration? Can you rewire your brain to respond differently to situations that in the past you found to be challenging?

Your mission today is to realize that *your imagination will create stories*. It *is* creating stories – and you can impact them by changing your physiology and reframing the meaning you give to these stories.

Breathe, reframe, and embrace the excitement of pushing beyond your limits. Your imagination is an "opportunity-creating" machine, so start guiding it!

TODAY'S ACTION STEPS:

- *What's something new that you can explore to take yourself more frequently into a state of relaxation and flow? Can you commit to trying out a yoga class or even add meditation into your morning or bedtime routine? Meditation has been an invaluable part of both Schuyler's and my routine. If you want to check out some of our favorite ones, we've linked them here: https://bit.ly/EpicMeditations (+2 Gold Stars)*
- *Now commit to stepping out into the world more aware of your physiology. When you walk into your next important meeting, are your shoulders back with your back straight? Are you making solid eye contact? Are you breathing deeply and even smiling? Stay aware of your physiology today and strive to keep up-leveling your game! (+3 Gold Stars)*
- *Bonus points if you plan for those moments when fear grips you. Can you plan to pause and assess: is this real danger? Is this unfamiliarity? Can I find a way to shift this and turn it into exhilaration? Create your plan now and set the intention to apply it the next time that you feel fear starting to creep in. (+3 Gold Stars) Booyah!*

TOTAL POSSIBLE STARS FROM TODAY: 8 STARS

Day 88 – IMAGINATION: Fear as Your Superpower: Embracing Fear to Crush the Impossible

If Fear isn't inevitable, if it's just a story that is told in an attempt to protect you, is it possible to use all of that Fear energy as your newly discovered superpower? Guess what?

The answer is YES! Fear can be your secret in the sauce, the stuff that helps you achieve incredible things and live a life you absolutely adore. I say this from experience because there have been many times in my life when I felt like the circumstances were overwhelming me with terror!

I never expected to discover that the bubbling energy beneath that emotion can be harnessed and guided to a place where it stops working against you and begins working *for you!*

So, let's dive into the power of fear as we uncover the secret to grit and resilience that makes us shine at our very best.

As I have talked about, I've lived years as a single mom and faced financial terror many, many times. However, the scariest time was when Schuyler's life seemed destined to end after being crushed by that boulder.

I still remember when the doctors walked into the ICU room to discuss Schuyler's injuries. They looked pale and stressed. They wouldn't even make eye contact, and I later learned that even for the most seasoned surgeons on the team, Schuy's injuries were perhaps the worst they had ever seen. They began listing all the risks, but I knew that the game I was playing wasn't going to be made stronger by obsessing over all the things that could go wrong.

Instead, I stopped them. I turned the conversation to my confidence in their brilliance.

"You are the best of the best. This hospital is one of the best in the world for treating this level of trauma. The medical field can achieve miracles, so there is no place that I would rather my daughter be right now and no other doctors that I would rather be helping her. My daughter will be fine – whatever that new fine is destined to be. We just have to get her there."

The room was silent for a moment as the doctors looked at me.

But in the following seconds, it was almost as if you could see these doctors stand taller. You could see the color return to their faces. It was almost as if the grip of fear and uncertainty was slipping off them.

You know the end of the story – or at least the end of that part of the story.

Those same doctors went on to achieve the "impossible." Schuyler survived injuries that medical precedent dating back thousands of years said would be unsurvivable. Miracles do happen, my dear chicks and gents. If you need a miracle at this moment, maybe that's why you're reading this very chapter today…?

Like Mike Tyson's manager Cus D'Amato, said, *fear is an energy*. Instead of allowing it to control us, *we can use that energy to fuel our drive*. Plato also said ages ago that courage means knowing what to fear. Armed with that wisdom, we can totally change the game on fear when it tries to entrap us.

So, here's the deal when fear creeps in: take a deep breath and use your focus, language, and imagination to get back in the zone. Think about who you know yourself to be, and remember your grit and resilience.

Be the coach firing up the team in the locker room halfway through the Super Bowl. Know that you ARE the winning team. This fear is part of the plan for your destiny. Your willingness to focus on your wins versus those passing defeats will allow you to overcome the fleeting "injuries" and achieve those big dreams.

This is your moment to BE the visionary. See beyond the hurdles and picture victory in your mind. Don't get me wrong; it doesn't mean there won't be moments when you think it would be easier just to throw in the towel; it's about staying positive and seeing those challenges as stepping stones to something even more epic.

Being resilient doesn't mean avoiding fear, and it doesn't mean that you won't encounter problems—it means using them to boost your progress. Like the players who hear the coach's words during halftime, we can use fear's energy to propel us forward.

So, get ready to rock fear as your superpower. Let it be your opponent that drives you and your team to greatness. You've got what it takes to achieve mind-blowing things. Commit to making fear your superpower – not your kryptonite.

Today, when fear comes knocking, don't run and hide. Face it head-on, channel its energy, and turn it into your secret weapon. Take that next step, crush the impossible, and turn obstacles into opportunities. With fear fueling your superpower, you'll discover a whole new level of strength and resilience, unlocking incredible possibilities beyond your wildest dreams.

Embrace the fear, rock it, and watch yourself soar! Your mission today? Show the world the champion you are capable of showing up BE-ing!

TODAY'S ACTION STEPS:

- *Go back to the fears you listed earlier. Imagine what it would look like if you could mold that energy into your driving force, just like one of the superheroes or lightsabers. (+2 Gold Stars)*
- *Now, write down a version of your new story around that fear. What would it look like if you could harness that fear into an energy that allowed you to do things that previously seemed unimaginable? Envision yourself feeling those physiological sensations, morphing into an energy and then using them to catapult you forward. (+3 Gold Stars)*
- *Bonus points if you create a physical action that you will associate with morphing your fear. Think of the Hulk and his pose as his mightiness transformed his body. Think of the Power Rangers – even Batman or Superwoman. What will be the Power Pose that reminds you of your potential? Practice it. See it in the mirror. Walk around your room feeling it. Recite to yourself, "When I strike this pose, Fear becomes my energy. I am a force to be reckoned with!" And the next time the sensation of fear starts to brew, go to your pose and master the power of your imagination! (+3 Gold Stars) Booyah!*

TOTAL POSSIBLE STARS FROM TODAY: 8 STARS

Day 89 – IMAGINATION: Inside Your Fears is a Dream Waiting to Make Itself Heard…

If boulders are inevitable, is fear inevitable as well? Sometimes, it certainly can feel that way. No matter how hard we try to avoid it, there are times when each of us will face times that feel crushing. And yes, that dreaded emotion: fear. We've talked a lot about Fear over the past few days, so hopefully, you're starting to relax into the realization that Fear *IS just a story.*

Fortunately, you are the author of this story – when you choose to be.

Life's inner weather can be unpredictable, ranging from sunny beach days to full-fledged tropical storms. When faced with challenging times, the temptation is to seek constant sunshine. Yet, we must remember that this glorious little planet would turn into a dry and desolate place without rain.

Years ago, as I woke up to face another cloudy and stressful morning, an unexpected thought popped into my head: "Inside your fears is a dream waiting to make itself heard." This tiny seed of epic hope sprouted in the midst of my dark thoughts, bringing a glimmer of sunshine to my inner world.

As I pondered this new perspective, I realized that Fear could hide the dreams I yearned to pursue, believing it was somehow protecting me. Instead of succumbing to that perfect storm of terrifying thoughts, I decided to embrace this belief as a new reality. I gingerly exercised my mind so that my thoughts focused on possibilities rather than despair. I used the adrenaline within the fear to hone my focus and amplify my clarity. Every molecule in my body seemed focused not only on the game but on playing the game *to win*. I lifted these thoughts like weights in that mental gym. I began to feel the tingles of optimism.

Could fear morph into a type of superpower?

This train of thought led me to remember the teachings of Abraham Hicks, which emphasize the value of keeping thoughts around emotionally difficult topics as "general" as possible. Sometimes, we just have to leave the "how" and "when" to the universe. I coaxed myself to focus solely on what felt good, what was already going well, and what I loved doing, even when the fear in my mind was screaming at its loudest.

I forced my train of thought to jump to the inspirational stories of successful individuals who overcame their challenges. Slowly but surely, my energy/ frequency shifted, and I began to feel ready to embrace the day with renewed hope and vision.

Then, a "cool, weird" thing happened. My phone rang, and a legal document I feared would take months to resolve was unexpectedly approved in just two weeks. Clients sent payments, and new opportunities emerged. The rain of fear had created new blooms of possibility.

Courage played a key role in this transformation—the courage to face the "flying monkeys" and discover the dream hidden within the fears. You see, when we finally give ourselves permission to bravely step forward, despite uncertainties, we allow our dreams to take flight and our fears to infuse those dreams with turbo-charged energy.

I may not have a single dream to end all dreams; they evolve with my inner ebb and flow. But through the dance with fear, I discovered renewed focus and hope. Perhaps courage lies in embracing the storms and the sunny days, knowing that inside our fears, a dream is waiting to bloom.

Today, your mission is to realize that fear is just one version of the imagination's story. If thinking about something specific feels scary or painful, try finding a more general thought that focuses on possibilities versus the impossible.

Look for stories of others who have faced similar challenges and emerged as bigger, bolder versions of themselves. Refuse to get sucked in by stories of defeat. Instead, give your attention to stories where tragedy transformed into triumph.

Today, find your moments of bliss and courage even as you navigate the ever-changing weather of life. Realize that our minds are destined to create stories, so when your mind creates a story based on fear, KNOW that maybe, just maybe, inside your fears is a dream waiting to make itself heard…

What sort of brilliant dreams will you, as your mind's sovereign, lovingly inspire that beautiful mind of yours to now create?

TODAY'S ACTION STEPS:

- *Find three stories of how other people achieved incredible things even when it required great courage. As you read or listen to these stories, acknowledge that because fear is just an energy and a call to prepare, you CAN take action beyond the fear. YOU are the master of the stories of the imagination. (+2 Gold Stars)*
- *Go back to some of those dreams or ideas you have put off because you feared you did not have all the answers. Seeing now that others who have faced fear also did not have all the answers – and yet the outcome they achieved was incredible. Make a note of what they had (if anything) that you don't have. Did they have mentors? Better resources? Also, make a note of what they did have that you do have. Resilience? Grit? Stubbornness? Wink! (+3 Gold Stars)*
- *Bonus points if you create a plan to take a look at some of those big aspirations. Imagine yourself succeeding, thriving, celebrating. What do you need to start being*

and doing to start transforming those dreams into your destiny? Start doing that today! (+3 Gold Stars) Booyah!

TOTAL POSSIBLE STARS FROM TODAY: 8 STARS

Day 90 – IMAGINATION: Embracing the Ordinary – Unleashing the Extraordinary

We're getting closer and closer to untangling the fears that have been holding you back from crafting your epic destiny. You've begun to be more deliberately aware of your focus. You've started listening to the words you've been choosing. We're now focusing on replacing some of those old stubborn fears with new, more empowering expectations. As we look beyond our old patterns, here's the question: Can something as simple as replacing old fears with the ability to envision new possibilities transform an "ordinary life" into one that feels EPIC?

What is "epic" anyway? The dictionary defines it as "extending beyond the usual or ordinary, especially in size or scope." Is there a part of you that would *love* to take your last breath knowing that you had lived a life that felt extraordinary?

This doesn't mean that you have to be rappelling down waterfalls or jumping out of planes (although for you, that might be your idea of great adventure–wink!). Sometimes, extending beyond the "ordinary" might mean daring to learn a new skill, shifting to a new career, or even making a phone call that has seemed terrifying. Or simply seeing yourself in a light you never allowed yourself to see…

In our Society of Epic Chicks, we look at "unleashing our E.P.I.C." as this: **the call to ignite your unique blend of empowerment, passion, inspiration, and confidence**. This we know – Life is filled with opportunities to create moments that feel extraordinary and meaningful *to you* – *AND AT THE END OF THE DAY, IT'S ONLY YOUR OPINION THAT MATTERS, isn't it?*

So, how do we align our focus, narrative, and imagination in a way that fastlanes us toward a truly epic life regardless of our circumstances? One of the most important skills is learning to *envision – the art of actively using your mind to deliberately imagine specific future possibilities.*

We'll get into the specific technique tomorrow. For now, simply know that envisioning involves deliberately projecting your focus to where you guide it to go. Rather than emptying your mind as you might do in meditation, you focus on cutting through the noise within your mind and creating a clear set point. As I mentioned earlier, compare it to resetting the thermostat of your mind.

How do we determine what that next set point will be? We have to get clarity on two things: who we will now allow ourselves to *be,* and how will we know when we've crossed our next "finish line"? What does epic look like *to you?*

Just a few months ago, I sat in a cozy office in an Orlando Air Bnb. I reflected on what makes life feel epic to me. When I thought about it, I realized that it's not just those miraculous moments when everything comes together "perfectly," but the collection of ordinary moments that hold true magic *thanks to learning how to maintain a focused state of flow and alignment.*

As a coach, the impact that this approach has had on my clients' personal and professional lives is why I do what I do. Remembering the fear and uncertainty that once plagued me, I now cherish the journey that led me to this point, where my decades of experience can benefit those I serve.

But can the way that we view ourselves truly transform the way that we envision our future unfolding?

Absolutely, but sometimes you do need someone or something to be the catalyst to help you shift the way that you see yourself. In our case, it truly was that boulder that amplified my own personal transformation. I hope that most of you won't need a literal boulder to break through some of the things you have been allowing to hold you back.

Recently, a highly accomplished C-suite client shared her transformation with me, expressing gratitude for having been the catalyst in her own career. The wisdom and understanding I was able to provide at a time in her life when things felt overwhelming and chaotic allowed her to gain the courage not only to find a new job that she loves but also to embrace that she is worthy of these great things.

Those heartfelt moments are profound. They validate not only the choices I made to pursue this path but that sometimes "the epic that we seek" arrives disguised, looking like the impossible. Life's twists and turns have taught me that success isn't in spite of challenges but *thanks to the bolder version of ourselves that these boulders inspire us to become.*

When we least expect it, these same boulders often become footholds to exquisite new heights. *But you must develop the muscle to envision beyond the moments of chaos and disruption. That's without a doubt THE KEY!*

Here's what I've seen– whether in our personal or professional lives, true leadership and confidence don't demand perfection; they thrive in the presence of boulders. When we learn that our superpowers can exist even amid our fears, we can then dare to commit to becoming the most epic version of ourselves every day, daring to dream even bigger.

It all begins with being willing to imagine yourself as the person you aspire to be.

Today, I would encourage you to go out into the day ready to look for clues that point to your own "superpowers." Let fear and the desire for growth be simply more tools in your GPS, guiding you to serve, lead, and achieve impact. When we learn that we can trust ourselves and trust the process, we take bolder and more inspired action, even if it starts with a single, tiny step.

Let this day be one of your most EPIC "ordinary" days yet! As the dust from whatever boulder you are now facing clears, what tall buildings can you envision yourself finally ready to leap?

TODAY'S ACTION STEPS:

- *Go out into the world today, living as if today is the one day in your life that will be remembered by generations to come. Look for clues of where your superpowers truly lie. Lean into them and embrace them. Imagine being the biographer who is watching you, writing the story of your life. Who would you like for this person to see you as being? (+2 Gold Stars)*
- *At the end of the day, take a moment to assess. What would the biographer have written? How does this give you clarity around who you now claim your right to show up being? What can you let go of to truly live as the version of yourself that you desire to be? What can you now embrace? (+2 Gold Stars)*
- *Bonus points if you take a moment to celebrate the transformation that you have ignited in the past 90 days! What is your favorite part of the evolving Epic You? (+4 Gold Stars) Booyah!*

TOTAL POSSIBLE STARS FROM TODAY: 8 STARS

Day 91 – IMAGINATION: The Power of Envision: Igniting Your Epic Future

On the flip side of fear is the power to envision…

Close your eyes for a moment and picture this: You are standing at the edge of a vast horizon, where limitless possibilities await you. As you take a deep breath, you feel the exhilarating energy of your dreams and aspirations coursing through your veins. This is not just any moment of meditation; it's the Art of Envisioning—an intentional, energizing declaration of your destiny.

In the Art of Envisioning, we go beyond calming emotions; we focus our imagination, igniting a powerful and exciting vision of our future selves. This process involves aligning our emotions with the reality we wish to create. It's like having a direct communication channel with that epic version of ourselves—the one that has achieved everything we've ever dreamed of.

I've seen the transformative power of envisioning in my own life and with my clients who are ready to break through stubborn barriers and achieve remarkable things. It is the language of an optimally performing imagination, capable of navigating beyond the boulders of fear and self-doubt that have accumulated over time.

When I gather my Society of Epic Chicks, we always start with envisioning. Our inner game is the foundation of our success, and developing the ability to envision is a game-changer. It becomes an unstoppable set point for the day, propelling us forward with purpose and clarity.

Envisioning is not just a fleeting daydream; it is focused, deliberate imagination. The ignition point recalibrates our trajectory, much like an airplane course-correcting to reach its desired destination.

You don't need to be an expert meditator to tap into the Power of Envision. It's more like a spiritual recalibration—a moment to connect with your higher self, deepest aspirations, and source of strength and elevate your frequency.

As you practice envisioning, you create a sacred space where you visualize, imagine, and, most importantly, feel the future version of yourself—the one beyond your current limitations. This is the Future You with boundless potential and extraordinary accomplishments.

Make the Art of Envision a daily ritual. When you feel your energy waning or negativity taking hold, turn to your visions to uplift and empower you. Harness your imagination deliberately and powerfully, and watch as life seemingly transforms to conform to your visions.

If you are religious, you can integrate this practice into your prayers, using it as an opportunity to align your aspirations with the divine guidance you seek.

Envisioning is your compass, guiding you toward the destination of your dreams. Embrace it as your superpower, your secret sauce to epic success. Take action today and begin your journey into the Art of Envision.

Embrace the limitless possibilities that lie ahead, and let the magic unfold as your visions become reality.

TODAY'S ACTION STEPS:

- *Explore the power of a 5-10 minute "Envision." Remember your "I am" statements? Close your eyes and focus on those statements while playing some soothing or energizing instrumental music in the background. Allow your inner game frequency to rise. Feel the tingle. Move your fingers. Start your engines, THEN GO OUT AND SEIZE YOUR EPIC DAY! (+3 Gold Stars)*
- *Plan how you will stack them onto another morning routine and incorporate a priming Envision into the next 14 days of your morning regimen. (+2 Gold Stars)*
- *Bonus points if you reach out to our team for your complimentary audio of one of our Society of Epic Chicks envisions:* team@gritmindsetacademy.com *(+3 Gold Stars)*
- *EXTRA BONUS: Share your biggest AHA! so far by emailing us at team@gritmindsetacademy.com . Who knows? There might be a special reward in it for you… just saying!!! (+3 Gold Stars) Booyah!*

TOTAL POSSIBLE STARS FROM TODAY: 11 STARS

Day 92 – IMAGINATION: Harnessing the Wings of Your Soulmate

Now that you have been introduced to the actual practice of what I call Envisioning, let's revisit the definition of the word envision. Dictionary.com defines envision as *"to picture mentally, especially some future event or event."*

We want to amplify this action's impact and power by fusing the power of meditation with the momentum of setting intentions. One of the best ways to do this is to frame your envisions around visualizations of the Epic Future You.

You may not be able to easily see yourself breaking through the barriers in your current circumstances, but often, your imagination is more receptive to creating a story of possibility that takes place in the future – especially when you begin to think of yourself in the future as a personality that is independent of the current You.

Approach this as if you are one of the Marvel superheroes. By day, you appear like the "normal" person on the street. That would be the current version of you. However, you also have the special power to transform into a bigger, bolder version of yourself. That would be the Epic Future You. With superheroes, possibilities are limitless, and "reality" often intersects with the miraculous.

With that in mind, consider this: what if the Epic Future You *is your ultimate soulmate*?

Think about it. Even the word hints at the potentially delicious relationship between your brilliant mind and glorious soul – some would call this your heart. When your heart and your mind find alignment, epic things become not only possible but inevitable.

No one knows you like your own soul. No one yearns to love you as much as your own soul. Much of our heartache and pain comes when we deny our heart "permission" to fall in love with who we are, who we are becoming, and with the stories we have been creating all our lives. Our heart craves the opportunity to truly love and appreciate ourselves. When we love who we are, we set the stage for that epic expression of ourselves that we can yet evolve into.

As we go through life, it seems natural to criticize ourselves, and we begin to mistake our jukebox voice for the voice of who we are. When we shift the focus from how we currently see ourselves to envisioning a more exhilarating future version of ourselves, we make it easier to reframe our language and use our imagination as a catalyst for escaping the hamster wheel of negativity.

In fact, here's an **Epic Ninja Tip** that has helped many of my clients who were dealing with a particularly persistent negative voice: as silly as it may sound, try naming it. Yes, give that ornery voice a name that makes it seem less ominous, even laughable. Poindexter, Myrtle, Dr.

Fear… any of those types of names can help your mind relinquish the belief that every statement in your mind represents YOU, or that it should be listened to.

In contrast, give your Future You a powerful name. One of my most epic clients named the future version of herself "Queen Sandy." For another client, it was "Sunshines and Balloons". The clue is in the way that this name makes you feel. When you feel your heart flutter or your skin gets "truth bumps, " you know you've found it.

Your mission is to embrace the Future You *as your soulmate,* the love of your life. Imagine this Future: You revel in everything you do – even the stumbles. This version of you is successful beyond your wildest dreams, and every ounce of success is thanks to the current YOU.

Call upon your "Queen Sandy" when you are down and know that this Epic Future You knows how the dots will all connect. This soulmate of yours delights in your path and sees you as someone who cannot fail. They unconditionally believe in you, encourage you, and see the beauty within you even when you fall.

Today is about embracing the future as your fuel. Realize that your imagination is the resource that powers your GPS. It can give you the ability to transform your kryptonite into your superpower. So, as you fully embrace this quest to experience your life at its most epic, know that your imagination is intended to be your deliberate tool. To use it only to worry and to doubt is like using a flame to set fire to your own house.

Your mind is a great resource, brimming over with opportunities, gifts, and tools. You have earned the right to choose to use them deliberately and wisely.

TODAY'S ACTION STEPS:

- *Have some delicious fun by naming those critical voices! And, of course, feel free to share! (+1 Gold Stars)*
- *Now that you've named it, why stop there? Can you imagine the hideous costume that this critical voice would wear? What do they look like? Do they have clown hair? Are they half beast? Get creative! And the next time that voice erupts, you can tell them you've had enough of their sharing. "Now go back into your abyss, Hildegarde. Your purple tutu is showing!" (+2 Gold Stars)*
- *Bonus points if you also acknowledge that sweet soulmate within that loves you unconditionally. That is the true Epic You! Together, there is no stopping you! (+4 Gold Stars) Booyah!*

TOTAL POSSIBLE STARS FROM TODAY: 7 STARS

Day 93 – IMAGINATION: The Appreciation Wheel – Antidote to Doubt and Pushback

As much as you would like to be able to flip the switch and immediately access a fully open, positively focused, and engaged imagination, you may find that you experience some pushback. Choosing to imagine a future infinitely larger than what you have envisioned in the past is definitely a change for most – and the knee-jerk reaction from your mind can be resistance.

If you think about that future version of yourself and come up with a bit of a blank, take a breath. If you've been struggling to even clearly vocalize what you're passionate about and what you consider to be your strengths, don't be too hard on yourself. Those who have spent much of our life laser-focused on keeping others happy tend to have an especially challenging time shifting into "thinking about ourselves" mode. That's totally natural. Remember that for many of us, both men and women, the more we sacrificed, the more accolades we received. If there were times when we "put ourselves first," it almost felt as if it had to be done apologetically or defiantly when we were close to a breaking point.

Many of us were trained into a very warped logic that sounded like this:

"You need to put all of your energy into making sure that I'm happy. I should not have to worry that you will fail at this. If you do not focus entirely on making sure that my nest is feathered the way that I like it, you are being incredibly selfish."

Can you see how bogus this logic is? Yet, especially when we are in "baby elephant mode" and our own happiness (and sometimes survival) depends on keeping the adults in the house happy, we get trained into believing that this is normal. We tend to continue this pattern even when we move into future relationships.

Is it any wonder that imagining yourself doing epic things feels selfish and strange? When you're feeling stuck or afraid, envisioning an empowered future version of yourself can feel like I'm asking you to believe in unicorns.

So what's the solution?

When I was really suffering from anxiety, struggling financially, and had just gotten myself out of that abusive relationship, it was all that I could do to believe any level of success was possible. I remember sitting outside one evening on my lanai and stumbling upon a technique quite by accident. As I mentioned, I have always found tremendous value in listening to the work of Abraham Hicks. Although, at first, I had a difficult time executing the strategy that they call the Focus Wheel, I discovered that things began to click when I could overlay it onto the practice that they called the Rampage of Appreciation.

This has become the key that has unlocked many a door in my mind that seemed initially to be shut. I have shared it with numerous clients who have experienced the same shift and relief. For me, it's the secret to clearing away any inner game log jam and regaining momentum.

I call it the Appreciation Wheel, and it goes like this:

1. Write down what it is that you are bumping up against now. For example, you might say, "I feel like no matter what I try, I always end up coming up short. I'm afraid that things will never change."
2. Next, write down where it is that you want to be. What do you want to be feeling? Example: [I want to be feeling that] I am destined for great things. Everything that can go well goes **even better for me.** I know that things are working out for me.
3. Here's the *ninja part– rather than start by thinking about your own life, shift to thinking about those who are where you aspire to be and ask yourself this:* is it logical to believe that the people who are now where I want to be were at any point feeling like I'm feeling now? If you can believe that this is a logical thing to believe, write it down.
4. Next, write down whether you believe it's logical to think they *all* had massive advantages and resources you don't have. If you can believe that at least some of them started from a similar place as you are right now, write that down.
5. Next, do you believe it was solely their access to secret hacks or "the right people" that explained their current success? Do you believe that every single one of them just had luck that you do not have? If you believe that it probably wasn't luck that made them all successful, write this down.
6. If you can believe that one of the big reasons they are where they are is their tenacity and resilience, write that down. If you think they probably refused to give up, write that down.
7. If you can believe that it's realistic to believe that when these folks were down, they too probably doubted themselves, write that down.
8. If you can see that being "down" and feeling doubt doesn't mean you are not destined for great things, write that down.
9. In fact, if you can see how getting knocked down and experiencing doubt are a common theme even on the road to great success, write that down.
10. So, it's logical to believe that the ability to keep getting back up and iterating is the true indication of future success. If you agree, write that down.
11. It's the common ability to keep focusing on the "dream" and be resilient when things get tough seems to be the secret to these folks' success. If you agree, write that down.
12. If you can think of a time when you found a way to get back up when things were tough, write that down.
13. If you can see that you do have the potential to be resilient when it's important to you, write that down.
14. So if you have the ability to get back up even when it's tough and find a way to be resilient when you need to, don't you share the same qualities as those people who are now doing so well? If you can see this, write this down.
15. So, even though you may feel worry and doubt right now, can you see how it's possible that this is just an earlier chapter in your own epic success story? If you can see that, write it down.
16. Is your future important enough that you are willing to be tenacious, resilient, and persistent since that seems to be the formula for epic success? If the answer is yes, write that down.

17. So, if it's accurate to say that those who consistently demonstrate tenacity, resilience, and adaptability, along with a commitment to learning and growth, often achieve epic success, wouldn't it be accurate also to say that when you do the same, you have an excellent shot at achieving the same? If you agree, write that down.
18. Isn't it, therefore, logical to believe that "I am destined for great things." Everything that can go well is poised to go **even better for me.** I know that things are working out for me. I have what it takes, so it's just a matter of staying consistent, agile, and resilient. I am on my way to epic success." If you agree, write that down.

Did you feel the gentle shift in your emotional frequency? Did you notice that when you can't quite believe something to be possible for you, start by looking at other people's stories? That can often be the way beyond the wall of doubt into the full force of your incredible ability to imagine.

Now it's your turn. Take time to create your focus wheel and start softening up some limiting beliefs! Booyah!

TODAY'S ACTION STEPS:

- *Following the instructions above, dive into crafting your Appreciation Wheel. (+5 Gold Stars)*
- *Bonus points if you take a moment to notice how this process works and how it shifts your inner game focus and, therefore, frequency. One tiny controllable thought at a time it takes on the journey of 1% so that your mind begins to believe. By seeing that others have been where you are and progressed to where you aspire to go, you begin to identify what your original (bad feeling) thought assumed was not necessarily true. (+5 Gold Stars) Booyah!*

TOTAL POSSIBLE STARS FROM TODAY: 10 STARS

Day 94 – IMAGINATION: Real Eyes for Real EPIC

Yesterday, we explored the Appreciation Wheel concept and stretched beyond where our beliefs stop us. As we project our imagination forward with a shifted perspective, it's important to take another look at those previous beliefs about ourselves. Is our current expectation about what's possible defined by old fears and doubts?

Think about it: When we are children, most of us are asked, "What do you want to be when you grow up?" They really mean, "What do you want to DO."

This teaches us to inadvertently measure our value based on the success (or lack of success) in our careers. For most of us, this often becomes a lifelong struggle between our need to succeed professionally and our personal quest to realize our "purpose" and passion. Can we harmonize the two and still make money? Let's face it: this quest can be frustrating, and it's hard to imagine how it can have a "fairy tale ending."

Initially, the majority of us start down the path of finding a "good" job. Considering that the average person will work at least 90,000 hours over their lifetime, this is a significant decision. However, the unspoken truth is that a "good job" usually refers to a job where you make "good money." The assumption is that if you are making "good money," you will be fulfilled and happy. Enter the white picket fence effect. Or not.

At some point, even when making "good money," most of us realize that we're not feeling happy or fulfilled. This time in our lives is often referred to as the "midlife crisis." This is when we start crawling into bed, feeling stuck, and we thought that life at this point would be different.

We have come to the fork in the road. Some of us start chasing a rerun of our youth. Others get bitter and resign themselves to feeling like they never lived.

But if you're here reading this on Day 90, you're different. You're willing to make changes and explore what makes you truly alive– even when these changes may feel awkward and challenging.

Here's the catch: we often expect a grand epiphany, but it may not arrive like a thunderbolt.

What if the realization of your true calling isn't meant to arrive with the clouds parting and a choir of angels singing? What if it has been subtly nudging you all along, trying to catch the attention of your "real eyes" for years? And what if it's not your "true" calling as much as it is intended to be your next calling? Can you give yourself permission to change directions throughout your life?

What if the biggest clues to your next exhilarating pursuit lie hidden among your greatest gifts and challenges? What if the boulders that life has thrown your way have been concealing the most precious gems in the crown of your existence?

And what if your hyper-focused pursuit of fitting into everyone else's expectations has caused you to lose touch with what is uniquely important to you? And what has deprioritizing your dreams been costing you?

Today, let's pretend that every cloud you need to part is already contained in your imagination. I invite you to make today a day of self-discovery, to look for the gems within the stones. Bury your fear of being judged. Instead, open your "real eyes" and "real eyes" the potential that surrounds you and resides within you. Take a moment to reflect: What brings you joy? What stirs your passion? What would you do more of if given the chance? What are the principles and concepts that ignite your soul?

Imagine you have a magic wand – what dreams would you bring to life? If you knew that you could not fail, what would be the path that you would choose?

Explore your skills, superpowers, gifts, and talents. They are THERE! What do others admire about you? What unique strengths do you possess? Are you a natural leader, a master storyteller, or a source of unwavering support for others?

Create a list of all these things. Embrace the essence of who you are – the true YOU. Epic individuals understand that by embracing their passions and skills, they not only find happiness but also empower others to discover and claim their unique strengths. They also realize that by honoring their strengths, they honor their past so that they can now deliberately create an even more compelling future.

Today, look at your world with your "real eyes" and "real eyes" your authentic self. Share with those around you the beauty that comes from seeing the world with a clear sense of appreciation. Envision yourself as a beacon of inspiration for your friends, family, community, and team.

So, let's "get REAL" today! Embrace your passions, envision your dreams, and let your "real eyes" guide you toward "realizing" your *next* true purpose. The journey may not always be a thunderous revelation but a gradual unfolding of clarity and insight. Embrace it, for within it lies the key to unlocking the sweet brilliance of your own unique (and sometimes quirky) version of EPIC!

TODAY'S ACTION STEPS:

- *Grab a sheet of paper or journal and complete the following sentence based on what you now know: "With iteration as my superpower, I intend to approach any future boulders in my life like this…" (+3 Gold Stars)*
- *Now complete the following: "I now declare and Real Eyes that I choose to live like this…." (+3 Gold Stars)*
- *Bonus points if you now write down three things that you are going to do differently from this moment forward so that you can begin creating the life that you envision starting today! (+3 Gold Stars) Booyah!*

TOTAL POSSIBLE STARS FROM TODAY: 9 STARS

Day 95 – IMAGINATION: Dancing With the Whales – Dive Into Your Ability to Play With the Big Fish

We've stressed the importance of integrating The Epic 3 into your daily life. By reshaping your habits and routines, you'll uncover where Fear and Doubt have lurked in the background, like unwelcome backseat drivers. When setting the bar high each morning becomes a habit, shedding the weight of past fears and doubts and propelling you toward days of epic creation.

This transformation isn't confined to your personal life. You can supercharge your career by applying the Epic 3 professionally, too. Most people settle for allowing the 90,000 hours minimum that most people work over their lifetime to be tolerated as "just a job" – a necessary evil that allows us to pay for the things that we really want to do and have. However, when you shift your perspective so that your career becomes part of the harmony that makes you YOU, the results can be life-changing. When you approach your work as an extension of who you choose to show up being, your professional life can be one of the most powerful ways that you can choose to iterate and express that infinite depth of potential within you.

So consider this: those fears and doubts that hopped aboard your life journey as a young traveler often reappear in full force as you navigate your career. By your 20s, they've become overzealous backseat drivers with their own plans for your GPS.

And it's not only when you toss and turn in bed at night that your fears and doubts urge you to lower your aspirations; they can haunt you at your desk, urging you to aim low, stay under the radar, and play it safe.

As we dive deeper into the art of envisioning and now that we've recalibrated our perspective on failure, let's look at our professional life and revisit the things we thought we'd never attempt due to the fear of rejection, ridicule and failure.

Sure, that level of caution might have been valid if you were contemplating skydiving without a parachute. But in most cases, the professional leaps - pursuing a high-profile client, asking for a promotion, exploring a different industry, or starting a new venture - can turbocharge your career when iterated strategically and correctly. Mastering the art of envisioning can be your secret weapon.

Let's revisit Henry Ford's wisdom: "Whether you think you can, or you think you can't--you're right." Envisioning is the key to believing you can.

Now, let's talk about the business terminology of "whale hunting" - or, as I prefer to call it, "dancing with the whales." Picture it: you're venturing into uncharted waters, pursuing the seemingly unattainable. It's about embracing unconventional ideas and seizing opportunities you might have considered beyond your reach. It's setting sail on a vast, beautiful blue ocean, ready for an extraordinary journey.

Many people's big breaks came when they were willing to do exactly that. One remarkable story of dancing with the whales is that of actor Dev Patel. An unknown actor at the time, Patel pursued the lead role in "Slumdog Millionaire." With limited acting experience, he knew it was a daunting task. But driven by passion and unwavering self-belief, he approached director Danny Boyle for an audition.

Despite the odds, Patel's determination and talent won him the lead role. "Slumdog Millionaire" went on to win numerous awards, catapulting Patel to international fame.

Countless similar stories emphasize how stepping outside your comfort zone and envisioning extraordinary outcomes can lead to remarkable opportunities. When you dare to pursue the seemingly unattainable, you open doors to transformative experiences.

Dancing with the whales starts with stretching your imagination. It challenges you to envision your untapped potential, thriving in roles and situations that may seem out of reach. It empowers you to believe in epic possibilities and relentlessly pursue your dreams.

Imagination shapes your beliefs, and beliefs drive your actions. The path to success may not be straightforward, but when you hold the vision of an epic life, you can navigate the challenges.

So, embark on your journey of dancing with the whales. Embrace the unfamiliar, take calculated risks, and envision the extraordinary. Trust in your ability to thrive among the whales, for within you lies the strength and vision to conquer the impossible, just as waves wash ashore.

TODAY'S ACTION STEPS:

- *What three ways can you "dance with the whales" professionally?   (+2 Gold Stars)*
- *To put this into action, what do you need to start doing? Stop doing? Do differently? (+3 Gold Stars)*
- *Bonus points if you now pick one "dancing with the whales" action that feels a bit scary. (Although now you know that the fear is just unfamiliarity. Wink!) Can you be bold, strategize a plan, and take action? If it comes back with a light bulb that doesn't light up, what's your next action? Iterate and try again! (+3 Gold Stars) Booyah!*

TOTAL POSSIBLE STARS FROM TODAY: 8 STARS

Day 96 – IMAGINATION: The Envisioner's Triumph - Defying the Naysayers

As you continue to create this transformative journey for yourself, you'll notice that not everyone welcomes your changes. That's perfectly normal. Stay steadfast in your course and make those changes regardless. Here's a little secret: some of the pushback might come from your very own mind.

I Confess! For years, I allowed the naysayers to win. Others' opinions and influences crushed several of my dreams. Worst of all, I allowed my sense of failure and inadequacy to become my own worst enemy. Eventually, I became the loudest naysayer in my life.

This meant I wandered through life without a true north, no compass to guide me.

Let's be honest: life seems to conspire against our dreams from time to time. In fifth grade, an art teacher's comment about my "bad sense of color and space" stung. (Ironically, in my twenties, I "accidentally" became a jewelry designer with my pieces adorning showcases in department stores and art museums!)

Remember my ballet dream? When I didn't get the lead role in "The Little Match Girl," I was humiliated and ashamed. I had believed I had "something special." That little voice inside me declared this was my calling. But when my teacher wouldn't even consider me in auditions, I was not only humiliated but secretly vowed never to trust that little voice again.

As mentioned, it wasn't until my fifties that I discovered my teacher's snub resulted from payment issues during my parents' divorce, not my lack of talent. The "evidence" I'd used to bury my dream and doubt my intuition had been utterly baseless.

The final blow came a few years later. During my senior year at prep school, I achieved something few others had. The English teacher, a legendary hard grader, admitted he'd given only five "A's" in 30+ years. I was the fifth, and it was a pinnacle moment.

So, when I started honors English at Georgetown, I submitted the "A" paper I'd written at prep school as a writing sample. On the first day of class, the professor returned those papers. She'd given me a "D" over a "C-," the same paper that had earned an "A."

This shook me to my core. I was known for being the type of student who panicked if I got a "B." The "D" triggered such severe writer's block that I never took another English class, and I never wrote for pleasure again until my fifties.

Why share this? Maybe you see a bit of yourself in these stories. They became my "baby elephant collars." I was too young to process these experiences accurately, so I allowed them to define my beliefs about what I could do.

I had no idea my ballet teacher had payment issues. I still don't know if that "D" at Georgetown was intended to motivate me. Regardless, I made judgments that had repercussions for years.

Luckily, deep down, a spark of imagination and creativity waited to reignite. After the boulder fell on Schuyler, I reassessed everything. Over time, I learned to cherish and embrace my gifts and let go of some of those "baby elephant collars."

If you've ever believed a past "failure" defines you, remember this: you're the master storyteller of your life. You hold the pen to rewrite your narrative and create a destiny that defies all odds. Doubt and skepticism will come; your imagination must become your ally in those moments. It's never too late to rewrite your story.

Where does this all lead? (Wink!) Our less-than-subtle message over these past 96 days is this: our mission is to begin giving you the tools, insights, and strategies to finally break free of the "life happening *to you*" syndrome. Our desire is to help you open a powerful new door through which you create a life that is happening and unfolding *FOR YOU as envisioned BY YOU*.

So yes! I'm challenging you to dream big and go out and get whatever you can imagine!

Embrace the Power of Imagination and let it lead you to the joy waiting for you. Embrace moments of bliss as breadcrumbs to your true path. The world may try to cast you in a predefined role, but you can step into the spotlight as the lead actor of your story. Imagine possibilities beyond others' limitations, and, most importantly, don't **be** the person in your story who says, "I can't."

That light within, your unique brilliance, can never be extinguished. Let your imagination break free from doubt and disbelief, even when you're the loudest naysayer. Use your ability to envision as a tool to paint a vivid canvas of your dreams, colored with hope and determination.

Setbacks do not define your journey; your imagination does. Trust in it, believe in yourself, and let it guide you toward fulfillment. As you face life's challenges and critics, never forget your imagination's power. It's your compass, pointing the way to your dreams' realization.

You are the author of your destiny. Embrace life's chapters with courage and an audacious imagination. The world may say you can't, but you know you can deep down. So, defy the odds, rise above the doubts, and let your imagination pave the way to the extraordinary life you are destined to live.

TODAY'S ACTION STEPS:

- *Take a look at some past naysayers from this new perspective: what if now they can be the characters in your story who inspired your most significant iterations? Can you list at least 3 of those individuals or events from your past and rewrite your story from the perspective of "Look how this inspired me to unfold and iterate?" (+3 Gold Stars)*
- *Are there currently some naysayers in your life? Rather than try to convince them to view you differently, can you refocus your tale so that you simply assign them the role of "catalyst for iteration"? If they are supporting characters versus villains in your story, how does that impact how you will respond to them? (+5 Gold Stars)*
- *Bonus points if you write down three things that you will do differently from this moment forward when you encounter a naysayer so that you can begin creating the destiny you envision starting today! (+5 Gold Stars) Booyah!*

TOTAL POSSIBLE STARS FROM TODAY: 13 STARS

Day 97 – IMAGINATION: 3 Things the Boulder Taught Me About Bad Times

Even though, of course, I want you to envision epic things ahead, let's be clear: all of the great envisionings in the world won't keep you from experiencing some boulders in your life. And when you're in the middle of an avalanche of falling boulders, it can be downright infuriating to have someone imply that you should be using your imagination to envision something encouraging and empowering, yes? Or even to suggest (as we lovingly have done here) that now is your opportunity to iterate!

It's like the well-intentioned friend telling you after one of your biggest moments of crisis that "everything happens for a reason" – while her life seems to be flowing along perfectly.

When faced with "bad times," it's easy to feel disheartened and fearful. It can be tempting to retreat and hide from the challenges. Those are the moments when our minds tend to revert to old habits and when that critical inner voice jeers, "See…I told you that this wouldn't work."

Especially when we were starting to believe that we were seeing progress, it can feel almost impossible to envision beyond an unanticipated "step backward." These might be the times when you run for Ben & Jerry's, binge on Netflix, head to the mall, or order that extra margarita at the tiki bar. I get it – but this time, *you owe it to yourself to resist.*

Remember, boulders often hold important clues to your next success – and it's hard to see those clues clearly if your head is buried in an ice cream bowl or if you're mad at yourself. There's no better day than TODAY to declare that 'that was how I *used to* react. But no more! Now, I'm choosing to show up in these moments as someone who *responds with her eyes focused on epic. I will NOT let my actions be ruled by Fear."*

As I talked with my daughter, reflecting on our lives since that boulder fell, I realized what the many boulders throughout my life taught me about navigating tough times:

1. Focus is everything – so it's critical to focus beyond the times that feel bad. Concentrate on the pain, and it magnifies, overwhelming you. But when you shift your focus to the lessons and opportunities, you begin to grow – often toward a place of newfound strength and love.

2. Don't navigate it alone – lean on others. Find your champions versus those who are simply willing to commiserate. It's often when you recharge your vision thanks to the unwavering vision of others that miracles are born.

3. True grit is when your desire to create a miracle is greater than your desire to give in. Persist and persist; you might just transform yesterday's "impossible" into the future's "new normal." As unwanted as these boulders may be, they are all part of the delicious path forward.

The truth is, when we're at the bottom of the abyss, as we explored earlier, the best strategy is to search for one thought that feels even a bit better than the thoughts that hold us down.

Today's epic mission is to go through your day holding these little lessons close and navigating through each moment like one more rep in your "inner game gym". Whether you feel like you're seeing victory or whether you're feeling knocked down, appreciate that this is all part of the growth curve. Fear is just another billboard along the highway. Stay true to your GPS and keep driving.

Focus on building your envisioning muscle so that it's just a little bit stronger and then a little bit stronger. Find language to guide your mind toward encouraging thoughts beyond your current obstacles. Know that when you continue the journey, your own epic story awaits.

Your boulders aren't a measure of your success. They are just part of the path *along the way* to success. Here's to a future where we boldly and joyously turn our "Fear-filled Impossibles" into "Fear Less I'm Possibles"!

TODAY'S ACTION STEPS:

- *Take a look at Schuyler's and my three takeaways from our boulder. How do they resonate with these past 97 days, and what might be some of your takeaways? (+3 Gold Stars)*
- *Get proactive, and based on what you have learned and experienced here, what are 3-5 strategies you will turn to when a boulder drops? What thoughts will you guide your mind to think? What declarations will you repeat to yourself? How will you get yourself to refocus? (+5 Gold Stars)*
- *Remember our Three Defining Questions? Bonus points if you now write down responses to these three questions regarding how you will choose to respond when the boulders drop: What can I control? What can my mind believe? What am I assuming that is not necessarily true? (+5 Gold Stars) Booyah!*

TOTAL POSSIBLE STARS FROM TODAY: 13 STARS

Day 98 – IMAGINATION: Embrace the Hero Within - Unleashing the Epic YOU

So what will it be? Are you going to imagine that life is doing things *to you* or that life is doing things *for you?* Personally and professionally, you get to choose whether you invest in the power of your imagination or whether you tell yourself that such things are only believed by the "gullible people" of the world.

Whatever you choose to tell yourself, your mind *will* create a story about it – so why wouldn't you want to have input about the content of that story?

Only you can give yourself permission and authority to consciously use the faculties of your wondrous imagination to create the future you love. Only you can agree that you are worthy of as epic of a future as your mind can imagine. "To imagine" is to admit that you have the right to think thoughts that make you happy *even if you have not yet "earned" these feelings based on what has already occurred in the past.*

So the big question today is how epic of a life story can you believe that you deserve? When you can begin to believe that you deserve it, you can begin to access the muscle within your imagination to create it.

Picture this: you're standing at the threshold of your epic story, just like Dorothy from "The Wizard of Oz" or Frodo from "Lord of the Rings." You might not yet see the ruby red slippers or the courage and power within you, but they're there, waiting to be discovered.

In every epic tale, the hero or shero starts off unaware of their true potential. Challenges and obstacles appear as flying monkeys or wicked witches, threatening to hold them back. But deep down, they possess the strength, resilience, and magic to overcome these hurdles and transform their lives.

What's stopping you from embracing your inner hero (or "shero-ness")? Could it be that your story is not yet written the way it deserves to be? Imagine if you could rewrite your beliefs and perceptions about this very moment. What if you could be bold enough to challenge the "impossible" and craft your destiny in the face of all evidence to the contrary?

As I sat in the Jackson Memorial Hospital chapel, as Schuyler fought for her life upstairs in the ICU, I had an epiphany. This brush with fate was a wake-up call, urging me to release the boulders of doubt and fear that had weighed me down. It was like when I stepped into a dewy morning, where a perfect spider web suddenly becomes visible with just one step further. At that moment, clarity washed over me, and I realized that I had the power to define my story.

You, too, possess that power within you. Your imagination is the gateway to your heroic transformation. In every epic tale, the hero faces challenges, undergoes growth, and discovers their true potential. Your life's journey is no different. You can rewrite your story, redefine yourself, and release the past "reasons" that have held you back.

The call to action is to embrace the art of envisioning. Playfully harness your imagination to envision the Future You – that epic version of yourself you know you're destined to become. It's not just about seeing it; it's about feeling it. Embrace the emotions of that Future You – the confidence, courage, and determination. Let these emotions ignite your actions and shape your reality.

It might not be an easy journey, but every step taken with intention and excitement brings you closer to the epic you. Reframe your challenges as opportunities for growth, just like heroes face their flying monkeys. Conquer your inner wicked witches of doubt and fear, knowing that the power to transform is within you.

It's time to play, not work. Allow yourself to embody that Future You today, in this very moment. Dare to reimagine yourself and break free from the shackles of limitation. Write your story of courage, resilience, and triumph, and step into the world as the epic version of yourself you know you are destined to be.

So, are you willing to put in the work and play to unlock the hero within? Are you ready to let go of the past and embrace your epic destiny? The path may not be crystal clear, but with your imagination as your guide, you will navigate the twists and turns, creating a destiny that defies all odds.

You have the pen in your hand; the story is yours to write. Embrace the hero within, and let your epic journey begin.

TODAY'S ACTION STEPS:

- *It's time! One of your last iterations (for now) of your new EPIC YOU STORY going forward. Today, "Write your story of courage, resilience, and triumph, and step into the world as the epic version of yourself you know you are destined to be." (+5 Gold Stars)*
- *Now stand in front of your mirror, shoulders back and strike your Joy-rrior pose. Proudly, harmoniously, and fully alive, read your new EPIC YOU STORY aloud. And of course, when you finish, let's hear a ROARING: BOOYAH!! (+3 Gold Stars)*
- *Bonus points if you practice walking around your house (and into your day) as the EPIC FUTURE YOU version of yourself. BE the version of yourself who knows that you ARE the boat. You ARE ITS CAPTAIN. And no one, especially you, will keep this boat from savoring its limitless blue ocean!! (+2 Gold Stars) Booyah!*

TOTAL POSSIBLE STARS FROM TODAY: 10 STARS

Day 99– THE EPIC 3: Nurturing the 12 Brilliances

Day 99, and it's time to bring it all together! In our 12-Month Epic Life Makeover program, we call it Nurturing the 12 Brilliances. These Brilliances are the significant life elements that comprise the inner and outer game. Our program focuses on one brilliance a month so that at the end of 12 months, you truly have experienced an entire life makeover.

So what are the 12 Brilliances?

1. Career/ Legacy
2. Financial Health
3. Physical Health
4. Social/ Community
5. Relationships
6. Family
7. The Epic 3
8. Energy & Alignment
9. Self-care/ Mindfulness

10. Positive Habits
11. Personal Development
12. Self-Image

At the beginning of every month, we focus on incorporating empowering regimens into each of these Brilliances within our life. The process begins by asking yourself these three questions:

- What's working?
- What's not working?
- What might we do differently?

From there we go back to the 3 Critical Questions:

- What can I control?
- What can my mind believe?
- What might I be assuming that is not necessarily true?

Now is the time to examine that brilliance through the lens of The Epic 3:

- What have I been focusing on (and what I've been making that mean)?
- What story have I been creating around that Brilliance?
- How have I envisioned the story around this Brilliance to go in the future?

Once we've done that, we map out a plan for:

- What are we going to start doing?
- What are we going to stop doing?
- What are we going to iterate and explore doing differently?

Of course, we always keep in mind that each day's target is simply the 1%!

Now is your time! Start crafting your own Personal Empowerment System™ around the 12 Brilliances so that you can start living your life from the perspective of someone fully alive!

TODAY'S ACTION STEPS:

- *Play with the questions we outline above to help you uplevel each of your 12 Brilliances. (+7 Gold Stars)*
- *Bonus points if you outline an action plan for your NEXT 100 days, keeping in mind the 1% rule that success comes more quickly through small achievable action steps! (+5 Gold Stars) Booyah!*

TOTAL POSSIBLE STARS FROM TODAY: 12 STARS

Day 100 – THE EPIC 3: Brilliant Habits

It's Day 100! Time to reinforce your road to future success! So today, let's help you solidify these new habits that keep you showing up as the EPIC YOU. Remember, the Personal Empowerment System™ that you create is only as good as the habits that support it. And let's face it, changing our habits demands determination, consistency, and quite a bit of self-discipline. So, how do we create rituals and regimens that we're most likely to keep?

Here are some of our favorite "epic ninja strategies" to make the process easier and more effective.

First, here are five important things to do when creating a new habit:

1. **Start Small:** Begin with a small, manageable change rather than tackling a big habit overhaul all at once. (Can you see how important the 1% rule is?) Starting small allows you to build confidence and increase your chances of success. For example, if you want to exercise more, start with a 10-minute daily walk before progressing to longer workouts.
2. **Set Clear and Specific Objectives:** Define your habit clearly and make it specific. Vague goals like "exercise more" are less effective than specific ones like "run for 30 minutes every morning at 7 a.m." Knowing exactly what you need to do makes it easier to stay on track.
3. **Create a Routine That Stacks Your New Habit onto an Existing One:** Incorporate your new habit into an existing routine or schedule. For example, if you want to listen to more inspiring podcasts, make listening to these podcasts part of your morning commute. Want to incorporate an Envisioning primer into your morning routine? Make it part of your cool-down routine after your morning exercise, or start slipping it in before your morning shower. Associating the new habit with an existing habit can make it more automatic.
4. **Track Your Progress:** Keep a record of your habits. Use a journal, app, or calendar to track your daily or weekly progress. This helps you stay accountable and provides a visual representation of your success. Yes, remember to **celebrate even the small successes!!**
5. **Stay Consistent:** Consistency is key when forming new habits. Aim to perform the habit at the same time and in the same context each day. The more consistent you are, the more likely the habit will become ingrained in your daily life. Remember our focus on commitment to the essence of the new habit, too. If, for example, you can't make it to the gym, commit to doing at least 15 minutes of exercise at home before dinner. Being able to trust yourself to stick with your commitments is critical.

To make it easier to shift into these new habits, consider these additional tips:

- **Start with one habit:** Focus on creating one habit at a time. Once it becomes established, you can move on to the next one.
- **Use reminders:** Set alarms, notifications, or visual cues (like placing your workout clothes by the door) to remind yourself to perform the habit.

- **Find an accountability partner and/or coach:** Share your objectives with someone who can hold you accountable and provide support and encouragement. Enlist the help of a mentor as needed.
- **Reward yourself:** Celebrate your successes, no matter how small. Rewarding yourself reinforces the habit loop by associating it with positive feelings.
- **Be patient:** Habits take time to develop. Don't be discouraged by setbacks or slow progress. Stay committed and keep moving forward.
- **Learn from failures:** If you slip up or miss a day, don't give up. Instead, analyze what went wrong and make adjustments to prevent the same mistake in the future.
- **Visualize success:** Use the power of imagination to visualize yourself successfully completing the habit. This can boost motivation and reinforce your commitment.

Remember that forming new habits is a process that requires time and effort. Be kind to yourself, stay persistent, and focus on the long-term benefits of your new habits. And, of course, remember that inner game habits are still habits! Upleveling your mind is always a win/win!!

There's no stopping you when you become the Master of The Epic 3!

TODAY'S ACTION STEPS:

- *Based on the above positive Ninja Epic Habit Hacks, what are 3-5 ways you can fortify your Day 99 strategies to ensure your success? (+5 Gold Stars)*
- *Bonus points if you start implementing them today! (+7 Gold Stars) Booyah!*

TOTAL POSSIBLE STARS FROM TODAY: 12 STARS

BUT WAIT! THERE'S MORE!

It's TRUE! No quest into EPICNESS would be complete without a few "super ninja" bonus strategies to fortify your path to success! So venture on into Bonus Days 101, 102, and 103! You'll be glad you did!!

BONUS: Day 101 – THE EPIC 3: Guiding Lights and Turbo-Chargers

WHO LOVES BONUSES? We sure do – so on these bonus days of the 100 Days of Epic quest, we're all about double and triple ensuring that you are set up to win. Our mission is to make it easy and smooth for you to hit your targets. We appreciate that you may find yourself navigating uncharted waters in your journey towards epic transformation.

We all realize that the path to epic success can feel challenging and filled with obstacles, self-doubt, and uncertainty. Yesterday, we discussed the integral role that new routines, energizing habits, and solid regimens can play when your goal is to turbo-charge your progress.

However, in your toughest moments, when you're tempted to let old habits seep in, having the right guiding lights can make all the difference. What I'm referring to is your chosen team.

Imagine embarking on a solo expedition to climb Mount Everest. Would you really attempt to make the climb without any guidance or support? It sounds daunting, doesn't it? The truth is that personal growth and success, whether in your personal life or professional endeavors, are no different. We often see game-changing results when we have experienced hands to guide us, mentors to show us the way, coaches to refine our skills, and the camaraderie of accountability partners, like-minded communities, or mastermind groups to keep us on track.

Because you are committed to unleashing the most epic version of yourself, there's no question that having the right team to help you will avoid the pitfalls and frustrations of trying to figure it out on your own or relying strictly on the internet or trial and error. As someone who, for the longest time, stubbornly thought I should be able to figure things out on my own, I speak from my own experience, not simply from the perspective of someone who has observed great results with my clients.

Here are just a few of the reasons why it's not just smart but absolutely essential when at all possible to enlist the help of coaches, mentors, and accountability partners on your journey to EPIC.:

1. Expertise and Experience: Coaches and mentors bring years of experience and expertise to the table. They've navigated the very challenges you're facing and can provide valuable insights, shortcuts, and strategies to help you achieve your goals faster. In my case, I have coached hundreds of clients, spent decades learning from the top experts in various genres, and invested hundreds of thousands of dollars in hands-on training in everything from the inner game to branding and marketing. Not only do my clients benefit from my expertise, but it spares them the overwhelm that most experience when trying to figure these things out independently.

2. Unbiased Feedback: When deeply immersed in your journey, it's easy to overlook blind spots and biases. Coaches and mentors provide honest, unbiased feedback, helping you see things from different perspectives and make informed decisions. Here's a testimonial from my client Karen J so that you can see how beneficial getting help with your blindspots can be: "What can I say about Meridith! She is amazing! Life long hang ups were solved in just a few sessions with her. She put it into perspective that gave me permission to not hold on anymore. She gave me freedom from the chains."

3. Clarity on Targets and Next Objectives: Working with a coach or mentor forces you to define your next steps with clarity. This process alone can be transformational, as it compels you to articulate what you truly want and how to get there. Here's another example of the benefit that my client Virginia experienced when we started working on her plan together. Before working together, she'd frustrated herself for months trying to figure out a new career path on her own: "Meridith is top notch. She has a marvelous mapping system and is great at helping you organize your thoughts and getting you motivated to invest your energy in your dream."

4. Accountability: Knowing you're answerable to someone else can be a powerful motivator. Accountability partners ensure you stay committed to your goals and take consistent action. My client, Tom S., expressed it this way. In his case, in addition to guidance, I was providing him with accountability to take action: "I have to say that my first session was way more profound and productive than my highest expectations…Meridith somehow perceived and then zeroed in with laser focus on the exact limiting factor in my mindset and personality…and all I can say now, reflecting on our first session is: Wow, this is real. This can work for me." The right coach can not only keep you from stalling, but they can make sure that your action is headed in the right direction.

5. Personalized Guidance: Coaches tailor their guidance to your unique needs and circumstances. They help you create a customized roadmap to success rather than offering one-size-fits-all solutions. When I have been coached, the mentoring element was priceless. Here's how my client Elizabeth K. explains it: "This has been one of those experiences that changes everything! I've just had a handful of sessions so far, but I can already tell that I'm feeling stronger and extremely encouraged! Motivation is up! Energy is up! Confidence is up! And best of all, my daily joy and thankfulness is changing the way I see my successes. My husband and kids are also very excited to see this version of me. I have been a stay at home mom for 14+ years and have always carried with me some big personal dreams! Meridith is helping me cut a new path to finally making those dreams a reality! I'm learning the tools and rediscovering my passions that will take me into the next stage of life. I did a lot of research on available coaching, therapy, etc … and I'm pleased to say, the 5 star reviews are true! Meridith is extremely talented and has a special gift of helping others see the value in themselves. With practical solutions and thought provoking discussions, she is truly helping me turn my fears into determination! I will be forever thankful for this experience! Meridith is a true gem!"

6. Overcoming Self-Doubt: Self-doubt can be a formidable obstacle. Coaches and mentors provide emotional support, helping you build confidence and self-belief even when you're facing setbacks. For my client, Kim O, the coaching was huge: "Meridith is life changing! Having her as a coach has been pivotal to my growth. I met with so many people before deciding to choose her and I am so thankful I did. You will not regret it!" A good coach can help you recalibrate the areas where you hold yourself back due to self-criticism or self-doubt.

7. Expanding Your Network: Coaches and mentors often have extensive networks. They can introduce you to valuable connections, opening doors to opportunities you might not have accessed otherwise. This is one of the big reasons I decided to create my Society of Epic Chicks as well as my retreats and weekend breakthrough experiences. Having a tr'amily (part tribe/ part family) can be the key to maintaining momentum in the rougher terrain. My client Julie C expresses it well, "It's fantastic to be in a community with such amazing and strong women. The atmosphere of the group is such that we can share openly and honestly. It's a great opportunity to let all of society's expectations just melt away and be real with each other!"

8. Learning from Mistakes: Failure is a part of growth, but it doesn't have to be the end. Coaches and mentors help you learn from your mistakes and turn them into stepping stones toward success. My client Fiaz A had been having zero luck getting hired by companies in the industry that he was passionate about. He knew that it was his lack of confidence and his poor interview delivery skills. Our time together helped him not only build a completely new sense of what he brought to the table but to talk about it in a compelling way. Imagine how rewarding it was for me when I got his text saying, "THEY HIRED ME!" Fiaz said this about his coaching experience: "The best investment I ever made!"

9. Time Efficiency: Trying to figure everything out on your own can be incredibly time-consuming. Coaches and mentors accelerate your progress by streamlining your efforts and focusing on what truly matters. As you can see from my client Alicia B, coaching can help you get through the log jams more quickly: "I was reluctant to hire a coach but I knew I needed to do something exceptional to get noticed and eventually hired! I considered it an investment. Well, from the minute we started working together, I have been OVERWHELMED with appreciation for Merideth! She is the epitome of a professional and a true expert! I have received invitations for several interviews after years of no responses whatsoever! She has given me the confidence boost I needed along with a great, eye-catching resume! I will continue to work with her (forever! Lol!) so I can continue to grow and improve myself. Worth every penny!"

10. Motivation and Inspiration: Coaches and mentors are a source of motivation and inspiration. They challenge you to stretch beyond your comfort zone and hold you to a higher standard. My client Jonathan W had been "staying busy", but in actuality, he had just been spinning his wheels. We were able to shift that and get him making real progress. He explained it here: "My experience with Meridith has been amazing. She has been super helpful with my journey to do more with my life. She has helped me to identify all my barriers and weaknesses. She helped me with setting better targets and objectives. More importantly she has helped me to take more actions towards my dream 😊 I would definitely recommend Meridith to anyone who is currently feeling lost but wants to take control of their life."

Celebrities including Oprah Winfrey, Hugh Jackman, Leonardo DiCaprio, Serena Williams, Elon Musk, Nia Long, Bill Clinton, Andre Agassi, Jen Sincero, and more often highlight the importance of mentors and coaches in their lives, noting that they've played a crucial role in their careers and personal development.

Whether striving for professional excellence, seeking personal growth, or aiming to harmonize both, remember that you don't have to embark on this journey alone. The road to epic transformation is often paved with the guidance and support of coaches, mentors, and accountability partners. They are your guiding lights, illuminating the path to success and helping you reach heights you never thought possible.

So, as you continue your epic journey, don't hesitate to seek out these guiding lights. As Warren Buffet said, "Generally speaking, investing in yourself is the best thing you can do." Because, now more than ever, you should realize that you *are worth investing in.* So, use today to explore the world of coaches, mentors, communities, and masterminds more deeply. Embrace their wisdom, accept their challenges, and let them be the wind beneath your wings as you soar toward your dreams. In your collective strength, you'll discover the power to turn your aspirations into reality.

Of course, if, after having spent these last 100 days together, you can now envision how much further and faster you would be able to progress if we could work together in person, I encourage you to head to www.gritmindsetacademy.com or flip to the final pages of this book where you can browse through just a few of the possibilities.

ALSO…. If you are willing to show us that you would be a client who truly intends to take action, you can reserve a complimentary 20-minute "Live the Dream" Graduation Strategy Call. Note that we are not offering this indefinitely, so now's the time to take action. Right now, I am reserving five slots weekly as graduation calls for my 100 Days of Epic readers. These are to help you fill in any gaps you may still be feeling and help you plan how to keep up your momentum for the NEXT 100 days (and beyond).

All you have to do is email our team with your top 3 takeaways from this book and the biggest shift that you feel you have seen in yourself. Email us at team@gritmindsetacademy.com. Once you have completed action, you can book your 20-minute "Live the Dream" Graduation Strategy Call here: https://bit.ly/MeetYourEpic.

Epic little disclaimer… we will not be able to honor your reservation for your strategy call until we see that you have taken action, so please be sure to email our team BEFORE booking your session. This is yet another way of rewarding you for taking massive action! Wink!

So, today's message is this: Whatever direction you take, know that you'll go faster if you set it up so that you don't have to face the quest to Epic alone!

There are many Joy-rriors here on this exquisite little planet. Find them. Embrace them. Engage with them. Join them! We in the G.R.I.T. team are definitely dedicated to seeing you set you up for success, so let us know how we can help you! We think that if you've read this far, IT'S YOUR TIME — yes????!!!

P.S. – While you are making note of your takeaways, just a friendly "hint" that we'd be EPICALLY grateful if you have a moment to mention them in a review for us on the platform where you bought this book. Our mission is to spread EPIC amounts of joy and harmony to at least 5 million people by 2025 and your review can help us get the word out there!

TODAY'S ACTION STEPS:

- *Set up an action plan for creating your inner circle of support. Who will that be, and where will you find them? Start connecting with them TODAY! (+6 Gold Stars)*
- *Bonus points if you accept our offer for the Action Takers! Take a moment to email our team with your top 3 takeaways from this book and the biggest shift that you feel you have seen in yourself. Email us at team@gritmindsetacademy.com. Once you have taken action, you can book your 20-minute "Live the Dream" Graduation Strategy Call here: https://bit.ly/MeetYourEpic. (+5 Gold Stars) Booyah!*

TOTAL POSSIBLE STARS FROM TODAY: 11 STARS

BONUS Day 102 – THE EPIC 3: Once Upon A Future Me – The Story Not the Fantasy

Here, you are on the cusp of possibility. You now have in your tool kit the resources of The EPIC 3. You are learning how to master the power of your Focus and how to use your Language to write the story about what you are choosing to make that Focus mean. You are learning to tap into the infinite potential of your imagination to create, iterate, and innovate. You are stepping into this moment as the newest member of this Epic Joy-rrior Movement. Now IS your time.

So, as you look into the mirror and contemplate your day, what will be your Future You Story? And it *is* a story – not a fantasy. Because you, my dear, have everything you need to create that story already within you, already here. You *are* the unicorn, the magical creature hidden in plain sight.

Personally, professionally, financially, spiritually, and physically, you are born to create. You are born to imagine, inspire, and grow.

It's time to put pen to paper, get out those post-it notes, design your masterpiece mindmap, and get that Joy-rrior mind going.

What *will* your next draft look like? What will it *feel* like? Remember that the potential of the words is in the frequency that they make you feel. And there is no "right answer". You are the author, so the story is yours to tell.

You might start at first with a story that centers around a few "fill in the blanks." Maybe that story might look something like this:

> Once upon a time (maybe within the next hour–wink!), I am waking up as the EPIC ME! As I open my eyes to feel the first delicious rays of sunshine across my face, I say to myself: _____. I am feeling _____!
> My life is _____. And I have so much to look forward to! I am so freaking proud of _____, and I'm so excited to think that today I get to _____, _____ and most of all that I get to _____! I am not _____ or _____. I no longer _____ or _____. I AM _____! I am _____, and I definitely am _____!
> When people look at me now, they see someone who _____, and that is freaking awesome! Epic even! And speaking of EPIC, when I look at myself now, I see immense beauty. And the beauty that I now embrace within myself is _____. I have a purpose, a passion, and a message that is too important not to share. And this will be how I share my new story:
> _____!
> Personally, I intend to _____. Professionally, I commit

to _____. And in all of the other aspects of my life I will now _____. I am a force to be reckoned with, and I step out into this day fully, lusciously, and EPICALLY ALIVE!

Or maybe, you might find yourself writing your Future You Story as your own "Tinkerbell Project Blog," ever evolving as you grow:

To Infinity and Beyond….!

Well, dear friends! Greetings from the delicious whirlwind! Isn't it amazing to be able to feel so exquisitely alive? With every breath and, yes, even during those blasted "challenges" that fine-tune the machine, we are moving/flowing/blossoming into an even richer brilliance!

Can you feel the pulse of this amazing planet? Can you feel the goodness and the promise that is taking hold? How lucky are our children to be born now when our beliefs truly seem to be shifting? How lucky are we to have the chance to ask, dream, and choose to move forward?!

I believe the odds are stacked in our favor, and it's hard not to become positively giddy when the world grants us a quick sneak peek of the greatness yet to come. Let's look at all the dazzling, brilliant minds and spirits that have created such amazing things on our planet. It becomes truly awe-inspiring…so imagine how this level of "awesomeness" will only increase as more and more of us learn to discard the beliefs that no longer serve us and replace them with ideas that destine us to thrive and "blissify"…!

Yes, tonight I am grateful to be part of this amazing dance called life.

… And so, my dear friends, as I listen to the frogs crooning their love songs to the moon…as my three furry friends congratulate themselves on having domesticated me into such a perfect pet…as my children dream of making their mark on the world…as I write the pages of my life into my grand story book, I rejoice at the honor of being able to simply explore my "ME-ness"…. And isn't it a luscious revelation that as we each discover our own "ME-ness" that we begin to understand that we can freely allow others to manifest their own "ME-ness" —and that this eternal "Easter Egg" hunt for our infinite collection of inner light is precisely the ingredient that gives our species its mightiest treasure…???!

As we twist and turn, sometimes in joy, sometimes in challenge, we create and create and create …and that is what, in my opinion, transforms life from a black-and-white experience to pure blue ray 3D high-def technicolor! Yowie! Zowie! I'm not "there" yet (wherever "there" might be), but I am grateful for this opportunity to live and love and explore (and even occasionally panic) and savor....thank you, dear friends, for being the positive souls that you are....thank you for spreading the bliss and the hope and the spiritual curiosity...it is a wonderful time to be alive...we are indeed blessed. Yet, I can't help but feel like the best is yet to come.... So venture on...run, dance, play, and even stumble, but venture on and on and on....for THIS is still the world that we saw through the eyes of our childhood... a mighty planet waiting to move forward together as one into eternity.....!

Today is a brand new day in the next chapter of the most EPIC story ever lived – YOUR story! So step mightily into this moment. Focus on the presence of all the abundance that Life has to offer. Weave your language; knowing these words will shape and nurture the planet and your very BE-ing from now through eternity. Dare to imagine a world worthy of the Joy-rrior's Creed. Use your ability to envision and create as a power that allows you to dance within the frequencies of Time.

Life is magical. *Your* life will be magical. Miracles are only considered miracles because they seem to defy Humanity's ability to explain them.

So, will there be boulders in your EPIC QUEST? Absolutely, but I know when they arrive, you will remember this:

It's not in spite of the boulders that we succeed. It's thanks to these boulders that we learn just how high we are capable of soaring. Now is your opportunity to choose: will your sky have limits – or will your limits evolve into just the beginning?

The choice is yours.

TODAY'S ACTION STEPS:

- *Drumroll: it's your turn to write your final version of YOUR "Once Upon a Future Me (The Story, Not the Fantasy)!" Step into that Epic You, embrace your 3 Masteries, and WRITE AS IF YOUR LIFE DEPENDS UPON IT... because your "coming aliveness" certainly does! (+7 Gold Stars)*
- *Bonus points if you start sharing this vision with the world. Own it! You have spent a lifetime creating this Shero's/ Hero's Story! And it's going to be a blockbuster! (+5 Gold Stars) Booyah!*

TOTAL POSSIBLE STARS FROM TODAY: 12 STARS

BONUS Day 103 – THE EPIC 3: The Journey of Epic Transformation: A New Beginning

Hello, you Epic Joy-rrior!! Wow! The summit of the mountain is in sight! As we stand together at this day's poignant threshold, let's reflect on the incredible voyage you've embarked upon over these past 100+ days. You've delved into the very essence of what it means to lead an epic life. Together, we've explored the transformative power of The Epic 3 – Focus, Language, and Imagination.

In this journey, you've discovered that what you focus on shapes your reality. And it does, doesn't it? How many times over the past 100 days have you seen that it's true? While most people dwell on the absence of their desires, you've learned to turn your gaze toward the presence of what you want. This shift in focus has unleashed an extraordinary force within you, enabling you to experience life in its fullest vibrancy.

Welcome to the community of those committed to not simply making a living but who insist on living life feeling totally and epically ALIVE.

But it's not just about where you direct your focus; it's what you make that focus mean in the grand tapestry of your life story. Your experiences, decisions, and how you perceive yourself and others are intricately woven into this narrative. You've witnessed firsthand the profound influence of language, for words are not merely symbols but vessels of meaning, carrying the potential to shape your destiny.

Your language crafts the very frequency of your thoughts, which, in turn, creates the feelings guiding your decisions. Through language, your beliefs come to life, manifesting as the symptoms/ indicators of your reality. The importance of deliberate word choice can never be overstated. Your words are the oxygen that breathes life into your personal stories, infusing them with vitality or constriction.

Through the exploration of imagination, you've harnessed a remarkable resource that, for many, remains dormant. While most minds are captivated by stories of fear, worry, and self-doubt, you've glimpsed the infinite potential of your imagination. You've learned to harness this incredible power not as a tool of limitation but as a force of creation, shaping a more powerful future across every facet of your existence.

Now, the choice lies before you. Will these 100+ days serve as a mere collection of intriguing insights and hacks, or will they become the cornerstone of a transformative creed? The Joy-rriors Creed invites you to step boldly into the world, committed to unleashing a life that radiates with the essence of the epic.

As we say "Ta Ta for now," remember the call to action that echoes through these pages. **It is up to YOU to choose the life you want to live and *dare yourself – boldly and deliciously – to go out there and CREATE IT!***

Will you continue to pursue even more mastery of The Epic 3 in your life? Will you use their typically overlooked potential to accomplish what once seemed impossible? Will you turn the boulders on your path into profound lessons on truly "aliving", not just surviving?

How will YOU choose to live? Who will YOU choose to show up BE-ing?

It's time to activate your new Personal Empowerment System™, this blueprint that will anchor you in empowered habits, priorities, and regimens. Embrace the unquenchable love of learning and the joy inherent in your growth.

As you step into this 103rd Day of Epic, what will you choose? The world awaits your brilliance, resilience, and unwavering commitment to an epic life. As the final chapter in this remarkable journey unfolds, remember that the story is never truly over – it's simply the beginning of a new and exhilarating chapter.

As you continue your mighty quest, know that you are not alone. Wink! Because yes, your tr'amily of Joy-rriors always wait in the wings with open arms. Reminder: If you find yourself yearning for further guidance in the pursuit of epic things, eager to delve deeper into the tr'amily (a tribe that is also family) of Joy-rriors, just beyond these pages, you'll find several juicy ways to get started…

For now, with your heart ablaze with the epic, step forward into this new beginning. Let your life be a testament to the transformative power of Focus, Language, and Imagination, and may it radiate with the resplendent glow of an existence truly lived.

Thank you for being a part of this remarkable journey. You are the embodiment of the epic, and your story is one of boundless inspiration.

In joy and epic wonder,

Meridith Alexander

TODAY'S ACTION STEPS:

- *Flip back through these pages from the past 103 days, and if you joined us with the gamification, now's the time to add up all those points!! Write that number in HUGE letters at the bottom of the last tracker page. What have been the highlights of this journey? Where were you when you started, and what new frontiers have you unleashed yourself into now? (+5 Gold Stars)*
- *Bonus points if you use today to continue the habit of regularly assessing what's working, what's not working, and what you will do differently. Remember that iteration is your differentiating factor– your superpower that allows you to transform the impossible into your I'm Possible! (+5 Gold Stars)*
- *EXTRA BONUS: Share your biggest takeaways, moments of inspiration, and new commitments thanks to these past 103 days by emailing us at*

<u>team@gritmindsetacademy.com</u>*. And if you played along with your tracker, be SURE to share with us your total number of points!! Who knows? There might be a special reward in it for you… just saying!!! (+5 Gold Stars) Booyah!*

TOTAL POSSIBLE STARS FROM TODAY: 15 STARS

CONCLUSION: THRIVING WITH THE EPIC 3

P.S. – Life has the potential to be so much fun! Personally and professionally, there are so many ways to grow, contribute and expand. It really is up to US to deliberately choose how we want to live *and then go live it!* And I sincerely believe that every single one of us has an epic version of ourself just waiting to be unleashed. We just need to learn to master the tools and strategies that will allow us to do that with more flow and ease.

In these past 100 days, I have done my absolute best to share the strategies and power of The Epic 3. Learning to master these three aspects of my own inner game has allowed me to navigate some of my most intense times of crisis and reinvent myself so that I could savor moments so wonderful that they exceeded my wildest dreams.

The Epic 3 strategies have also allowed me to serve and positively impact others. This inner game approach has helped hundreds of professional clients excel professionally and evolve into more impactful, happier versions of themselves. Although the strategies in this book can absolutely help you maximize the resources within your mind, if you are serious about cementing what you have learned into your lifestyle, , I do recommend investing in coaches, trainers, and mentors to expedite your progress. Those who tried to "save" by figuring out things on their own can attest that trial and error and the Plan Bs (that quickly become Plan Zs) not only waste valuable time but usually cost you even more dollars in the long run. These days, the challenge is not the lack of information. It's that there is so much information that it's hard to know what strategy will work best for you and when the best time is to apply it.

At the end of the day, it all comes down to YOU! Will you choose to live your life fully alive? Will you brave the unfamiliar to discover the EPIC? Personally and professionally, there are no limits to what you have the potential to achieve. Your impact and influence can touch millions. And you *can* do things that currently may seem impossible. I'm confident that by mastering The Epic 3, you'll not only live a life that feels happier, but you'll become a better leader, better team member, better family member, better friend, and better member of humankind. So the incentive is there!! You just need to commit to doing it!

"How to choose to live" really is THE question, isn't it?

Finding the answer that works *for you* is the joyous quest of a lifetime! So my wish for you today is a heart filled with wonder and delight. And when it comes time for you to be taking that final breath, may you be one of the special Joy-rriors who takes one last look at this majestic world saying, "Oh my gosh, this was an EPIC adventure! I hope I get to do this again some time!!"

And my sweet daughter, Schuyler?

She continues to do amazing things. She is working hard to be able to regain her balance so that she can stand on her own and even aspire to walk. There is never a day when the walls of our home aren't resounding with her infectious laughter. Her smile can get an entire room grinning. On a regular basis we are stopped by people on the street who have either followed her story or read our *The Sky is The Limit* book.

She reminds me every day that my "play" is just beginning. And that our boulder came not as a lesson in how to face death. Our boulder came as a powerful lesson in how to choose to live –and to come fully alive in the process!

Booyah!

See you in the tr'amily!!

xoxo

Meridith

BONUS: HAPPINESS Re-Capping the JOY-RRIORS CREED

[A Final Excerpt From The Tinkerbell Project Blog]

Hello, dear wonderful friends! Tonight, I sit immersed in the exquisite silence of our planet at night….one dog curled on my lap…, and two others nestled into the pillows of the futon chair by my side…all I hear is the gentle intake of their breath and the all-embracing beauty of a world at peace….

Ok, so perhaps it wasn't the easiest day on the planet…life has a way of throwing curve balls into one's path..but nevertheless, in the perfection of this moment, I am finding my way back to the peace and quiet of inner contentment….I am changing, and this change is good…

For most of my life, I have been questing for happiness…yes, "the secret"… the ultimate prize that will "trouble-proof" my world and ensure that my world is light and fluffy. I have gone to great lengths to try to discover how to claim Happiness as mine–and yet, in spite of my efforts, these little snafus always seemed to appear. I would grow perplexed and discouraged. What could I be missing? Why could I not achieve it–and even more often, why could I not maintain it—harness it—disaster-proof it so that I could always call it "mine"?

And then one day, I began to see…. like a bird, Happiness is not something that one captures, but nor is it something that will fly away if one is not careful. Happiness is not something that one can claim or even hold stagnant. Happiness is around us…alive and beating like a heart in love… Happiness is a brilliance that one breathes into the depths of one's soul—usually by choice and by design. Although some things make it easier to allow that glorious Happiness into one's heart, Happiness needs nothing other than a willing soul. Happiness doesn't demand perfection.

Happiness doesn't require company or prosperity or even a series of carefully woven events.

Happiness is totally and completely free…complex in its simplicity. Happiness offers its essence to anyone at any moment. The fruit on the tree of happiness is always ripe. All we have to do is to decide to pluck it.

And so, dear friends, as we scurry through our busy days, let's not chide ourselves too badly for the occasional foul mood or momentary frustration. It is all part of the colorful palate that creates the masterpiece. And yet, as we play at this game called Life, let's remember that happiness is the sound of our lover's breath. Happiness is the perfect shade of green. Happiness is the perfect song at the perfect moment. Happiness is the first taste of that perfectly chilled nectar. Happiness is the sounds of laughter along a street. Happiness is the ability to giggle for no reason.

Happiness is here—waiting to be unleashed. Happiness is important and powerful, and always ready when we are.

Maybe there is no secret…maybe Happiness is like the missing pair of glasses that sits waiting to be discovered on top of our head…

[Newsflash! If you loved The Tinkerbell Project excerpts, you are not alone! We're FINALLY going to be making the entire collection available in book form. Whether you need a Joy-rrior Boost or just a reason to smile at the beauty on this epic little planet, you'll soon be able to gift it, hold it, or download it on Kindle.

Want to be kept "in the know"? Email us at <u>team@gritmindsetacademy.com</u> .

~~THE END~~

"The New Epic Beginning"

(Because this is definitely not where the important stuff ends...!)

ACKNOWLEDGEMENTS

To EPICALLY Acknowledge Some of the Heroes and Sheroes Who Have Helped Make This Book Come Alive!

Sandy Nordstrom — OMG! There is a reason why I call you my Epic Side Chick! Thank you for being not only one of my earliest and long-term clients but thank you for tirelessly dedicating the hours to proofread, edit, and infuse the epic "power whooshes" into this book. Thank you for adding the "Epi" into our golden Epichicks! Thank you for your creativity, your imagination, your generosity, your overall genius, your faith in me, and, of course, your overall shine! Thank you for always showing up and nurturing those around you. Thank you for being bold enough to go beyond your own familiar zone. And last but not least, in addition to thanking you for all that you are and all that you do, I would be totally remiss if I did not publicly thank you for creating probably the world's first Epichick walker for Schuyler and for making sure that I never go to sleep without a pair of ruby reds at my side! Love you, and SO APPRECIATE YOU, my dear! "Oh, the places WE will go..." This story is just beginning!! Xoxo

---

Rob Ramsey — My Epic Friend and Graphic Guru! Thank you for the DECADES of stunningly gorgeous graphics, websites, and designs! Whether we are talking chocolate or chickens or "Can you make this look more sparkly?", you know how to transform my (often vague) visions into something spectacular! You've done EPIC things with our videos, made irresistible landing pages, and, of course, the ultimate Booyah Epic Chick graphic! I appreciate not only your talent and your skills but also your decade-long friendship and faith! Xoxo

---

Marisa Murgatroyd and the Live Your Message Coaches and Team — Booyah! Where do I begin? Thank you all for the past two years of EPIC mentoring, guiding, and teaching me how to truly go out into the world and LIVE MY MESSAGE! From the whips to the flight decks, from the opportunity to get out in front of your Mentos and share my craft, my world has blossomed and grown thanks to you. Marisa and literally every single coach that I have worked with (and, of course, everyone on your "behind the scenes" team) have been instrumental in my progress. You inspire me, challenge me, and encourage me to get even bolder and grow! Much love to my most impactful genius mentor of all time (and I have had many a great mentor, so that's saying a lot!!)! Looking forward to ASCENDING toward more epicness in the future! Xoxo

---

Schuyler — Where do I even begin? My sweet, amazing daughter... To say that you have been the catalyst for the biggest AHAs in this life adventure is selling you short. Your grit, your love, your tenacity — and, of course, that fiercely infectious laugh and smile... no wonder happiness is your middle name! Thank you for handling the disruption of this boulder in your eternally graceful, awe inspiring way! Thanks for holing up in your sunflower chamber while I spent hour after hour writing this book. Thank you for enduring my bouts of pirate tongue when technology misbehaved, and thank you for those delicious hugs to celebrate a job well done! To many more dinners at House of Vegano, to many more stages where we can share our story together, to many more abilities that we have yet to discover, thank you for being the "mini Me" and inspiring me to become Fearless! And maybe it's actually me who is the "mini" version of YOU!! I love you — and always will, sweet child!! Xoxo

My Family — Wow! Just Wow! I could definitely write another book just detailing how much I appreciate all of you! And when I say all of you, I include my epic daughter-in-law and son-in-law (and grandkiddies), who make this family even more loving and complete. To Mom, who has been my lifelong cheerleader and source of unconditional love and encouragement, who Facetimes Schuy religiously every single day, whose generosity never wavered through all those years when I struggled financially as a single mom, I love you more than a thousand skies. To Saya, again, how do I capture all that you have been to me? From the flowers celebrating my first podcast to visiting Schuy every single weekend in the hospital to the wife/mom you have now become, I cherish you, and I appreciate you. You are a marvel, a beauty and on and on and on… To Ryu (Linden), you have always been the rock in our family. Your incredible mix of strength and empathy has nurtured me more than you know. Your statement as a child when being a single mom was so tough "We may not be a typical family, but we are a perfect one" is a statement that I will carry close to my heart forever. You have no idea how that one sentence buoyed me up on nights when I felt terrified, not sure how I would get up the courage to face the next "impossible." Now, to see you as a father, a husband, a man… wow… just wow… Dad and Kathy, thank you for your never-ending "special touches" — the cards, the thoughtful gifts, the posts, the personalized "fun stuff" — all shared with such love and generosity. Clearly, the list is too full to share… Thank you to every single one of you (and yes, even to my furry Diva dachshunds who snuggled into the wee hours as I found stolen moments to write). You all are my champions, my beacons, my source of joy and delight! Thank you for believing in me, encouraging me, and sometimes being there to catch me when my "great idea' didn't quite work out…! I love you all so much! Xoxo

Steph and Michelle — Booyah, Baby!! Thank you, ladies, for being the behind-the-scenes angels/ superheroes during this process. Thank you for taking Schuy to movies, to doctors, to Altar'd State, and wherever our princess desired to go! Thank you for keeping my "Beauty Cub" happy and pushing forward so that I could focus on 100 Days! Xoxo

My Society of Epic Chicks, Coaching and Speaking Clients — You are "the why" behind this book! Thank you all for showing up 1000%! Thank you for making me fall in love with what I do. Thank you for venturing well beyond your "familiar zones" and for believing that "the impossible" is a matter of opinion, training, and perspective. Thank you for encouraging me to share the insights that our crazy boulder brought with it, and thank you for all for simply being YOU! Xoxo

And of course….

MIKE!!! — This man…. ♥
Some things in life are worth the wait, and these past years have taught me that some PEOPLE are also DEFINITELY worth the wait! You are my hero, my muse, my source of inspiration, my joy, my champion, my love, and yes, of course, my supplier of endless fresh avocados…Wink! You challenge me, encourage me, support me, and help me to keep discovering the bliss of EPIC in so many ways!! You have helped me build my career and my soul, my security, and my sense of self… I love you, acknowledge you, and celebrate this incredible man that I know to be YOU!! Thank you, thank you, thank you!!! Xoxo

About the Author

A featured coach on Forbes Magazine's Council of Coaches, one of Creative Click Media's Successful Women of 2019, and Influence Digest Media's Top 15 Coaches in Tampa in 2022, Meridith Alexander is a sought after expert on resiliency, optimal performance and grit .

As CEO of G.R.I.T. Mindset Academy, Meridith has helped hundreds of clients makeover their lives both personally and professionally by shifting to entirely new careers, launching new businesses, reinventing themselves and most importantly discovering just how possible it is to live a life that speaks to both your purpose and your passion. Even when life's boulders start falling.

Her first book "The Sky is the Limit" that shared her actual Facebook posts from the first months after the boulder struck her daughter hit the #1 slot among Amazon's "hot new releases" in November 2017. Critics called it a "mandatory read if you want to become the best version of yourself."

Having launched her current business in the shadow of unexpected tragedy, Meridith embodies the new genre of 60+ year old "grandfluencers" who remind us that it's never too late to reinvent ourselves or to make a positive impact on the world around us.

Meridith's story has been featured in media including ABC, NBC, Fox and Prevention Magazine. Her passion for the "inner game" can be traced back to her days at Georgetown University when she first discovered the philosophies of Plato and Socrates. Meridith believes that each and every one of us carries within us the seeds of EPIC. A brilliance that separates the Human Genius from anything else outside of Mankind. Sometimes that EPIC comes naturally. At other times EPIC is thrust upon us when we find ourselves in the role of what she calls the reluctant hero.

And it's these tiny individual seeds of EPIC that live waiting to be cultivated within our own minds. Then, as we master our own mindset and discover the real beauty within our own story, we become free to empower others. So when bringing together all of our individual EPIC-ness into a massive "Wholeness", she believes that we can create a momentum that will ultimately transform the world.

Meridith loves exploring the new vegan hot spots with her daughter Schuyler, playing Superhero Charades with her grandsons Jackson, Caden and Liam -- and of course watching her three diva dachshunds patrol their Queendom to keep the Florida squirrels at bay.

Read more about Meridith and Schuyler at www.gritmindsetacademy.com/about-us . For EPIC TIPS, follow us on your favorite social media channel!

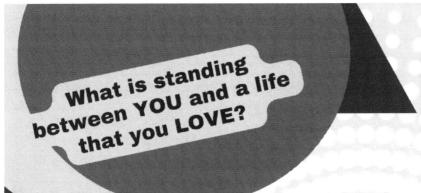

Read

Meridith and Schuyler's Story

On Amazon: Paperback, Audio or Kindle

www.bit.ly/OrderSkyStory

Loved Meridith's Excerpts from her Tinkerbell Project blog? Get the entire collection here!

Email:
team@meridithalexander.com

GET MORE EPIC IN YOUR LIFE!

 @meridithgrit

 @UnleashTheEpicYou

 @meridithalexander

 @meridith.grit.alexander

 @meridith-alexander-skylimit

 aboutepicchicks.com

 meridithalexandar.com

 gritmindsetacademy.com

 The Sky is the Limit book

 team@meridithalexander.com

WE HOPE TO SEE YOU SOON!

Made in the USA
Columbia, SC
08 October 2023

24126488R00150